Adjacent

to the

Argonauts

a voyage of discovery in Greece

Adjacent
to the
Argonauts

a voyage of discovery in Greece

Julian Blatchley

Matador
5 Weir Road
Kibworth Beauchamp
Leicester LE8 0LQ, UK
Tel: (+44) 116 279 2299
Fax: (+44) 116 279 2277
Email: books@troubador.co.uk
Web: www.troubador.co.uk/matador

ISBN 978 1848762 947

British Library Cataloguing in Publication Data.
A catalogue record for this book is available from the British Library.

Cover painting by William T. Rohe
wtrohe-art.eu

Typeset in 11pt Perpetua by Troubador Publishing Ltd, Leicester, UK

Matador is an imprint of Troubador Publishing Ltd

Printed in Great Britain by the MPG Books Group, Bodmin and King's Lynn

This book is dedicated to my generous hosts:
The people of Greece.

CONTENTS

Chapter One - Beginnings   1

Chapter Two - Down to the Sea   16

Chapter Three - An Introduction to the Islands   40

Chapter Four - Daliance and Decadence   69

Chapter Five - The Noble Art of Parking   98

Chapter Six - Abroad on the Main   134

Chapter Seven - The Back Nine   174

Chapter Eight - The End of the Beginning   196

PostScript   209

Glossary   211

CHAPTER ONE

BEGINNINGS

In which we make an ominous start... A voyage is planned... The perils of promotion...The voyage despaired of...An unlikely crew... Reflections on ethics... Doubts suppressed... Morals suppressed...The game afoot... Dramatis Personae... A grim encounter.

When Malcolm, Rex and I first encountered the old Athens airport, our initial impression was that coming to Greece had been a serious mistake. Consisting of grimy concrete, dark glass in scratched frames, grungy, grey pillars, faded wall paint, scuffed floors and murky shadows, Hellenikon airport was a rather dingy affair at the best of times. In the gloom of a late October night in the Eighties, when we first entered the Eastern terminal's brooding portal, it resembled the Lubyanka in nuclear winter.

Entering the dimly-lit arrival hall had all the allure of walking down an unlit alleyway into a ghetto, but we mustered our courage and pressed onwards. Under the sickly light of numerous diseased-looking yellow electric signs, we proffered our passports to the sinister shadows in the immigration booths and then progressed via an arthritic escalator into the shabby baggage reclaim area. Here we found that at least two flights were sharing one luggage-belt. We jostled on cracked and stained linoleum with a mêlée of Orientals to retrieve our baggage, a task made Herculean by the fact that the Easterners evidently included a fully-equipped orchestra. Obstructed by obstreperous oboes, turbulent tubas and contumelious cellos, we barged bassoons, trampled timpani and diced with double basses as we heaved and hewed our way through the maggot-like mass towards the queues for the customs desks. These lines moved forward with all the alacrity of a cat entering Crufts, the delay being due to the custom officials doggedly recording the serial number of every musical instrument in the owner's passport. It seemed that we would see daybreak before we managed to clear the terminal building... until they saw Malcolm. Dressed in green denim hat, combat jacket and trousers, with lank, collar-length hair, thin beard, sallow complexion and wearing an army-surplus back-pack, he was liable to attract the eye of the officials at the best of times. What made his being singled-out a matter of granite certainty was the four-foot length of green tubing he carried, with some stencilling on the outside and end-caps taped in place. He looked for all the world like a Middle-Eastern revolutionary armed with an anti-tank rocket. Unfortunately I chose to speak to him at the very moment two humourless, blue-uniformed officers came for him, and so I was also invited to jump the queue and enter a dismal little cubicle. Rex, the third man of our trio, ignored us pointedly, and stayed in line. As the door of the booth closed behind us, a customs man opened a drawer, in which I happened to notice a holstered pistol and a set of hand-cuffs, and took out a pair of latex gloves. As he grimly donned them with a practiced 'snap', I took a moment to ponder the rather complex sequence of events which had led me to this invidious circumstance.

* * *

Our story really starts about six weeks before the grim encounter at Hellenikon in a bar in Singapore, whence I had been drawn by my occupation as a navigating officer in the Merchant Navy. Finding myself at liberty from the duties of a Second Mate for a few hours, I and two kindred spirits in the persons of the Third Engineer and the Radio Officer were relaxing over a cold Tiger beer in the open-air hawker-stall by the Singapore River. Jim, Lester and I, three stalwart bachelors in our mid-to-late twenties, were relaxing and greatly enjoying the fashion show which occurs here like clockwork at around mid-day, five days of every week... a time when each of the towering office blocks in the vicinity spews about a thousand elegantly-dressed secretaries onto the sidewalks for lunch. As we enjoyed our Tigers and contentedly wallowed in the surge and ebb of tailored, perfumed loveliness which flowed around our little mosaic table, we concluded that this sort of outing was all too rare in our quasi-monastic existence*. We decided, on the spur of the moment, to do something about this lamentable state of affairs, and as all three of us were shortly due for leave the suggestion was made that we might join forces in a suitable environment to pursue our mutual interests jointly.

With the spontaneity which often accompanies youth, companionship and ale, we instantly drafted a plan. We wanted sunshine, cheap booze, mobility, a reasonable chance of female company whom we could understand, and a climate which would attract them *en dishabille*. We did not want beaches or overly commercialised tourist-traps and, being averagely bigoted seamen neither did we want overmuch contact with the population of the fortunate nation upon which we chose to bestow our custom. It seemed that some sort of mobile accommodation might be our oyster... and as I had done rather a lot of sailing in my youth, Lester and Jim went along with my suggestion that we could do worse than chartering a yacht.

The venue was our next consideration. The British weather was instantly ruled out as being too fickle for our purposes, and unlikely to attract the more scantily-clad variety of the female species. Seamen are generally reluctant to travel abroad when not getting paid for it, but it seemed that our needs could not otherwise be satisfied and so we resigned ourselves to going foreign, and considered our options. Spain was thought too commercial, and Italy too refined. The Caribbean seemed a little beyond our purses, the South Pacific too remote, and Turkey too Levantine. However, a friend of Jim's had recently reported positively on the Aegean and this, combined with hazy childhood impressions of the Aegean as depicted in the Iliad and the Odyssey, led us to believe that Greece was a land suitable for sailing, favoured with good weather and moderate prices. It was also, apparently, well stocked with female back-packers, and supposed to be lacking the more extreme manifestations of commercial tourism. By the time the last Singaporean secretary had parked her chopsticks and undulated back into her tower-block, the common consensus had focused on taking a yachting holiday in the Aegean in early September.

---

* I wouldn't want to stretch credulity too far in metaphorically relating our life at sea with that in cloisters; the restricted opportunity to mingle with the opposite sex was probably... indeed, hopefully... about the limit of it.

I could expound at length on the plans we made; the time that went into planning the maximisation of duty-free allowances, the poring over charts, the planning of routes which, given their complexity relative to the boozy haze in which we intended to conduct the exercise, never had much chance of coming to fruition. I could write separate books entirely on the characters of my two would-be shipmates; Of Lester, the exiled Polish radio-officer, with his unbelievable capacity for neat vodka and his firm conviction in those pre-perestroika days that this introduction to sailing was the key to a fantastic plan to extract the rest of his family from behind the Iron Curtain; or of Jim the third, a Geordie of no fixed parentage, a man who considered the term 'alcoholic excess' to be definitively oxymoronic. All this and more I could write, but there wouldn't be any point. Fate reared its ugly head, and the trip never happened. Lester and Jim were relieved in mid-August, and we agreed to meet up at the beginning of September, when I was due for repatriation; but fate, in the form of a nasty marital row exacerbated by a sadly convenient frying-pan, left the company bereft of a Chief Mate at short notice. I was promoted, and had to stay on the ship a month longer.

By the time I flew home from Cape Town, it was the beginning of October. Lester was already back at sea and Jim had taken a barmaid to a beer festival in Belgium. I had been very much looking forward to the sailing trip, but the lack of a crew appeared to have killed the project. As I sat out a foul Lake District autumn day in the public bar of the Hole in the Wall I reflected that the weather in Greece was probably also starting to break now, anyway. I heaved a sigh… the ale was good, the bar was snug, and with rain lashing the window I could feel my disappointment evaporating rapidly. Within another ten minutes or so, the plan would probably have passed peacefully away in its sleep, buried at least until another year.

The door slammed open, admitting in order of arrival a blast of cold air, a burst of rain, and a disreputable coat of the green, knee-length, waxed-cotton variety containing a bearded and fiercely cursing creature. Having forced the door closed against the blattering bellicosity of an English autumn, the inhabitant of the coat began to remove it in a shower of water and foul language. The gist of his deranged invective was that the nation was generally fit for inhabitation by aquatic and amphibian life-forms only; that he was not such a life-form himself; and that in his humble opinion, no country was entitled to call itself either civilised or developed when it's benighted citizens were condemned to eternal inundation and eventual lingering death of galloping bronchial pneumonia, rheumatism and trench-foot. Settling on the barstool next to me, the newcomer, now recognisable as the proprietor of a local guest-house and an old school contemporary of mine, muttered on into incoherence. Then, as he accepted a pint from the barmaid, he turned to direct a malevolent glare at my good self.

"Just back from somewhere warm, are you?" he asked, rather maliciously. I nodded.

"South Africa, actually"

"Ah, that's nice. South Africa, eh? Rain a lot there, did it?"

"Not so's you'd notice"

"Hot, was it? Sun beating down out of clear, azure skies? Tigers gasping in the shade of the jungle? Hippos scratching desperately to find a damp patch to lie in?"

"I think," I replied to this, "that the presence of a tiger or a jungle in South Africa might alarm environmentalists, but zoological pedantry aside, your general impression is correct, yes."

"And furthermore," remarked this gloom-monger, whose name I now remembered was Malcolm, "I doubt if you pay poll-tax in this bloody aquarium we call a country?" I smiled smugly in response to this, which provoked a bitter laugh.

"Thought not. You must be bloody touched to come back here at all."

I don't quite know why I said it: I'd like to think it was a consequence of an overdeveloped generosity gland, but I suspect that I just wanted to goad him further when I said, "Well, it's only for a day or two. I'm off to Greece on a sailing holiday soon".

Instead of railing further, he slumped dejectedly over his beer and muttered, "Bloody good idea. I'll come with you."

"Can you sail?" I asked idly. He gave a short bark of laughter and gestured wildly at the rain-lashed window and the sodden grey overcast beyond.

"Oh, I'm a bloody expert at water sports, mate!"

Now, I like to think that impulsiveness and spontaneity are features of my character, and so it was with almost no thought on the matter that I said, "Well, come along if you like. We've got a spare place."

It swiftly became apparent that spontaneity was also a feature of Malcolm's nature, because within ten seconds he had accepted my offer, bought me a pint, asked me when we were leaving, how much it would cost and what the weather was like in Greece at this time of year.

"Not that it matters," he added, "it can't be bloody worse than here!"

I cannot for the life of me remember what I replied to these questions, and neither with any luck can Malcolm, but it is surely eloquent testimony to the ravages of an entire summer dealing with tourists, followed by the prospect of a long, bleak winter, on the soul of this B and B proprietor (not on the whole a species known for capricious profligacy) that he marched straight down to the cash-dispenser and handed me a wad of notes. We parted, with me making a mental note to check up on the October climate in Greece, whilst Malcolm maintained a contentedly pessimistic note in his peroration.

"It'll probably be a cock-up," he predicted, jauntily. "But anything's better than Tener-bloody-rife again." As I walked home, I reflected on this statement, and it occurred to me that at least Malcolm would be easy to please, since to do so all one had to do was displease him, thus confirming his gloomy forecasts. Such elevated logic is a natural by-product of fine ales.

I also turned over in my mind how compatible a companion he would make for a couple of weeks, and slightly surprised myself by concluding that he would probably be good company. I hadn't been close to him at school but subsequent brief encounters had generally been pleasant. Malcolm was something of a wit, in a cynical way; he was also an adept banterer, and professed himself a decent cook, at least by bachelor standards. As I passed the newsagents, I made the decision that I would pursue the venture, and bought a copy of *Yachting Monthly*.

* * *

That afternoon I was quite unusually active, despite my lunch-time ale. A swift consultation of an ageing Atlas informed me that Eastern Mediterranean temperatures and rainfall were still quite civilised, whilst the sea-temperatures were positively inviting. Thus heartened, I went on to read in an ancient guide, quaintly titled *The Gentleman's Moorea*, that wine festivals were common in

Greece at this season, which was most encouraging, and an encyclopaedia informed me that great celebrations at the end of the month attended the anniversary of the day General Metaxa told Mussolini to take a running jump in 1940. Better and better!

At this point a sailing trip was again on the cards, but I felt it would be prudent to have one more person who knew something about sailing in our party. I rang several acquaintances with a vaguely nautical background, but with no takers until I telephoned a pub in Dorset, where a friend who sailed competitively on the south coast was wont to hoist a glass in an idle hour. The publican, whom I had met once or twice, said he felt it highly unlikely that my friend would be interested since he was currently on honeymoon. This landlord, whose name was Rex, went on to say, however, that he would willingly take a place himself if it were offered, as the season had been a torrid one. He felt himself to be on the point of wreaking carnage and mayhem amongst his staff, whom he described as a 'coven' of bar-maids. Recalling him as a sandy-haired, ruddy-faced individual possessed of a cheerfully cynical sense of humour akin to my own, I cautiously enquired as to his sailing ability.

"Got my own boat," came the reply. "Sail it most days during the summer". This I cheerfully accepted at face value, without further enquiry. No further crew candidates were forthcoming, but I felt that the inclusion of this veritable Horatio in our party had made us a technically competent crew. We had our quorum, so I settled down to book a boat.

Locating our argosy was suspiciously easy. The third telephone number extracted from the back of *Yachting Monthly* led me to a lady with a Greek name and a Geordie accent in Croydon who confirmed a twenty-five foot boat available in Kalamaki Marina for the weekend, and my local travel agent found me three very reasonable flights to Athens for some ungodly hour on Friday night. All this was accomplished under the residual warming glow of the lunch-time ale, and it was not until the following morning as I stood in the bank transferring money for the boat deposit that a sense of vague unease began to stir in the back of my mind.

There have been many great explorers who, over the centuries, have ventured upon the oceans of the world and discovered new lands, or nicked those discovered by others. In tiny and often ill-wrought vessels they sailed with crews prised from the gallows and the gaol. Nourished by faith in God, lunatic self-belief and salt beef with the consistency of an oak floorboard, and displaying strength of resolve that nowadays would be called obsessive-compulsive, these *conquistadores* realised their dreams of discovery and conquest. They brought their wealth home, and colonised not only new lands but also the very pages of history. Their deeds are admiringly recorded in impressive tomes and national lore, their names bequeathed to geographical features across the world, and their features preserved in sternly-posed statuary. But consider... the fame these men enjoy alone was possible only because of the unsung crews they sailed with. What, then, of me, sailing off into foreign and unknown waters with a crew about whom I knew little? Naturally, I saw myself in the central role, but who would be the Vespucci to my Magellan, the Oates to my Scott, (or, as it turned out, the Christian to my Bligh?) In short, did either of these turkeys have the slightest bloody idea what they were undertaking, or how to undertake it? I quickly concluded probably not; and then, with the characteristically optimistic reflection that all great men are assailed by doubt at times, I simply ignored the issue of their ability*.

Having settled the question of the suitability of my crew by mentally transferring it directly from the 'In' tray to the 'Out' tray of what passes for my mind, I found I was faced with a moral problem. I had a sneaking suspicion that, left to their own devices, Rex and Malcolm would probably not have elected to go on a yachting holiday. There was the further suspicion that had they done so, they would probably not have chosen Greece in October as the venue; and since one of them lived in the Lake District, the other in Dorset, and they had never even heard of each other before, it appeared statistically unlikely that they would have chosen to go on holiday with each other. This left me, in a rare moment of self-examination, with some qualms that I might be creating a holiday for me, using someone else's valuable time and money. Was I not hijacking these hard-working people's precious leisure time for my own ends, and was my position in any way morally defensible? This time I concluded almost certainly not... but since neither Rex nor Malcolm boasted notable muscular development, nor were given to violence to the best of my

---

* No such procrastination affected the remainder of Malcolm's family, with whom he shared his business, I later discovered. It was with some chagrin that I heard their assessment of my ability was such that they hustled him round to a solicitor and made him draw up his will.

knowledge, I shelved that question too, with a mental note that I really must do something about my ethics one of these days; second thing on the list after procrastination.

* * *

Thus it was that, on a grey and drizzly Friday evening, Malcolm and I met on Windermere station.

When he arrived, I thought hard and long, but could not think of any selection of apparel which would have been quite so completely un-suitable for sailing, unless he had been able to lay his hands on a suit of armour. Malcolm's form is a slightly corpulent one, marginally below average height, and it manifests itself beneath an incipient double chin. His face is smoothly fleshy with large, sensitive-looking lips, and is fringed with shoulder-length hair and a thin brown beard. His eyes are bright, keen, active buttons in an otherwise indolent frame, sole indicators of an active intelligence which excels in observation and cynical comment. At any time intolerant of fashion, and a devotee of the 'first three things out of the drawer' school of sartorial coordination, he was on this occasion dressed by the maker of a well-known brand of country-sport wear in drab waxed cotton. Even his hat had the form of a battered trilby in this material, and beneath the voluminous knee-length overcoat I could glimpse a lamentably shabby olive-drab combat jacket. His feet were encased in the scruffiest pair of baseball boots imaginable and he carried his chattels in an army haversack.

Given the appearance of him, I was hardly surprised to note that he carried over his shoulder the aforementioned green plastic tube, with its uncanny resemblance to an anti-tank rocket. I felt constrained to point out that if he intended putting up some guttering, he had better look sharp about it as the train left in ten minutes.

He took all this with disdainful calm, explaining that the pipe contained his fishing-rods, without which he could never consider travelling (angling, cats and curry being his only confessed passions). The coat and hat were his best waterproofs, he said, and he understood that these were carried by all yachtsmen. Now, the idea of Malcolm in this Middle-Eastern terrorist guise standing on the deck of a Whitbread round-the-worlder surrounded by a crew in designer ocean-racing waterproofs struck me as being so richly comic that for a moment I dissolved into mirth, but Malcolm appeared unperturbed by this, and addressed himself to a can of elephant-strength cider. He was evidently unruffled by either his singularity of appearance or my reaction to it, so against the fact that he manifestly knew nothing whatsoever about sailing, I was thankful to note that he was not overly sensitive to ridicule. Someone once said (and I rather think it may have been me, actually) that if you wish never to appear ridiculous, you should stay away from fast women, slow horses and any sort of boat; Malcolm seemed able to smile in the face of friendly mockery, which boded well for his suitability for sailing… but then, at this stage, I little suspected that the holiday was to test my own sense of humour somewhat more sharply than his.

During our journey to Manchester Airport we amused ourselves innocently by making loud and derogatory comments about the types of people who read certain newspapers, and surreptitiously watching the knuckles go white with rage on the edges of the papers in question. It was a great success. One man actually tore his paper turning the page in fury.

We had arranged to meet Rex at the bar in the departure lounge, but quite by chance we arrived almost simultaneously at the check-in queue. Rex is on the tall side of average height, comfortably fleshy all over. With his fair complexion, reddish-sandy mop of hair and a bristling sandy moustache, and made bulkier still by the chunky, red-brown Guernsey he was wearing, it was not a notable feat of observation to identify him.

British-ness is perhaps the key to a description of Rex. It is certainly so in appearance… his demeanour and complexion have something of Empire about them and it takes little imagination to see him in wing collar and tie, scotch and water in hand, gazing out across the plantation from his veranda and making a mental note to have the number seven elephant serviced. His manners are quintessentially Edwardian British… very understated and reserved until in comfortably familiar society. He then becomes the disseminator of a satirical wit which flowers especially brightly when exercised upon the French and Spanish fishermen who maraud the coasts of his beloved Dorset. He has had a university education, to which many attribute his cutting line in repartee… I don't quite understand why, since he studied agriculture, but there you are.

Having found Rex our fellowship was complete, and I reflected momentarily that any hope I may have had that his sailing experience might have balanced out Malcolm's appalling lack of nautical nous was abruptly dashed by Rex's dress. The jumper was fine, pure Devon fisherman. The tweed trousers and brogues were not, pure Scottish deerstalker. The belted raincoat was pure Gestapo. And the large-ish suitcase meant that he had never been on a yacht before in his life, otherwise he would have known that there is nowhere to stow the blasted things. As the introductions were performed, my heart was in my boots. Well, I temporised to myself; perhaps we can just stay very close to Athens. Then I ignored the problem until my roller-coaster confidence cycle had time to return to the imbecilic positive phase again.

* * *

Assembled and checked in, we hied ourselves into the shopping area to purchase our duty-free supplies. Malcolm stocked up with good brandy, I took gin, and Rex loaded himself amply with carefully selected white wine. We also took a couple of cartons of cigarettes because, although non of us smoked, I had been through Suez a time or two and knew the value of a swiftly palmed packet of Marlboro at a crucial moment. And if we felt it possible that we might encounter corruption in Greek officialdom, we were damned sure we would come across it in the food. To prepare for this aspect of the holiday, we repaired to the pharmacy.

At this point, as I casually confess to having harboured such dark preconceptions of our Greek hosts... the founders, after all, of Democracy and cradle of Western civilisation... I suppose that some sort of explanation is appropriate. I should perhaps briefly digress to examine our perceptions of foreigners.

Rex, Malcolm and I had, I believe, no presumption of the deficiencies of other nations, but we certainly shared a sense of the superiority of the English mind. It was a benign prejudice; a nebulous, even a subliminal, bigotry which was not intentional. Had we been taken to task about it, we would have denied it, indignantly and sincerely... yet protest as we might that we conceived ourselves no better than citizens of other nations, it cannot be denied that we certainly considered ourselves first-amongst-equals.

This comfortable conviction probably emanated from a hysteretic (and highly selective) consciousness of Waterloo and the Spanish Armada, steam trains, flushing lavatories and the East India Company; a doubtlessly empirical state of mind, certainly flying in the face of any sporting evidence, which expressed itself not in dislike or distrust of foreigners but rather in the mildly patrician, tolerant manner of a kindly uncle to a not-overly-bright-but-good-hearted nephew. It led us elegantly to a number of dubious presumptions about Greece, based, I suppose, on Mediterranean stereotypes. It certainly wasn't based on experience... Malcolm and Rex had never met a Greek outside a restaurant, and my exposure to them had been limited to a night ashore in Piraeus port when still a cadet[*]. But, however derived, hindsight reveals that we entered Greece in a state of mind which dictated that we expected to find the Greeks and their food dodgy. There was absolutely nothing personal in this, we knew they were only poor, foreign chaps, and unable to help it.

In the pharmacy there was some disagreement as to what our individual needs would be, so we bought a small common stock and then set about laying in personal supplies. Rex, being fair-skinned with reddish hair, wisely stocked up fairly lavishly with sun-block and zinc cream. Worried about the quality of his greens, he also took a startlingly hued selection of vitamin tablets. He topped off his selection with an assortment of laxatives and purgatives in bottles.

In common with his disillusion with all other aspects of life, Malcolm's outlook on the subject of health was pessimistic in the extreme; his purchases in the intestinal care department were legion. He also bought water purification tablets, antiseptic cream, and (I was alarmed to note) some athletes foot powder. He was collecting a range of anti-acid tablets from the shelves when I asked him just a touch sarcastically whether he didn't think it would be best to get a body-bag and some formalin whilst he was at it.

Next he went on to attend to more pleasurable aspects of the trip. First he picked up a bottle of suntan lotion, and then wandered over to the 'embarrassing things' counter. Raking his hand through a basket full of condoms, he loudly asked the girl at the till on the opposite side of the shop, "Are these slim-fit or full-cut, love?"

---

[*] On which occasion I patronised two establishments called The John Bull Bar and the unforgettably-named Clap Cabana, enterprises whose particular aspect of Greek culture is imparted principally by young ladies from the Philippines!

Unbelievably, the girl replied that she didn't know, and came round to examine the labels. When she was eventually forced to admit that she couldn't tell, Malcolm said not to worry; he could stretch them in hot water. He purchased an amount of the things which made me wonder whether he intended spending much time on the boat at all, and thinking that he might be contemplating inflating them, I reassured him that lifejackets were provided onboard. He followed Rex off to the bookstall, leaving me to make my purchases.

In common with seaman as a whole, I had no truck with laxatives and the like. After travelling a fair bit, I was firmly of the opinion that I was made of sterner stuff than mere foreign bacteria. (Never once did it occur to me that my freedom from intestinal disorder was actually due to the fact that the countries I visited were, on the whole, perfectly sanitary and healthy.) I was damned if I would be seen dead using suntan lotion. In the Merchant Navy, that is reserved for a breed called 'Hollywood Sailors'. I limited myself to a bumper-sized family pack of alka-seltzers, and some insect repellent lotion. As an afterthought, I picked up a spare toothbrush, because I have a habit of losing them at an alarming rate when travelling, and a much less ambitious number of condoms, because after all, you never know when a short-sighted, slow-moving nymphomaniac is going to blunder like an amorous rhino across your path.

* * *

Our take-off from Manchester was a model of smooth execution. Rex loudly remarked "Bit twitchy on the stick, this chap, isn't he?" just to enjoy the reaction of those around him, but any expansion he may have cared to make on this topic was drowned by an announcement concerning seat-belts, seat-belt signs, and smoking in the toilets.

There is little to say about the actual flight. It was very cramped, and the three and a half hours passed fairly sluggishly. The food was served, not as bad as I had expected, and certainly nowhere near resembling the plastic-packed banquet of botulism that Malcolm had gleefully predicted. Rex disgraced himself by scrounging the dregs of everyone else's bottles of white wine, and Malcolm ended up wearing his egg mayonnaise (or egg with malaise, as he referred to it). Apart from this, we proceeded smoothly to the duty-free vending stage of the flight. Have you ever noticed that this process is always timed to block all aisles and movement in the cabin just after dinner and the effects of altitude have strained one hundred and twenty bladders to bursting-point?

The last hour was spent reading and chatting idly across the aisle. During one such conversation, Malcolm noticed that a lady next to him was reading *Moby Dick*. He tapped her on the shoulder and stage-whispered in her ear, "The whale did it!"

Flight attendants were pretty busy during the last hour, keeping apace of the demand for drinks, and the holiday atmosphere was growing tangibly throughout the cabin. Snatches of song and loud bursts of laughter punctuated the hum of excited conversation and the 'Fasten Seatbelts' light had been on for about ten minutes before most people were back in their seats, the last velour track-suited soul being frog-marched back to her seat by a flight attendant whilst the runway lights were already rushing past the windows. As she went she performed an impromptu flamenco followed by a loud "Ole!", which caused me to wonder if she was on the correct flight.

Seconds later, we were down as smoothly as we had gone up, and the engines roared thunderously in reverse thrust as the plane braked. Moments later, all was quiet.

What happened next was so horrible that I can barely bring myself to relate it here. Even in retrospect, it was grotesque, hideous, unnatural and indecent, an affront to the dignity of the British nation.

They cheered!

I was speechless, stunned. I had never flown on a charter flight before, and the experience of British passengers applauding the pilot in the manner of a South American football supporters outing shook me to the very core. Where the reserve? Where the stiff upper lip? Where the vaunted understatement in time of adversity? Were these people going to behave like this in front of *foreigners?* They were, and I have never quite recovered from the shame. Rex commented in the bus on the way to the terminal that such a lack of *sangfroid* made his blood run cold, but I was too far gone in shock to appreciate witticisms, particularly on a subject so inappropriate for levity. It was as a man whose world has been not just turned upside-down but also given 20 minutes in a tumble-dryer that I entered the terminal building.

When we first entered the Eastern terminal's brooding portal, it resembled the Lubyanka in nuclear winter...

* * *

...And so it was that we came to be sequestered in the customs office at Hellenikon, in a scene disturbingly reminiscent of Midnight Express and made more sinister by the total silence of the customs officers. Once in the cubicle, one officer with three stripes on his shoulder closed the door firmly, and leaned against it. The other, a two-striper, walked behind a steel desk, donned the latex gloves in the ominous manner already described, and beckoned us forward. He took my passport from my nerveless fingers, glanced briefly at it, and tossed it casually onto the desk in a manner highly suggestive to my hyper-active imagination that no matter what Her Majesty's Secretary of State for Foreign and Commonwealth Affairs requested and required, he was not going to be able to prevent THIS particular entity from letting or hindering me in the most objectionable way possible. Still without a word, The Gloved Nemesis disposed similarly of Malcolm's passport, and then beckoned for the drainpipe. I will not try to hide the conflicting emotions which possessed me as he flipped open a penknife and deftly slit the tape from the end-cap. Outraged innocence boiled in my breast, whilst an altogether baser emotion invoked by terror at the possible significance of the gloves churned my stomach. Somewhere in between the two, I also found room for an earnest desire to eviscerate Malcolm, who, having got us into this situation was now doing his best to exacerbate it by ignoring the officials and studiously examining the contents of an infamous handkerchief. As the officer peered into the tube, Malcolm became engrossed in a poster about currency importation and had to be recalled to the present to answer the first question of the interrogation.

"Feeshing?" enquired the officer, who received a chummy grin and a "Yup!" from Malcolm in reply. My fingers curled, and in that instant I wanted more than anything in the world... apart, that is, from being spared closer acquaintance with the gloves... to feel Malcolm's windpipe collapsing under my thumbs. Surely now we were for it...

I had not heard the customs man at the door move, but suddenly a hand descended heavily on my shoulder from behind. I mentally prepared myself for the ultimate indignity... and in my ear hissed a low, menacing voice.

"Sir," it growled, "...welcome to Greece. You may leave by this door."

I left so fast I had to go back for my passport.

15

CHAPTER TWO

DOWN TO THE SEA

In which we encounter a Greek taxi driver...The quest for Kalamaki...A Greek hotel...The villainy of the taxi-driver revealed...We meet Spiro...The good ship Nissos...The hand-over...We meet Ouzo...Bureaucracy dished, and the making of a monster...The Captain asserts his authority...Disaster narrowly avoided.

It was well after midnight when we sallied forth into the airport taxi-rank. Our arrival coincided with that of a shattered Volvo estate driven by a short, spherical man with a moustache that looked as if he had a small musk-ox emerging from his nose. On the front seat of the car a child lay asleep, curled up like a dog in a basket, and in the back was a shapeless heap covered with an old piece of carpet, which I furtively discovered to be the earthly remains of a large, superannuated motorbike engine. We put our bags on top of it and squeezed into the back seat all together so that junior didn't miss any of his beauty-sleep; if the driver was his father, he certainly needed all the help he could get in that department. With our three corpulent frames wedged across the back seat, the drainpipe was gingerly positioned over Malcolm's shoulder, and the doors forced shut against a surplus of the roast beef of old England.

We were in possession of a letter from the charter company in England which informed us that our boat awaited our pleasure in Alimos Marina, Kalamaki. The letter went on to say that this was about ten minutes drive from the airport by taxi. We tried asking for the marina in English, but this elicited only an indifferent shrug from the driver by way of reply. Prepared for this, I triumphantly produced an English-Greek dictionary, one which included a selection of those ready-made phrases without which one feels so lost in a foreign land*. Some preparatory study on the aircraft now allowed me to tentatively announce:

"Thello pauw kotero limani Kalamaki, parakalo."

Normally when one tries this sort of thing, one receives an odd look, a pound of raw horse-liver and some lavatory detergent. However, on this occasion, in a noteworthy break with tradition, the gambit worked a treat. The taciturnity of the driver vanished in a flood of accented but perfectly comprehensible English as he roared off down a dual carriageway. The gist of this flood was that he had never heard of the Marina, but he would take us to Kalamaki town where he was sure we would find the place we sought. But it was awfully late, wouldn't we prefer to take a pleasant hotel for the night and find the boat in the morning? He indicated the Hotel Odysseus, which we happened to be passing, and which he said he had heard was cheap and clean. We politely said that we preferred to find the marina, and so we sped on into the night.

It is a general rule of travel books (in which genre it is my earnest wish that this tome is counted; I should hate to be accused of peddling trivia!) that they tend to dwell at some stage on the atrocities committed on the roads of the countries concerned. Most of them single out taxi-drivers for special comment. I have my own fund of taxi stories. They range from the chap who drove us from Callao to Lima in Peru, who in lieu of anything in the way of braking facilities scraped his nearside down a rock face when going downhill, to a sad collision I once witnessed in Sri Lanka between a speed-crazed taxi-driver and a bullock cart; the sight of the enraged bullock making good his escape through a busy fruit market with a few of the fundamental members of his cart still in tow is one that I still find hard to erase. The various strange driving habits of foreigners are worthy of a book in their own right. The custom of bolting substantial bars across the front of Australian cars as a token to ward off the evil of low-flying kangaroos springs to mind. Likewise the Saudi Arabian law that if a foreigner is involved in a road accident with a Saudi, it is the fault of the foreigner on the very reasonable grounds that if the foreigner hadn't come to Saudi Arabia, the accident definitely would not have

---

* Such as "Regrettably, the principles of my holiday company have done a runner... would you accept my wristwatch/passport/girlfriend?"

happened. And in many Pacific islands, if you run someone else over, you become financially liable for his medical treatment and the maintenance of his family until he can work again. Unfortunately, since medical treatment is a lot more expensive than a funeral, it is reputedly common practice to limit one's financial liability by reversing over the victim to make sure of him, especially if his wife is pretty. I am sure that minimal research will unearth much more bizarre examples of automotive lunacy. Thus, it is not my intention to dwell either upon highway hooliganism or to represent our trip to Kalamaki as an outstandingly harrowing one. I will content myself by mentioning that the three of us were petrified in our seats as the Volvo squealed, honked and weaved in maniacal abandon through the light traffic.

We must have been quite preoccupied with the driving. because it was some time before we noticed that as fast as our taxi went, there was one thing which went faster; the meter. This large, dated, semi-mechanical contrivance resembling a one-armed bandit* was precariously suspended over the head of the sleeping child. As we sped through the Athenian suburbs, its windows blurred as the numbers whizzed round so fast that we were only able to read them during rare moments when the driver braked. Even when we left the highway and proceeded to curb-crawl around the lesser roads looking for the marina, I couldn't see much slackening in the awesome pace of the brute machine. I had an ace up my sleeve, however, as the letter also told me how much the taxi should cost, so I let the matter ride for the time being, even though we had already spectacularly passed the correct amount.

After perhaps half an hour in the taxi, we passed the Hotel Odysseus again, and the driver once more pleaded with us to take a hotel for the night. We declined. After a further five minutes, during which the driver apologized profusely, questioned pedestrians and consulted a tatty map, he declared himself desolated to have failed us, but he could help us no more. Were we sure of the name? We showed him the letter. He wondered if the charter company hadn't perhaps made a mistake? We didn't say so, but we began to suspect this might be the case. Thus, when he suggested a hotel for the third time, we accepted on the grounds that whatever it cost could not begin to approach the Central American national debt which the meter was

---

* and therefore differing from its owner only in number of appendages

industriously accumulating. The driver contentedly whisked us a remarkably short distance to arrive outside...the Hotel Odysseus!

Over the discussion about the fare, the driver's bonhomie evaporated a touch as he and I went into a duet of grandiloquent bargaining, each pleading poverty and large, starving families in support of our conflicting claims. To be fair to the driver, the meter was referred to only at the outset of negotiations, its purpose being nothing more than the setting of an arbitrary, if Olympian, starting-point. We roared on into the night, the driver acquitting himself magnificently as befits a son of the nation where drama originated. I was in good form myself, having recently been through the Suez Canal a couple of times. Finally, feeling that this had gone on long enough, I played the joker: reverting to my phrasebook, I demanded the presence of the *Touristiki Astynomea*... the tourist police. A spot of preparatory reading on the country before departure had elicited the information that this stalwart body of men exist to champion the beleaguered tourist*. It worked! The driver went into a spasm of hysterics which amounted to his death-throes before agreeing a price around one quarter of the metered amount. He explained that he was doing this purely because he did not want to wake the child, but the child slept through the theatrics so soundly that a more suspicious person than my good self might have supposed that he was not unfamiliar with such performances.

The price settled and paid, the driver became affable again. He proposed a new deal. We were to sleep, and whilst we did so, he would scour the waterfront, leaving no stone unturned, and find the marina. He would then come back to take us there in the morning. He would search all night, if necessary. We declined, and bade him farewell.

We checked into the hotel, which was fairly reasonably priced even if it did seem strange that, at such a late period of the season, the hotel was so full that only the more expensive luxury rooms were available. The morale of the crew was high, with the taxi-driver firmly handled and a good night's sleep in prospect, so we shared a bottle of wine in the foyer before retiring. Malcolm

---

* Having since had the experience of giving a statement to one of these worthies, I now know that I was bloody lucky that none happened to be in the vicinity that night, or I would have seen the dawn break without doubt.

and Rex performed a critique of my bargaining techniques. It was at this moment that the rascally driver himself entered the hotel and was greeted by the receptionist with a familiarity and warmth which had been lacking in our own welcome, and there was the suspicion of money changing hands. This left us with the strong suspicion that we had been royally hoodwinked, and we went to bed in a slightly deflated mood.

* * *

Despite retiring at a late hour, we were up at six thirty prompt. This was due to the airport re-opening at that time, and we were left in little doubt of the fact by the thunder of mighty engines apparently in our wardrobes.

Looking out of my window, it was somewhat annoying to find that, however far we had driven the night before, the terminal buildings were clearly visible less than a mile away, and the runway appeared to start in the hotel car-park. As bitter a testimonial to the perfidy of the taxi-driver as this was, it paled into insignificance by comparison with the evidence visible from Rex's window. The driver had stated, you will recall, that to find the marina he would "Search all night if necessary!" It wouldn't have taken all night. Below Rex's balcony, separated from the hotel only by a lethally busy three lane highway, lay a veritable forest of masts and a large sign saying 'Marina'.

These revelations were hard to swallow. Our quiet pride in the no-nonsense policy adopted in dealing with the locals, a pride which had waxed unchecked during the argument about the taxi fare, now waned to negligible proportions. With every glance at the masts across the teeming road, the magnitude of our gullibility was flaunted in our faces. Even with our eyes closed, the constant roar of the traffic and the regular crescendo of aircraft passing our balconies made it impossible to forget, or to sleep any longer.

Breakfast was taken, more because we had already paid for it than for any gastronomic allure created by its presentation or flavour. Rex and Malcolm then went for a wash and brush up at my suggestion, as I pointed out that any access to fresh water that doesn't have to be carried by hand is, to the yachtsman, as a season-ticket on a banana-boat is to a gorilla. In the meantime I made a reconnaissance of the marina, which confirmed beyond all possible doubt that it was the one we sought. The recce further taught me a lesson about the policy of Athenian motorists towards pedestrians... a lesson that I very nearly did not got the chance to pass on[*]. The experience of crossing the highway un-nerved me to the extent of inducing me to take a cup of coffee with a stiff brandy in it before attempting the return trip. I recommended to the others that they do the same before trying to get across with the luggage, and so it was that we became acquainted with Metaxa. It was our unanimous view that disparaging comments made about Greek brandy are slanderous. We quickly acquired the taste, and by the time we reached the marina office, the combination of brandy at eight o'clock in the morning and a cloudless, clear blue sky had greatly improved the jaundiced view of the host nation we had developed the previous evening.

I was in something of a quandary as to how best to approach the authorities with regard to finding out where, in this mass of glass-fibre and aluminium, we were to find our boat. In a sense, however, it found us. We drew near to the marina office complex (and 'complex' is a very good word to use in connection with anything to do with an office in Greece) and searched in vain for any sign in English which might offer useful guidance. We found no such thing, but by the side of the office, which was the heart (albeit badly in need of a pacemaker) of the marina, we came across a dilapidated jeep the colour of aged concrete. As we drew nigh, it began to rock violently. The door flew open, under considerable pressure from some internal force, and after a final violent contraction, the vehicle gave birth to a swarthy, rotund and exceedingly hairy individual. His face split into the sort of toothy smile that put one in mind of someone un-zipping a brown bag packed to bursting point with wedding-dresses. As he advanced towards us, he tripped slightly on the curb, but recovered without deflection of the smile whilst the arms he flung out to help preserve his balance remained spread, either in greeting, or in imminent threat of a Greek dance ensuing.

"Mr. Blatchley?" he asked in faultless, Oxford English, "You have come for my *Nissos?*"

---

[*] The lesson is that the highway is exclusively reserved for the use of motorists, and the pavement is for overtaking on the inside and parking.

We agreed, little caring what his *Nissos* might be as we retreated behind one another in case the wide-flung arms should presage one of those deplorable hugs or cheek-kissing exhibitions so beloved of the continentals. The threat, however, did not materialise; one hand swung down into a firm handshake, the other did no worse than pat the target on the shoulder. The recipient of this fulsome greeting was Rex, who had retreated marginally slower than Malcolm and I.

The man went on to introduce himself as Spiro, the representative of the charter company, and he began energetically packing our bags into the back of the moribund jeep. All the while, he kept up a relentless barrage of boisterous, over-the-shoulder statements, which were mutually unconnected and which we were beginning to suspect were what passed in Greece for conversation. By the time we were all shoehorned into the jeep, with Malcolm perched precariously on top of the bags and Rex on my lap in the front seat, we had followed Spiro's life history from a surprisingly gallant national service (he appeared to have seen action with at least three arms of the Greek forces), through his university education in Sussex (which explained the accent), to various responsible positions high up in industry. His current job, he made it apparent, was the crowning achievement of a glittering career, one which he esteemed a vocation, scorning all thought of financial or personal gain. His greatest reward was the spreading of happiness, he confided, and we were given to understand that he was virtually a charitable organisation. Rex later commented that, at this point in the monologue, he had furtively dug into his pocket for some small change for the collection-plate when it came round.

By the time the sadly overloaded jeep had been coaxed into the somnolent, funereal pace which passed for its cruising speed, Spiro had begun a eulogy to the beauty of the Greek Islands. This lasted the length of a quay full of gleaming gin-palaces, large, ostentatious motor-yachts which shone in the morning sun and dazzled the beholder with a mixture of burnished chrome and naked opulence.

The next quay, nuzzled by a fleet of large, sleek and new-looking charter yachts, passed by to the accompaniment of a soliloquy about the wisdom of choosing October for a sailing holiday in Greece. This left me, as the instigator, with a pretty smug feeling.

A finger-pier garlanded with rather older and smaller yachts slid by as we were treated to a prolonged dissertation on the surprisingly many fine qualities of the English nation. These Spiro illustrated with unfavourable comparisons to other nations, particularly the Germans and French. He even confided that other nationalities were not always honest, and that consequently he occasionally returned the favour. Yes! Even He! But never with the English. No, the English one could deal with as gentlemen. Given our confessed faith in the English primacy, we were, by this time, emitting tangible waves of warmth and appreciation for this perceptive and erudite foreigner.

We passed the penultimate finger-pier to a diatribe on the subject of charterers who left their boats dirty (mainly French), who complained about trifles such as uncleaned ashtrays (Germans), who were insensitive to established local customs such as flexible timekeeping (Swiss), and who became such enthusiastic socialisers on encountering the cheap Greek booze that their boat-handling suffered as a result (Scandinavian). These sweeping slanders on the seamanship of entire nations ended with a heartfelt gratitude on Spiro's part to be dealing mainly with the English. He closed with the offhand comment that some of the other vile nationalities would complain even when given a *larger* boat than the one they had paid for...Incredible!

At last, we had reached the outside wall of the vast, concrete marina. Like so many constructions in Greece, it was difficult to tell whether it was already in ruins, or had simply never been completed. Alimos Marina in the 'Eighties was as ugly as it was functional, and the vast concrete sea-walls and piers more resembled something built to keep Messrs Eisenhower and Montgomery off the continent in 1944 than any sane person's concept of a chic leisure facility for the well-to-do. The berths on the outer wall needed only Maximillian Schell and a few extras in coal-scuttle helmets to create a most unsettling vision of the past, and a single, shouted *Achtung!* would have been enough to send any veteran diving for cover.

Looking down from the height of the wall, we found ourselves perched some feet above a rather drab, grey little boat with the touch of age definitely on her brow. I scanned both ways up and down the quay, looking for any sign of the brand-new twenty-five footer that we had booked, but the already obvious conclusion was confirmed when Spiro stepped rather gingerly down the steep gang-plank connecting the boat to the quay and held up his arms for the bags. Seeing my hesitation, he struck an elaborate attitude of surprise.

"They did tell you that we had arranged a larger boat for you, didn't they?"

We said 'they' had not. Spiro opened wide his arms, mouth and eyes to the heavens in amazement. "Typical! These office people! Well, we are not so busy at this time of year, so I have given you one of our larger boats."

As he said this, he reached up to the edge of the quay and pulled the drain-pipe towards him. Sadly, this was now attached to Malcolm's grip, and whether Spiro would have expounded further on the substitution of an old twenty-seven foot boat for a new twenty-five foot one without prompting remains a mystery. He was quite unprepared for the heavy grip which followed the drain-pipe happily over the edge of the quay. This struck him an un-balancing blow in the chest, and he staggered backwards until his knees made contact with the cockpit push-pit rail*. He wind-milled his arms for a second before his knees buckled and his feet shot out from under him, sliding the plank off the coaming in the process; then Spiro cart-wheeled backwards into the cockpit as the grip and drainpipe followed the gang-plank into the water. Simultaneously Rex stepped confidently into mid-air where the gang-plank had been a moment before and with one startlingly loud obscenity plunged, flailing madly, into the dock.

The next few moments were pandemonium. Spiro groaned and thrashed in the cockpit, Rex breached and sounded in the water, and I, trying to retrieve Rex's passport and wallet, became slightly entangled with Malcolm, who was intent solely on the preservation of his baggage and the bloody drain-pipe to the total exclusion of all extraneous concerns. He quickly gave up trying to reach from the quay and cast wildly about for some other means to recover his bag. Finding nothing, and observing a particularly large fart of air escape from the grip, which presumably heralded the imminent final plunge, he cast the sedentary ways of a lifetime to the winds and made an elephantine leap for the back of the boat. His inelegant arrival coincided with a spasm of Spiro's boots, which dislodged his feet from their precarious landing-place on the tiny ledge of deck behind the cockpit and Malcolm glissaded effortlessly

---

* Fear not, reader of lubberly origins. A glossary is included at the back of the book. I frequently need it myself.

down the sloped stern. He ended up hanging from the back-stay with his legs in the water to the knee, from which position he kicked Rex's wallet and passport out of his hands. I managed to catch the passport as it arced through the air and Rex dived like a grampus to recover the sinking wallet, surfacing under Malcolm's bag and probably delaying it's sinking just long enough for Spiro to recover his equilibrium and get a boat-hook on it. Having dragged the sodden dead-weight into the cockpit, Spiro set good-humouredly about helping Malcolm back up the transom, and then let down the swimming ladder for Rex to climb out.

"Could you pass the plank up first, please?" he politely asked Rex, as calmly as if this had all been quite the normal way to board a boat.

Such mayhem, and all over in the blink of an eye. Seemingly seconds after the debacle began, the four of us were sat in the cockpit roaring with laughter: Spiro ruefully rubbed his bruised ribs, Malcolm rummaged in his bag trying to separate the wet items from the dry ones, and Rex spread his passport and the contents of his wallet out in the sun. Immense good will filled the air as the various feats and indignities were re-told, and, most significantly, the issue of the boat-switch was completely forgotten. The just reader will surely conclude that much of the blame accredited to my good self regarding the various failings of our stout vessel over the following weeks may justly be laid at the door of the Gladiator Piscatorial and his portable armoury.

* * *

Having lowered the remainder of the baggage onto the boat in a somewhat more controlled manner, we sent Rex below to dry and change. Then, after hanging Malcolm's wet gear out on the rails to dry, we followed Rex into the cabin.

It is an observation that I have made many times over my years on the unacceptable fringe of the yachting world that, whenever confronted with a strange boat, people behave like frightened rabbits; that is to say, they bolt below at the first possible opportunity. The outstanding manifestation of this troglodyte behaviour can be readily observed at any reputable boat-show, where row after row of gleaming boats stand apparently deserted apart from piles of unsavoury footwear around the access ladders. A quick scan around the deck and cockpit, for the sake of form, is swiftly followed by a headlong plunge into the bowels of the vessel to see how much room there is in the heads* of this year's model. Or perhaps it is the necessity of convincing the lady of the family that life without the craft in question can no longer be borne that drives the hopefuls below decks. Whatever the motive, it is as effective as an air-raid siren. Only rarely can a thoughtful viewer be seen gazing at the chain-plates which will hold up his mast in the dreaded 'bit of a blow in Biscay'. Seldom is the salesman's knowledge of the sail inventory options tested, or his comprehension of the effect on the boat's centre of effort of reefing the main before the genoa. "The anchor weight and chain calibre, Sir? Er, well it'll be in the brochure." But let him once forget the exact number of velour upholstery coverings offered, or stumble over the availability of the optional extra egg-cup holder in teak, and he might as well accept a commission-only contract to sell pork chops in Tel Aviv on the Sabbath as hope to make a crust at the yacht-sales game.

Once in the cabin, we found a standard four-berth layout, with a vee-berth in the forward cabin. Settee berths were sited on both sides of the main saloon, with a small galley immediately aft of the port one and a miniscule chart table perched on the end of the starboard. The varnish had seen considerably better days, and the Formica in the galley was sufficiently decrepit as to make one suspect that biological warfare researchers could have done worse with their time than to investigate a culture or two from under its lifting corners. A quick look in the icebox was a glimpse of Hell itself. There was a tatty old mat on the cabin-sole, and the companionway steps (which doubled as the engine-compartment cover) were partly coated with chipped and blackened varnish and liberally coated with a protective layer of spilled liquids of suspicious provenance. The head-lining of the cabin was sagging, off-white plastic, resembling that found in abandoned cars, and the upholstery was a decidedly jaded tartan in which red and coffee-stains fought for predominance. Rex described the pattern as, "Royal Stuart meets asylum dining-room wall."

---

*Toilets. Sorry, but there is simply no point becoming a sailor if you are happy with the English language just the way it is

The effect of the whole was dingy, made murkier still by the limited amount of light that entered by the hatchway and the opaque, scratched blueish Plexiglas of the cabin skylight. In short, to my two bachelor compadres, and to me — familiar with the very old charter-yachts to be found on the Norfolk Broads — the tatty old *Nissos* was a snug little home from home!

We took in the interior splendours of our vessel. Each to his own, Malcolm made a bee-line to the ludicrously small toilet compartment to test the facilities. Rex, now somewhat drier, started poking a discerning finger into mattresses to test their composition, and I, deciding that I had better look captain-ish, started rooting through the charts and navigating instruments. Spiro presented a broad back to the cabin as he rummaged deeply in the several cavernous and un-inviting looking lockers that were cunningly built into the galley-area. After a moment or two, he un-earthed a grubby-looking clear bottle, half-full of a water-like liquid. The label was a naïve design, as if it had been written by a child with a crayon. Spiro brandished the bottle triumphantly in his right hand, and with his left offered four narrow glasses of dubious cleanliness, each one slotted neatly onto one of his sausage-like fingers.

"I knew it..." he declared with a flash of the film-star smile that quite brightened in the gloomy cabin, "...they always leave a bottle of Ouzo somewhere!"

With the glasses filled and distributed, Spiro informed us that the Greek word for cheers is *Yamas*, and proposed a toast to the holiday. Looking back on the moment, I can see that it was a grave error not to have asked whether he meant ours or his, but hindsight is of course a very precise science. Ouzo is an aniseed aperitif closely related to the French *pastis* and, to my palate, nowhere near as welcome at this early hour as the brandy had been, but one man's meat is another man's poison, and Malcolm and Rex swiftly returned to the seedy-looking bottle for a refill.

With the second glass of aniseed death in my hand, I turned my back on the pleasantries in the cabin and went out on deck with the outward intent of having a look at the rigging, and the covert aim of getting rid of the ouzo over the side. Having deposited the stuff in the thoroughly undeserving water, I stomped heavily around on deck to lend verisimilitude to my stated quest, and, in doing so, did in fact spend a moment or two identifying the various halyards and winches. In the good old-fashioned style, these were all at the foot of the mast. Having done this, I proceeded to swing lustily in the standing-rigging with my substantial weight to test its tension. Unfortunately, the spare genoa halyard was also wire, and was made fast to the toe-rail in the vicinity of the shrouds, but the tail was unsecured and was held to the mast only by the friction imposed by the neck of the mainsail cover. Possibly influenced by the early assimilation of both brandy and ouzo, I mistook this for the adjacent shroud, and swinging carelessly on the wrong wire resulted in an undignified and noisy fall onto the coach roof as the halyard rendered through its head-block. From inside the boat came a raucous gust of laughter, but I rightly surmised that it's cause was the contents of the ouzo bottle rather than my discomfiture, so after a sly glance around to ensure that I had not been observed by outside agents, I started unlacing the sail-cover to have a look at the mainsail. Sadly, the moment I released the tension of the lacing at the neck of the cover, the spare genoa halyard which had recently been my downfall now completed it's humiliation of the proud skipper. Released from the clutches of the sail-cover, it raced eagerly up the mast, squiggled through its head-block and fell at my feet on the deck.

Like any quick-thinking criminal, I swiftly gathered the serpentine mass of the halyard into an inelegant coil, stepped back to the cockpit, and buried the evidence deep in a cockpit locker after a sidelong look to see that no-one was watching me from the cabin. I needn't have worried; my crew and the voluble Spiro were seated around a book at the table with the nearly empty ouzo bottle firmly between them, showing absolutely no interest in my nautical fossicking.

Finding myself at the blunt end of the boat, I resumed my investigations with a rummage through the contents of the lockers and surveyed the sheets, winches and other cockpit impedimenta. Then my beady little eye came to rest on the engine controls lurking behind a coil of genoa-furling line. Just give that a quick try, I thought, and with that, I advanced the throttle a touch in neutral, shouted a warning of my intentions down the hatch, and turned the key.

The first impression, as the engine rumbled easily to life, was that vibration of this magnitude should surely only be experienced when crossing an unstable rope-bridge in a steamroller with an eccentric fly-wheel and an intoxicated driver. The second impression was that an impression was all that one was left with… the drab marina, the lack-lustre concrete buildings, the haze-softened background of olive-green and white hills, even the brilliant blue of the sky, were all engulfed in a choking cloud of soot-black smoke.

One would not wish, at this early stage in the narrative, to achieve a reputation for exaggeration, so obvious comparisons such as the eruption of Mount Washington will be dispensed with in the interests of strict comparative accuracy; suffice it to say only that were any destroyer, upon coming face to face with an enemy battleship of evil intent, capable of enveloping itself in impenetrable smoke with anything like the speed and efficiency of the good ship *Nissos*, its crew would have been entitled to reduced insurance premiums. I wasn't quite left gasping for breath, but it became a matter of urgency to find the controls in the murk and stop the infernal machine again. As the death-rattle of the engine shuddered through the boat, eclipsing even the tooth-jarring reverberations of 'normal' operation, the tinkle of a glass shaken clean off the saloon table was heard through the hatchway. This was followed by a short, expressive word from Malcolm, which frankly did him no credit at all.

Within seconds, the evil cloud had disappeared, whipped away seawards by the fresh breeze blowing over the bow, and leaving only the transom dappled with oily soot as evidence of its passing. Rex emerged first from the cabin, cheeks a rosy red from the ravages of either the ouzo or the smoke. Malcolm and Spiro followed with an alacrity that spoke clearly of a good quantity of exhaust having eddied its way below, and a good, hearty fit of coughing was indulged in by all. It appeared that in the confines of the cabin, the effect of the nebulosity had been quite smothering, but even so I felt that Malcolm's hacking was a touch forced. True to form, it was Spiro who first re-acquired the power of comprehensible speech, saying, "It starts very easily, you see!"

To emphasise the point, he patted the coaming in an approving manner.

"It smokes a bit," I felt compelled to comment, but Spiro dismissed this lightly, saying that, "They all smoke a bit until they warm up."

I felt constrained to test this theory, so we re-started the engine. After a moment or two, the smoke-emissions reduced from the spectacular to the merely annoying, which, knowing at that time very little indeed about the function of diesel engines in general or injectors in particular, I decided was probably acceptable. There was no noticeable reduction in the incredible level of vibration, but Spiro explained that this was characteristic of the single-cylinder diesel engine, and quite normal. (So, of course, it is: later investigations, coupled with a basic ability in the lower levels of mathematics, however, revealed that this was a twin-cylinder model).

Spiro showed us quickly around the fuel, lubrication and cooling systems, and gestured grandly to a large plastic box inside the chart-table seat, remarking as he did so that there was a "very good toolbox". When we later came to open it and found only a cheap screwdriver, two rusty spanners, a light-bulb, a jubilee-clip and an oily rag, we could not on oath have said that he lied, since he had made no comment at all about the contents.

The hand-over of the deck was unremarkable. We raised the mainsail, which seemed to be in good condition (which transpired to be the case) and we rolled out the genoa, which flapped vigorously in the strengthening wind and also appeared sound (which transpired *not* to be the case). We were also introduced to the scarred, battered and superannuated anchor-winch, which appeared to be the oldest, most dilapidated, misused, ill-conceived and poorly-maintained piece of Victoriana on the entire hoary vessel.

* * *

And so it came to pass, some hour or so after we had first set eyes on the good ship *Nissos*, that we found ourselves seated once more around the cabin table, ouzo glasses replenished with the last of the bottle, and signing papers concerning inventories and cash-deposits. Outside, the sound of halyards tapping on a thousand masts rose slowly but steadily as the wind strengthened. Inside, where I could no longer throw it away, I found that my ouzo was not unpalatable after the first shock, and my complacency waxed majestically. My ship was stout, my crew stalwart (or perhaps the other way around) and Spiro was proving to be no end of a fine chap, with his anecdotes about less accomplished sailors than ourselves interspersed with some well-meaning do's and don'ts about local conditions, and advice on ports to visit. Perhaps there seemed to be rather a lot of don'ts, but so what... Oh, you found another one! Yes, please, Spiro, just a splash... and he did seem to be recommending ports within a very close distance of the marina, but perhaps he just didn't want to tire us... OOPS! Good job it was empty...well, just one more, then...Yes, yes,

Spiro. We'll be careful to listen to the weather-forecast every morning. What time did you say it was in English? *Six thirty!!!* God! Yes, all right, we'll do that…

After some time in this vein, Spiro stood up and stretched.

"Well, time for the Port Police. Can I just have your certificate, please?" he asked.

There was a moment's silence, during which I glanced round to see who this last request had been directed at before realising that I was the intended recipient. It transpired that to hire a boat in Greece, the skipper and one of the crew require certificates of competency, not unreasonably, but no-one had informed us of the fact. Our spirits sank as, with typically British respect for the sanctity and omnipotence of documents, we saw an insurmountable problem arising. We reckoned without Spiro, however, who produced from under the seat of his jeep a small, portable typewriter, and from a wallet of papers drew an impressively headed piece of notepaper purporting to be from a prestigious English yacht club. With these, he swiftly composed a testimonial that made me appear to be Grace Darling with a willy. Without batting an eyelid, he added a postscript naming Rex as a competent crew and got Malcolm to sign it, thus distancing himself from any evidence of involvement. He showed his true artistry with the application of a seal, made by imprinting a coat of arms on the reverse of a large coin onto sealing-wax. The finished forgery was then carefully folded and creased with a dampened thumb to 'age' it. Armed with this document, which as an instrument of infamous falsehood rivalled even Chamberlain's letter from Munich, I set off with Spiro to complete the formalities.

The officer on duty at the Port Police office was, to say the least, disinterested. He completed the official charter agreement and crew-list without apparently looking at them, and the lack of interest he showed in Spiro's masterpiece lead me to believe that he would have been just as happy with a piece of newspaper, perhaps even more so had it had fish and chips in it. He did open my passport, but since he at no time looked at my face, I couldn't really see the point of the exercise, and he spoke only twice during the transaction; the first time to fire a staccato question at Spiro, and the second when he treated the telephone receiver to what seemed like a particularly vicious reprimand for having the temerity to ring during his 'busy' period. Finally, he set about laboriously and heavily stamping every piece of paper within his reach with the circular blue and white stamp, without which nothing can happen, does happen or has ever happened in the Hellenic Democracy since the last Turk was evicted. All this he accomplished without once taking his eyes off a small black-and-white television. Finally, he handed a sheaf of multi-coloured papers back to Spiro, and without looking more than obliquely away from the lugubrious singer on the set, he muttered something about 'Captain'. By the time we had turned away, he was again watching the television with a diligence which, had he been watching a radar screen, would have been highly laudable.

It was just as we were getting back into Spiro's chariot that the significance of the policeman's parting word struck home. He had called me 'Captain'!

As the sudden realization that I had been elevated from the status of mere tourist to the exalted rank of Captain sank in, I felt my chest expand and my chin rise irresistibly. My folder of ship's papers tucked purposefully under my arm, I climbed authoritatively into the tatty little jeep as though it were an admiral's barge at Spithead, and gazed disdainfully at the mere people about me as we drove back to the boat. Oh, if only the policeman had known how that one little word had unleashed my ego, had he conceived what dreams, what aspirations came to fruition in those two innocent syllables, had he realised what a flood of self-confidence he had unleashed in my breast, he would surely have spoken with greater circumspection. (I had yet to learn that in a country which has more boats than people, any man who is *not* a captain of something is either dead or locked up.)

There came to my mind a rather pompous shipmaster with whom I had once sailed; a man of whom it was said that, in his own opinion, the only difference between himself and God was that God could not use a sextant. At the time, I laughed and scorned. Now, Oh! How I appreciated the burden on those casually-epauletted shoulders; how I felt the responsibilities and lofty concerns concealed behind those wrinkle-free brows. I could finally comprehend the magnificence and solitude of command. With one casual word, on a lazy, windy, autumnal Greek morning, a monster was created.

By the time we arrived back at the boat, I had been subjected to a further litany of cautions, warnings and conservative counsel from Spiro, but apart from the mechanical responses of "Mm... Ah ha... Yes... I see... No, of course not, Spiro...", these elicited nothing from me. I knew he meant well, of course, but he wasn't a *captain*, was he, poor chap? My ambition waxed alarmingly, and diverged sharply from that of Spiro... and, I fear, from reality too. A glance at my watch showed that it was still not midday, with a pleasant stiff-ish breeze and good visibility. On board, the ruddy complexions and depleted ouzo bottle might have indicated to a person less self-concerned than me the true state of my crew, but I was blind to all but the chart and compass. As Spiro began recommending good bars and tavernas in the neighbourhood of the marina, I busied myself with dividers and parallel rules. Spiro started on a round of farewells and invited us to have an ouzo with him in the marina café that evening. Quietly, I remarked, "Thanks very much, Spiro, but I think we'll get a bit of shopping in and then get going for Aegina."

The effect of this statement on our Greek friend was somewhat similar to that on a devout nun who has just been informed that the Pope's daughter has been caught buying condoms. He looked open-mouthed at me for a moment as he digested the fact that I hadn't taken a blind bit of notice of anything he had said in the last hour or so, and then, composing his face into a rather hurt *Et tu, Brute* look, began to explain why it would not be a good idea to voyage forth today... wind bound to get stronger... catch up on a bit of sleep... wind often goes westerly in the afternoons... gets cold in the evening at this time of year... much better to go in the morning. It was an impassioned speech, and it had evidently won over my two compatriots. It would have won over most people, I suspect, for he was a gifted orator, was our Spiro, as befits a citizen of Athens. But it didn't convince me: I was a Captain!

"It's only three or four hours... good sailing wind, shame to waste it... nice to get to an island tonight," I countered. The nautical side of Rex wavered and then began to swing to my side of the argument. Spiro, realising that he had to convince the jury as the maniac Captain was beyond reason, addressed himself to Malcolm and Rex and became quite impassioned. After a short address during which he cunningly played the 'importance of democracy in a successful holiday' card rather heavily, he suddenly sensed that the argument had swung his way. Feeling that Malcolm and Rex were now firmly on his side, he played his masterstroke; suddenly becoming airy and unconcerned.

"Oh, well, why don't I run you up to one of the bars and let you decide amongst yourselves?" he said. (He really *didn't* want that boat to go to sea!) Any move to a bar was instantly approved by my two desperadoes, and shortly we were comfortably ensconced in a jovial little establishment quite a long way from the marina, up a maze of backstreets. Seeing us established there, and knowing that we would have a hell of a job to find our way back to the boat, Spiro recommended a bottle of wine and left us with a cheery wave and a 'Bon Voyage'. He was probably quite confident that he had scotched any thought of sailing that day; after all, he must have thought, Rex and Malcolm were well of his way of thinking. He was well mistaken. I had only just got my first captaincy, and I was damned if I was going to sit back and watch it degenerate into mere democracy!

* * *

We drank our bottle in the bar, and then I commenced my counter-attack by suggesting some food. In the company of three stalwart trenchermen like ourselves, such a motion was ever likely to pass the house with an overwhelming majority, and as I lead them towards the taverna opposite I congratulated myself that I had started the process of sobering my crew by getting them out of the bar into a restaurant.

Fifteen All, Spiro!

It so happened that the taverna in question was offering on that particular afternoon something slightly short of a cornucopia of good things. The choice, in fact, came down to some rather sad-looking meat balls called '*sounzoukakia*' or a wilting moussaka. The unanimous points decision went to the former. This proved to be an excellent choice, since their flavour was good and in no way represented by their appearance. They were swiftly swilled down with a bottle of white wine which Rex, our oenophile, pronounced to be disgustingly drinkable despite having no label. We emerged after a mere half hour with The Motley ecstatic at the quality and price of the meal, and the captain chortling inwardly as the contented crew were lead docilely into a small general store a few yards down the road.

Fifteen-Thirty, Spiro.

With glee, I found that the younger son of the lady in the store spoke rather better English than I did myself. Whilst Rex and Malcolm were rooting diligently through the saturated fats and high carbohydrates section of the shop, I made a Machiavellian little deal with the urchin that we would buy at least five thousand drachmae worth of grub if he could organise some transport back to the boat for it. This neatly solved the problem of finding our way back to the marina, whilst at the same time ensuring that The Motley were not sidetracked into any more hostelries on the way. Mentally noting that it also bypassed the need to cross that bloody road on foot again, I was well pleased with my chicanery. My two dupes presented themselves at the till with three thousand drachmae worth of assorted calories, which I made up to five thousand with a quick raid of the wine and spirits department. A case of beer tossed in with an airy remark about not running short hiked the total nearer to six thousand, which brought a devastated death-trap of a Citroen to the door.

So daunting was the idea of committing their lives to the safekeeping of this migratory monument to incurable oxidisation that Malcolm and Rex were only persuaded to get into it by playing on their instinctive fear of physical exercise. The wizened driver (Rex suggested that as his primary skill lay in keeping his charge all together in one piece, he should properly be termed a 'herder' rather than a driver) grinned at us through a disaster of dental work which eclipsed even the state of his vehicle as he kangarooed through the tangle of backstreets and junctions in which Spiro had sought to en-maze us. Apart from the steering wheel, the only part of the thing that seemed to function adequately was the asthmatic horn. Gear-changes involved fearful wrestling matches, sometimes requiring the use of two hands, whilst braking was apparently achieved by our desiccated chauffeur gripping the rim of the wheel tightly in his gnarled hands and sucking mightily on his one intact tooth. This habit led Malcolm to christen him Fang-io.

Eventually we lurched across 'Hell's Highway' with our eyes tightly closed and slid to a halt in a cloud of rust-particles, dust and bilingual profanity at the end of our quay. Rex thanked Fang-io politely for some interesting cardiac arhythms, which thanks he reciprocated enthusiastically with a manic cackle and further abuse of the horn, and we trotted up the pier to the boat. With all the bottles in our shopping-bags, we jingled along the quay like a troop of household cavalry trotting down the mall.

Fifteen-Forty, Spiro!

Back onboard the good ship lollipop, I set the two of them to work stowing the victuals in the galley. By common consent on my part, arising out of absolutely no discussion whatsoever, Malcolm was appointed Chef for the voyage (due to his infallible ability to select exactly the right packet sauce mix to complement a meal *after* another had already proved unsatisfactory), whilst Rex assumed responsibility for the onerous post of cellar-master (because he was possessed of the uncanny knack of segregating wines into even more classifications than Red, White and Rosé). For myself, I had reserved responsibility for 'The Deck', although what actual duties this might have entailed was unclear even in my mind, since I sure as hell had cleaning it allocated to The Motley. Anyway, I assembled the crew at the helm and made these dispositions loftily, my ego swelling a further few impossible points at the ease of their acceptance. They ambled off below, and, thus emboldened, I determined that the moment was ripe for the final act which would establish beyond doubt my authority as Master Before God of the Good Ship *Nissos*.

Everything was in my favour; the wind was fair, blowing a good stiff force four by now and the island of Aegina lay expectantly fourteen miles to leeward, just visible over our *Festung Europa* seawall. I sneaked forward, and let-go the lazy-line which moored our bows. It sank swiftly into the murky water. I then walked nonchalantly aft, unlashed the tiller, discreetly pulled in the plank that served as our precarious garden path, and slipped the stern-lines. The boat, securely nestled between the two adjacent ones, was still reluctant to leave the quay, which gave me a moment or two to tidy up the stern-lines before taking up position at the tiller. I advanced the throttle, started the engine, rammed it into gear and shot forward into the harbour to a chorus of "What the Hell!" and "'Ere!" from down below. I swung the boat to port, which had the dual advantage of pointing me towards the exit and extricating me from the cloud of smoke which was, like the poor, ever with us.

FAULT!

Just as the boat was gathering speed, the engine surged once, spat an unusually dense gob of smoke, and stopped dead. Coincidentally, this occurred just as Rex appeared in the hatchway to enquire what was I under the impression that I was doing? (That, at least, was the fundamental import of his query, although the actual wording, I felt, did little credit to an educated man.)

Unfortunately, I was unable to satisfy his curiosity directly since I now found myself broadside-on to the wind and drifting rapidly down onto the boats on the quay to leeward. Amongst these boats were two with enormous bowsprits, which now appeared to me as, no doubt, the cocktail-stick appears to the hapless olive at five minutes to martini-time. Gibbering, "The Genny, the Genny!" I dived across the cockpit to release the genoa furling-line and then, bracing my foot on the lee side of the cockpit, I heaved mightily on the genoa sheet.

As the sail began to unroll, I realized that the weather sheet was still coiled around the port winch and, in hastily casting it off, I missed my chance to check the furling line as it ran out. The genoa slammed out uncontrolled and filled with a thunderclap which effectively cut short Rex's query as to who Jenny was. It also sent seismic spasms through the rigging, brought half a hundred heads in the marina whipping round or out of hatchways to see what was going on, and ripped the sheet out of my hand. The sail flogged like gunfire, people on boats to leeward howled advice, threats and imprecations laced the air. Malcolm joined in from below and the engine buzzer started buzzing helpfully to let me know that the engine had stopped. All things considered, I don't think I have ever heard such a volume of conflicting sound. As I heaved mightily on the sheet to tame the sail, I roared at Rex to get me a winch-handle. In a small and miraculously uncluttered part of my brain, I recorded that neither of my companions had any clue as to what a winch-handle might be, or where it might make its nest, so gibbering wildly without due care and attention once again, I abandoned the genoa to the staccato cracking act that it did so well and heaved Rex out of the way to get at the winch-handles just inside the hatchway.

By the time I was heaving at the sheet again, having mentally excluded from my mind some terse, pithy and no doubt pertinent questions from my 'competent crew', we were disappointingly close to the boats to leeward. In fact, I could see as I started to get the sheet under control that one of the helpful chappies giving advice with such startlingly red faces was Spiro himself. After what seemed like a geological age or two, the genoa filled. But could it fill gradually, like a civilised piece of Terylene? Oh, no! Not this spiteful rag. Taking full advantage of a small wind-shift, the genoa did its Thor sound-effect again, only this time I had hold of the sheet. Consequently, the rigging orgasmed once again, the boat heeled savagely, and shot off like a rocket. From below, a bellow of rage coinciding with the crash of tumbling stores and heavy objects indicated that Malcolm was getting some impromptu training in the art of stowing the sea-going galley, but my attention was riveted to the spectacle of a threatening bowsprit passing at five knots speed and about five inches distance from Rex's left ear. It kissed the top of the life-buoy, missed the backstay by a fraction, and was gone from our lives as rapidly as it had entered them.

It is virtually anticlimactic to record that we cleared the end of the pier by a comfortable eighteen inches. (Rex is of the opinion that the term 'missed the end of the pier' would be more appropriate here, but I have explained to him that this would imply that we had at some stage been out of control of the situation.)

With the genoa drawing splendidly, I wrestled the tiller to bring us on course for the exit, only to find that the boarding plank, which I had omitted to lash down, was now contesting the windward side of the cockpit with me. By the time I had sorted *that* out, we were creaming across the middle basin of the marina at five or six knots.

Not very far in front of us, on the eastern wall, were some *awfully* expensive-looking gin-palaces. To my left, upwind, lay the basin of the marina, and to my right the exit. To negotiate the way out to sea required that I make what I can only describe as a 'U' turn between two fifteen foot concrete walls. I was left with three generous options. The first was to come head to wind and anchor, but I doubted whether I would have the time to get forward, unlash and drop the anchor before drifting back onto the wall. In any case, anchoring would have been the act of a desperate madman, because once an anchor was down in that maze of heavy ground-tackle, we would have had about as much chance of lifting it again as we would have of winning the Grand National on a clothes-horse. The second option was to perform a gybe right in the exit and run out to sea, a manoeuvre in which the fifteen-foot concrete walls were designed to heavily penalise the imprecise helmsman. Neither of these alternatives was attractive, but the third was too horrible to contemplate, and so as I saw it coming closer, I put the helm over and went for number two.

The next few seconds were all a bit confused. The genoa went into its Wagnerian timpani routine again with all the gusto of Pavarotti hearing the opening bars of *Nessun Dorma*, the engine-alarm wailed plaintively on, Malcolm's face appeared at the companionway to contribute some understandable but hardly constructive advice which seemed to have a lot to do with ancestry and anatomy, and I shouted, "Ready to gybe!"

I did this in my finest Stentorian voice before the thought flitted across my mind that this crew thought 'gybing' was a style of dancing originating in the 'Fifties, and changed it to the more proletarian, "Get your bloody heads down!"

I heaved the tiller up, and we shot round in a dizzying arc which removed Malcolm from the companionway and prostrated Rex across the Port sheet-winch. The sail filled, and we found ourselves broad-reaching furiously down a concrete channel, causing consternation amongst the serried ranks of anglers lining the inner wall. Abuse, threats, lead weights and putrescent bait were liberally hurled at us as we tore past, and Malcolm emerged once again to shout, "Sorry, mate," at each of his spiritual brothers. Rex so far recovered himself as to stand erect and alternately give a stately bow or a regal wave to anglers puce with outrage.

We were expectorated suddenly from the end of the channel, taking a few years off the life-expectancy of a motor-boat skipper who was just entering, and I headed the boat away down-wind for the distant, hazy shape of what I thought was probably Aegina. I trimmed the sail, switched off the engine ignition, and sat down. All this I accompanied with a casual whistle which belied my sweaty palms and churning belly. My heart felt like it was fitted with a three-volt pacemaker into which the surgeon had carelessly put a twelve-volt battery, and I appeared to have developed a nasty twitch in the left eye, but I kept my voice casual.

"'Bout three hours to Aegina, then, eh? Malcolm, me old son, you'll have to learn to get the galley really well secured when we go to sea."

The stream of expressive words which followed this friendly advice appeared to have little mutual connection, except that you would hope not to hear any of them on children's T.V.

Game, Set and Match, Spiro!

CHAPTER THREE

AN INTRODUCTION TO THE ISLANDS

In which we contemplate ruins ancient and modern... The triumph of the Engineer... Democracy at the point of a tome... Perdika... A cultural introduction... The sirens of the night... Our first ruin... Our first wreck... An encounter related... The approach to Poros.

Relative calm having been re-established on board the boat, there was time to take stock. On the positive side, we were sailing splendidly with the wind well aft of the starboard beam, the magnificent vista could hold no secrets from us in the crystal-clear air, and Malcolm had reluctantly informed us that no irreparable damages (by which I assumed that he meant booze) had been sustained in our departure from Alimos. We had, apparently, ample time to reach Aegina before nightfall, and Rex had proved himself sufficiently capable at steering to allow me to go forward to raise the mainsail. Malcolm had completed stowing the provisions, albeit with much seditious muttering about someone he called Ahab, which I chose to ignore. At least he didn't seem to get seasick below decks, which augured well for his appointment as cook. Not that I envisaged much cooking at sea, or even in port for that matter, but I had lofty ambitions about the frequency and variety of tasty little snacks which would hopefully accompany a copious flow of cool beers to help *me* enjoy *my* sailing! I spared a moment to congratulate myself heartily on my shrewd selection of the crew.

On the negative side was the relatively minor problem that, apart from the general designation of 'Aegina', I had absolutely no idea where we were going. Then there was the rather more pertinent question of the engine; unless I could contrive to learn something about diesel engines fairly swiftly, I was going to have to sail into whatever harbour we arrived at. Oh, joy! I began to mentally sift through everything I knew about faults in small diesels, but that took a depressingly short time, so I resorted instead to a private mental catalogue of engine failures. Within a very short period, I had worked myself into an internal state of seething rage as I recalled the myriad of instances of mechanical treachery when my enjoyment, life or dignity had been imperilled by these jumped-up, misanthropic amalgamations of oscillating alloy, these fickle and faithless fiends. Why I am discriminated against by what are generally accepted to be insensate, soulless *things*, I cannot tell; yet a brief perusal of the case-histories will convince the staunchest sceptic that it is so, and, God knows, there is certainly no shortage of witnesses! Not only do engines fail me in their multitudes, they do it for the most obscure reasons and with a sense of timing that argues genuine malice.

Take, for example, the day when, eager to impress a young lady of flawless feature, I borrowed a small boat with an outboard motor to visit some of the islands on the lake. I had never set eyes on the blasted machine before in my life, but it had it in for me from the word go. Only one miserable island had we visited before the engine declined any further interest in the proceedings. I adjusted its choke, I checked its fuel-cock, I sweated and laboured at the pull-start. Nothing. I removed its blaguardly spark-plug, dried it, and tested it for a spark, whereupon it joyously electrocuted me. I pumped the little wotsit on the carburettor, and it threw up onto my shirt. I exhausted whatever mechanical supplications I was capable of, but not a splutter would it utter. Finally, tormented beyond reason by its smug inertia, I gave one last titanic heave on the starter-rope, which promptly broke and lashed the young lady quite severely across the cheek. I was left to row a heavy boat some two miles home in the company of a hysterical girl who believed that her looks were ruined forever. I don't believe I ever saw her again. Needless to say, having repaired the pull-start, the bloody machine started first swing. There was never any explanation for it, other than wickedness. If it hadn't belonged to a friend, I would have taken my revenge by putting sand in its fuel.

It is not only nautical machinery which is hostile to me. I had a car once. A French one, which might account for the quite extraordinarily unpredictable service I was accustomed to receiving from it. The engine was nurtured as rarely an engine has been nurtured. It had regular doses of oil, water and fuel, in the correct qualities and quantities, at the correct times, and even in the correct orifices. The reward for this devotion? It ran moderately well most of the time, and at others simply would not start. This happened at any time, although it definitely didn't like rain. At the slightest hint of precipitation… cough, splutter… and silence! It did not require to be actually struck by rain… a darkish cloud on the horizon, or a pessimistic look from a weather-forecaster was enough to induce inertia in some bleak and desolate moorland waste. Then, after an hour or so, it would simply start again. One day, one of those Lake District days when the rain comes up at you, the false Gallic contraption failed about thirty yards short of the crest of a hill. I was incensed with rage! Another thirty yards and I could have coasted down the other side to my destination, but oh, no! I sat for some seconds at the wheel, spitting with rage. I explained the distance to the crest in metres, in case the thing had misunderstood how short a distance it was, and then I started swearing at the damn thing, in French, just in case it should be in any doubt as to my feelings. Had there been a telephone nearby, I would have invested some time and money in abusing the French embassy. Finally, deciding that, whatever it cost me, I was not going to get soaked yet again, I engaged first gear and drove it over the crest of the hill with the starter-motor, screaming at the top of my voice "Take that, you sod!" as it whined and lurched piteously. Two weeks later, I sold the thing for scrap, on the condition that I could watch it die in the crusher.

I could go on for hours like this, anecdote after anecdote, time and again at crucial moments, treachery after perfidy after stab in the back. And now within minutes of starting a new voyage with a new crew, here we were again in a foreign country, on a foreign boat, with a foreign engine and travelling down a road so familiar that I half expected to find the Hole in the Wall at the end of it. I foamed at the mouth in convulsions of rage, but quietly, lest The Motley realise that I was at a stand.

Into these dark thoughts, the voice of Rex intruded.

"That must be the Acropolis up there," he said, and pointed out over the starboard quarter to where the city of Athens proper lay behind the strip of sprawling coastal suburbs. Sure enough, perched upon a mighty slab of rock over the city, the columns of the great temple were easily discernable in the bright sunlight, and we all three sat entranced in the cockpit passing the binoculars back and forth.

"How old is it, anyway?" I asked. Malcolm shrugged, but Rex looked thoughtful.

"It must be Hellenistic, late Hellenistic, I would say," he ventured. Malcolm looked sceptical.

"Would that be before or after Pearl Harbour, then?"

Rex grinned. "Oh, it was built about five or six hundred B.C., I think. It's not actually all that old... about two and a half thousand years or so."

"So pardon my hignorance, yer honour, but what exactly would you call 'old' then?"

Rex pursed his lips in exaggerated thought. "Well, Mycanae is older, about a thousand B.C.... and the Minoan stuff in Crete goes back to about fifteen hundred."

"Fifteen hundred!" cried Malcolm. "...You mean they finished it just after lunch!"

"G.M.T. of course."

"Ah. Bit of luck, they'll be back to fix the roof tomorrow."

"I'll take it that's your Parthenon shot?"

I chipped in at this stage, sufficiently impressed by Rex's classical knowledge to forget that I was supposed to be the omniscient guiding light of this odyssey. "Are we likely to be seeing any ruins this trip, then?" I asked. Malcolm was onto this like a mongoose onto a rheumatic cobra.

"Oh, *you* are asking *us* now, are you Bligh?"

"Well," I temporized, "... if there's a few ruins about, it might be as well to work them into the general scheme of things."

Malcolm pointed down the companion steps. "Listen, Hornblower. The only Greek ruin you need to concern yourself with right now is that alleged engine. And whatever miracle you are about to perform, I have a sneaking suspicion that you are going to need a bit more in the way of technical support than this." He produced the toolbox, open to display its contents, (or, rather, lack of them) and then closed it and threw it into my lap. "Will you make the initial incision at the iliac point, Doctor?" he enquired, with a wolfish grin.

"You'll get a bloody incision in a minute," was the best I could manage in reply.

Here it was, the moment of truth. What was I going to do about the damn machine? If I couldn't fix it, we couldn't sail back into Alimos, and getting Spiro to come to Aegina would probably take ages. I resigned myself to crawling into the dirty, oily hole under the steps where the thing lived. Mustering an air of martyrdom, I opened my mouth to make the announcement.

"I'll have a look at that."

I closed my mouth again, hastily. It was Rex who had spoken.

That's it, of course, delegate, you mug!

"Know a bit about diesels, do you Rex?" I enquired as casually as possible.

"Oh, we did a course on them during the ag. degree, and my car's a diesel anyway."

Thank you, God!

"O.K, then, you have a look," I breezed, "…I'm better with petrol engines really."

Malcolm wasn't having that. "You must have bloody big spark-plugs on these ships of yours then."

We were separated by Rex driving Malcolm back into the cabin so that he could get at the engine, which ended that little bout of acrimony. Shortly, I could hear the sounds of the engine cover and steps being removed, followed by Rex asking Malcolm for a light. There then ensued several brutal slaps as the torch was shown the path of righteousness, and then a long silence, broken only by position-changing grunts as the preliminary investigation began. I settled back, luxuriating in the fact that I was in command of a fine vessel, sailing pleasant waters, with a fair wind, a cook in the galley, and an engineer (university trained, no less!) in the engine-room. A great feeling of peace came over me. A beer would just have set the seal on it, but with both of my stalwart fellows half inside the engine compartment, I didn't think asking for one would be the finest idea in the world. I just got on with enjoying my sailing.

I looked ahead. The island of Aegina was clearer now, with the larger buildings discernable. Behind me, the coastal buildings of the metropolis were merging into an amorphous concretion with the distance. We were really getting somewhere! But where? Other than the fact that the chart showed four harbours on Aegina, I knew about as much about the place as Christopher

Columbus had known about his destination. Well, that's not quite true; I could actually see my goal, so I knew that it existed, and I had a sneaking suspicion that Greek drachmae were accepted there. But beyond that, nothing. And on reflection, there wasn't much I could do about that, with the chart stuck below. I mentally filed the choice of course and port under 'too hard, try again later', and set about comfortably contemplating what sort of magnificent seafood spread the drachmae in my pocket would buy.

These agreeable ponderings were interrupted by a muffled voice from below demanding, "I need a pair of pliers!" Malcolm replied that, regrettably, pliers did not fall within the scope of our comprehensive toolbox, and would some barbecue tongs do? Rex said that he doubted it, but I was complacent. If the chap knew enough to recognise that a particular tool was required, I was quietly confident that he was also sufficiently ingenious to find something else to substitute for it. I was right.

"That's no good," came the voice. "Have you got a pair of scissors?"

Out of the hatchway spun an indescribably mangled pair of cheap tin salad tongs. They were followed shortly by an equally shattered pair of scissors. Then a thought stuck me. Time to take a hand, and show a bit of skipperly omniscience.

"What do you need, Rex?" I called.

"Some bloody pliers. There's a hose loose in here. The fuel-pipe's in a bloody awful condition."

Malcolm is not slow to take up a cue. "Oh, Danny boy, the pipe, the pipe's appalling," he sang in an atrocious Irish accent. He received no lasting applause for this sally, and had the decency to look penitent for a second or so.

"Have a look in the end of my red bag," I told him. He did, emerging with an unsavoury cocktail of socks and underwear from the previous day. I redirected him to the other end of the bag, where he found a leather scabbard, which I had belatedly remembered packing. One tries to forget about these items: they are the sort of thing given to yachtsmen for Christmas, containing a selection of rarely-used but highly nautical-looking tools. They are worn in a scabbard on a belt, so that one can conveniently forget to take them off before walking into the yacht-club bar, where it is the belief of the wearer that they will convey to the awed topers therein the impression that here is a horny-handed mariner of some renown. The esteem in which the wearer is actually held is indicated by the fact that, in one yacht-club with which I am familiar, these sets are known as 'prat-packs', and so it was with some diffidence that I admitted to owning one. However, amongst the tools in the portable compendium were an incredibly stiff pair of pliers and a nasty, cheap, Chinese adjustable spanner. The pliers were handed in to Rex in his oily grotto, and the sporadic grunting resumed.

Time passed most pleasantly, and with little sense of its passing, for me at any rate. As we cleared away from the lee of the shore to windward, the seas began to build. The wind held, so that the boat raced along with the rigging thrumming and the water swooshing satisfactorily past as we half-surfed down the quartering waves. I was in hog-heaven and, to my discredit, I so lost track of the time that I cannot tell whether Rex was in the engine-compartment for a minute, an hour or more. To my even greater discredit, I didn't care then, and am only feeling bad about it now by trying very hard. Those morals again… one day, I swear! Ah, well. Let us just say that it was some time later when Rex appeared in the scarred wooden frame of the hatchway. He looked suitably tousled, a touch sweaty, and had a most authentic smudge of oil on his cheek. I resisted the urge to applaud.

"Give her a turn, and keep going 'till I tell you," he said. I did. The engine ground and whirred, it coughed and then it spluttered. Next it just whirred. The buzzer buzzed with its peculiarly mocking note.

"Give it some bloody throttle!" came a muffled cry from the cabin. Cocking my right leg over the tiller to control it, I went into a curious legs-spread, head-down position reminiscent of Rodin's Vomiter, and managed to manipulate ignition and throttle simultaneously whilst maintaining a semblance of a course.

The engine ground and whirred. It coughed. It farted. And suddenly, just as I tried the throttle-lever hard forward against the stop, it sprang to juddering life and spewed out the customary choking black cumulonimbus. This roiled briefly into the lee side of the cockpit before streaming away down-wind. The engine roared insanely until I retarded the throttle a bit, whereupon it settled down to gurgle, shudder and rattle in a contentedly asthmatic manner. The exhaust died to a mere miasma, and when I engaged the gear-lever, I was gratified to see a healthy prop-wash neatly bisecting the wake.

A dishevelled Rex emerged from the hatch.

"Sounds good," I enthused. He raised an eyebrow. If my concept of 'sounding good' resembled the death-rattle of a bull-buffalo with emphysema, he could concur, he said; otherwise, he thought the engine to be in the final stages of a terminal illness, but given light usage and a good portion of luck, he did not totally despair of it's lasting the fortnight. Coming from a cynical pessimist like Rex, I took this to be an excellent prognosis, and, promptly dismissing the engine from my mind, I proposed a beer. Rex proposed re-interring the engine, and Malcolm proposed deciding where the hell we were going.

The 'prat-pack' was re-assembled and, for the first time in the voyage, I received a modicum of recognition for my contribution. It didn't stop Malcolm from ceremoniously cleaning his nails with the marlin-spike, but the set had proved its worth, and was hereafter accorded a special stowage within easy reach of cabin or cockpit. It was hung in the hatchway, where it remained all voyage, inflicting lacerations of the upper thigh on returning drunks.

***

Beers materialised, the steps were returned from whence they came and the chart brought into the cockpit. With a nasty whiff of recurring democracy, the first planning session of the voyage was called to order.

The planning of a route with regard to absolutely every consideration of navigation is a principle enshrined in the teachings of maritime lore. Confusion will easily occur at sea when details and minutiae are neglected in 'passage planning'. I know it for a fact... I speak as one who has sailed all day only to arrive at an island where the only pub was closed for a week for restoration. What a fine feast of condensed milk and sardines we had that night!

But, to the story. A wooden, multi-articulated thing lurking in a cabin locker had been plausibly identified by Malcolm as a cockpit table, and after a few incredibly frustrating moments, this parody of a dwarf's deck-chair was transformed into a small, barely functional table large enough to make all operations in the cockpit impossible, whilst not being quite large enough to be useful. Onto this Malcolm put a book I was unfamiliar with, and the chart. The latter he weighted down with the three cold beers. Initially these held the chart against wind and roll admirably, although their efficiency declined rapidly throughout the meeting until their replacement became a matter of urgency. The chart itself had spent its entire life folded into quarter-size to fit on the less than extravagant chart-table, and consequently had disintegrated along the folds. This made it a trifle difficult plotting courses over the furry-edged creases, which clung to the rubber feet of the parallel rules with the tenacity of Velcro on a poodle, but I was eventually able to determine that we seemed to be on a rough course for the south side of Aegina. This was most encouraging, as visually we were in fact heading for the south side of an island... although Rex, who was sitting on the other side of the chart, took a moment or two to agree with this assessment.

I proceeded, therefore, to address the meeting on the subject of a suitable haven for the night, managing to drown out some muttered motion from Malcolm about 'setting some ground rules'. Waffling mightily to stop Malcolm getting any more of his proportional representation rubbish in, I searched the chart out of the corner of my eye for a suitable harbour.

"What we need," I prevaricated boldly, "...is good shelter from the North and East, a taverna for dinner, and a quay to moor to. I'm buggered if I'm going to blow up the dinghy if I can help it..."

"Perdika," interjected Malcolm. It sounded like one of his outlandish oaths, so I democratically ignored him.

"...Then we need a bit of cash in the morning and some fresh water if possible. I suppose you two are going to insist on cleanliness..."

"Perdika's got showers." Malcolm again.

"...And last but not least," I concluded, "somewhere where we can have a morning dip... that's the way to keep clean without wasting fresh water."

"Bloody Perdika, I've told you, Ahab!"

"What do you mean, Perdition?" I demanded in exasperation. Malcolm shook his head, more in sorrow than anger, it seemed.

"Not perdition," he explained, "Perdika."

"What the hell is a Perdika?" I demanded with some heat. Malcolm stabbed the chart with a rather oily finger in the general vicinity of the South-West corner of Aegina Island.

"Not *a* Perdika, Queeg. Perdika is the place we're going tonight. It's got a tourist office which changes money, a quay, good shelter from everything except a west wind, something called 'moderate holding', whatever that might be, water on the quay, swimming outside the mole, showers and telephone facilities, a bus to Aegina town and an ancient monument, taxis, ice... and most importantly, a good selection of fish-tavernas. He paused for a moment before adding casually, "The south side of the harbour is a restricted area... military."

I stared in desperation at the chart. Sure enough, there, partly covered by an oily fingerprint, was a small bay marked 'Perdika', but nothing, not even one of those little magenta yacht symbols, to confirm or deny Malcolm's information. I was desperately searching the margin for some pencilled notes that I had missed when Rex chipped in, "It's described as very pleasant."

I gave in. "How do you know?" I asked, and was treated to my first example of one of Malcolm's rather unpleasant, foxy smiles of victory. It was accompanied by the reappearance of the book I had not taken much notice of earlier. This was flourished under my nose, open at a page clearly marked 'Perdika', and showing several lines of text with a small plan. I grabbed for the book, but it was swiftly whipped back out of my reach.

"Oh, no, Bligh! This is for us!" The grin became even more wickedly vulpine. "Then we won't be having any more surprises like this afternoon, now, will we?"

That seemed pretty much to be that. The table was 'struck below', as I believe Sir Horatio would have put it, and the beer flowed slowly but steadily. To starboard, to coin another nautical expression, the whitish rugged rocks and olive scrub of Aegina drew nigh, and then started to slip past us. The steep cliffs plunged unhesitatingly into a fringe of pure cobalt water, and the wind bent obligingly to follow the coast of the island, giving Rex his first go at goose-winging the boat and running straight down-wind with an easy following sea. Malcolm achieved contentment, if not fish, by trailing a lure astern.

***

Gradually, about half way along the south side of the island, the sun sank behind the rearing rock of Methana, and the jerseys came out. The wind dropped steadily until, in an almost flat calm off the headland behind which lay Perdika, we stowed the sails. In the gathering dusk, the lights of the town and the white walls stood out most romantically. It was with the greatest reluctance that I started the engine, spoiling the peace and the view.

Despite my misgivings about the Mediterranean style of mooring with the anchor out forward and the stern to the quay, there was ample space on the end of the roughly-built finger-pier and, after circling once whilst the warps were prepared and The Motley instructed, we made a superb job of the mooring. Rex handled the anchor, snubbing the chain with the windlass-brake to control our approach, whilst I steered and Malcolm sprang ashore with the ropes like a veritable gazelle… well, like an elderly, recently well-fed gazelle, at any rate. With no wind and the whole of the end of the pier to aim for, it was hardly an exacting manoeuvre, but Rex and Malcolm picked up the technique immediately and the performance was a gratifying one. I glanced around to see whether our efforts had been appreciated, but the waterfront was deserted.

With the engine off, and peace once again on the harbour, I nipped ashore for a quick look at the ropes against a background of brightly-lit tavernas and to the accompaniment of several muted but competing bouzoukis issuing from them. The place was quite perfect, and I was in such a state of grace that I thought nothing of the fishing-line leading tautly from the push-pit rail across the transom in the general direction of the propeller.

The small cupboard which housed our shower and toilet now came under scrutiny, and, for gentlemen of our portly build, appeared somewhat lacking to say the least. Rex declined, on the grounds that no English gentleman would deign to demean himself in such undignified contortionism, and shunning the *oubliette* as he termed it, he loaded up with towel and wash-bag and headed off in search of the advertised 'facilities'.

Malcolm, who has fewer pretensions to gentle birth or dignity, decided to take his chance in the Iron Maiden, although I suspect that he had to strip naked and coat himself with soap to get into it. I hid on deck whilst he entered, but once he was inside with the door closed, I started surreptitiously searching for the mysterious book. At first, I was the embodiment of stealth itself, but as I drew blank after blank, and as the squelching, slopping and thudding from the shower crescendoed, I became less careful and more irate until Malcolm suddenly halted his ablutions to call out, "You won't find it, Bligh!"

He then continued his shower, creating in the process a noise which put me in mind of someone disembowelling a whale with a powerful vacuum-cleaner. I slunk out into the cockpit to take a manly sailor's shower with salt water, which damn nearly caused my death of pneumonia. The heat goes out of the Greek day faster than I had realised in October.

After my shower, I sat down in the cabin for five minutes to wait for the others and awoke at a quarter-to-ten by the cabin-clock. Anyone who has done a spot of sailing will know that the first day can do that to you quite easily even without spending the previous night on an aeroplane. It took me a moment to work out where I was, and why. That accomplished, I had to sort out who the other two people asleep on the other side of the cabin were. Having done that, I panicked. This awoke The Motley, who panicked too. To those conditioned by British hostelries, there didn't seem much chance of finding a restaurant open at such a late hour, and three stout trenchermen such as we viewed the prospect of missing a meal with about the same enthusiasm with which heavy cavalry viewed the invention of the machine-gun. Despite our sedentary natures, we actually jogged up to the raised road along the harbour-front where the tavernas look down on the fish-quay.

As any Greek will tell you, we need scarcely have worried. Everywhere was brightly lit and patently very open as we arrived, only slightly out of breath, and we soon found ourselves the object of considerable attention from the restaurateurs. The late season clientele was sufficiently reduced that our custom was eagerly sought, which was exactly what we expected of volatile Hellenes. It was with a superior air that we ambled in and out of restaurants, disdainfully ignoring the commercial patter and chairs held for us to sit on as we inspected cool box after refrigerator full of fresh fish. It was a stately progression along the waterfront, attended by a cloud of mosquito-like waiters, until we came to the second to last restaurant. Here, under an awning, a very Greek-looking chap in waiter's black-and-whites leaned casually against a pillar inspecting his nails. He paid no attention to us at all until we had almost passed by, and then he called out without looking up,

"Better youse eats here, guys!" He favoured us with a quick glance, which was friendly without being excessively so, and then returned to the contemplation of his cuticles. We stopped. The Greek changed hands. The onus of conversation seemed to have passed to us, so Rex took up the gauntlet.

"Ah, and your food is better than the others, I dare say?"

Our man shrugged, exactly as one would expect a Greek to shrug, a deep, exaggerated shrug in which the palms turned heavenwards and the chin thrust out below pursed lips and half-hooded eyes.

"Foods the same," he said, "an' price the same. But is more comfortable the chairs here." He gestured economically at the steel-framed, red-upholstered seats, and then jerked a dismissive thumb at the other tavernas. A quick inspection revealed that they all possessed rickety wooden chairs with woven rush seats. The Greek shrugged again, and went back to his nails. "Them others, 's gonna kill your ass!" was his final word on the matter. What would you do? We sat down.

Looking back on it now, I very much doubt if we could have picked a finer establishment for our introduction to Greek cuisine and culture. Having lured us off the street with a masterly air of studied indifference, Stavros, our host, became a most attentive and instructive guide to the menu, the form of the Greek meal, and to many other partially or wholly unrelated aspects of Greek life. We were shown a menu, the standard type of Tourist Authority menu which had the entire cornucopia of Hellenic cuisine printed on it in incomprehensible lower-case Greek, with translations in excruciatingly bad English, French and German. On these tributes to rampant bureaucracy, the restaurateur filled in, in pencil, the prices of the dishes he offered, leaving the others blank. Stavros let us peruse them for half a minute or so in utter incomprehension... I could have been reading the starting line-up for the Athens Gold Cup for all I could make out. Our host smiled, and retrieved his menus. "No worry. I choose for you. You likes fish?" We said we likes. "O.K. I fix. S' terrible, this menus, no? Zassolze!"

We asked for wine. Stavros smiled, the sort of smile that makes one suspect that one is about to make the final instalment to the smiler's pension-scheme. We tried to get an idea of the price of the wine by asking for the wine-list, but he wouldn't hear of it.

"I gives you best wine, *my* wine. This bottles, is mostly RRRRRubbish! Zassolze!"

The way he rolled the R at the last caused Rex to murmur, "If you have dentures, prepare to shed them now!"

The wine came in a tin carafe with no spout; it was cool, dry, and brought a respectful murmur from Rex. Stavros began our introduction to the Greek tongue.

"*Krassi*. Is wine. *Krassi apo varelli*...is wine from a barrel. *Retsina!*" He gestured to the caraffe, and helped himself to a hearty slug. We stared at it... there was just the very faintest hint of resin in the flavour... a very pleasant, crisp, white table wine. Another myth about the unsophisticated nature of Greek alcohol dashed. Stavros was well into his lesson now, evidently enjoying himself.

"*Aspros Patos*... is 'cheers'. Means 'white bottom'... you make a white bottom in your glass... so, drink all." He downed another tumbler full in one go and watched benevolently as we took a while longer to do it. "Zassolze!" he beamed.

The food began to arrive. Small dishes of starters, luke-warm or even cold, but definitely tasty. These, he told us, were *mezedes*, small snacks served as appetizers. This started a punning-match amongst us along the lines of "Mercedes?"..."Audi 'ell do you know that?"... "Can you a-Ford it?"... "Datsun awful joke!"... "Well, it's a bit Austin-tatious!"... and so on. It gives us a simple pleasure. It puzzled Stavros, though; he waited until we had exhausted our tiny minds of groan-making cracks, and then shook his head in bewilderment.

"Strange," he said. "Zassolze!"

Stavros was certainly on form as regards the food. The starters gave way to rather more elaborate dishes of fried marrow, charcoal-grilled calamari, and some spicy little meatballs. By this time, a waiter had taken over the service; Stavros drifted around his other tables, sometimes sitting to take a glass but always returning to our table, where he now had two glasses in commission, and a full place-setting. Malcolm did at one point ask Stavros whether moussaka was available, but our host tossed his head emphatically in the gesture the Greeks have for 'no'.

"'S for tourists. Zassolze!"

It seemed, as the gradual flow of more palatable dishes continued to percolate inexorably onto our table, that this was the meal itself, a selection of appetizers; not so. We were surrounded by a litter of empty plates, and well into... well, let's call it the third jug of wine, for the sake of argument... and I think we were already feeling fairly well-fed. In fact, I think Rex had suggested calling for the bill when Stavros arrived bearing a large stainless dish held chest-high. He plonked it down in the middle of the table, clearing a space for it with a sweep of his forearm, and made a rather rude and annoying rasping sound with his lips. I think he thought that it sounded like a trumpet fanfare, and I wished he wouldn't do it. When I saw what was on the plate, I wished I hadn't eaten the other food.

On the salver was a splendid fish, two crayfish and a crab. Each gap between the seafood was filled with a dip or sauce, and the whole drew a fair amount of attention from the other tables, even from the adjacent restaurants. Glancing across the table at Rex and Malcolm, I saw that my own feelings were perfectly mirrored… the mere lack of appetite was not in any way going to degrade the pleasure of eating this dish. A momentary concern about the cost flitted to the nether-world before it was truly formed. Stavros took up an alloy knife and fork with the gravitas of a royal chef hefting gleaming utensils over the carcass of a spitted stag, and deftly filleted and served the fish.

I could say that the fish was glorious, the crays superb, and that the crab had rarely been surpassed. It wouldn't be true… the fish was very good, the crays were good but were (and to my way of thinking, always will be) inferior to a real lobster, and the crab was a spider, and therefore as sparse and bony as he was undoubtedly tasty. But the whole feel of the thing was incredibly right, even down to the addition to the table of Stavros and his wife who helped us to finish off the plate by rending and devouring with most un-British gusto those parts of the seafood that delicate people at home decline to give to the cat. I confess that my account of the night proceeds from this point with only the flimsiest of recollection, but I do seem to remember that wine continued to arrive. Slowly our table extended to include few locals, and then some tourists, and late on Stavros brought out some lamb chops. There is some fleeting impression of coffee and fruit.

Evidence after the coffee and fruit is scarce and entirely circumstantial; I know I walked home to the boat, because I woke up in my bunk, and I suspected that I had been singing because, amongst the more abraded parts of my body, was my throat.

***

The painful process of waking-up the next morning commenced early. By my watch, it was two-thirty, but I was fairly sure that I hadn't altered it since leaving Manchester, so call it four-thirty a.m. Greek time. At any rate, it seemed a bloody uncivilised hour to hold a brontosaurus-strangling competition right next to the boat. My head was splitting as I awoke with a desperate, hollow, rasping bellow filling the boat. Evidently, the noise portended a dreadful fate about to befall some hapless soul, because faintly through the unearthly bronchial booming could be heard the frantic screams of a human voice. I lurched to where my feet are customarily to be found, only to find that someone had moved the floor to a position about three inches lower than I was accustomed to finding it. I pivoted on my buttocks, crashed headlong through the insubstantial fore-cabin door, and ended up doubled over the forward end of the saloon table. In disentangling myself from this obstacle, I managed to interact with Rex, who was engaged in a life-and-death struggle of epic proportions trying to escape his predatory bedding. We emerged into the cockpit in what must have been a most intriguing agglomeration of naked flesh and tartan blanket.

The brontosaurus was a small tanker with an asthmatic whistle; the screaming voice belonged to its captain, and it wanted very much to park where we were parked.

I think I said a naughty word.

We started the engine. Rex went forward to the anchor-winch, and I hopped arthritically ashore to loose the stern-ropes. Unfortunately, in my abstracted condition, the happy thought of doubling the mooring-lines back to the boat so that I could release them from onboard did not occur to me, so when I released the first line, the boat slewed sideways as the tension came on the other. This caused the end of the gangplank to fall in the water, and as I made a grab to retrieve it, I lost my hold on the second stern-line. The tension of the anchor-chain took over, and the boat shot away from the quay… which was a dreadful shame, since I had just grabbed hold of the push-pit rail to preserve my balance. There could only be one end to this, and whilst the water was cool, it was superbly refreshing. I felt quite good as I climbed out up the rugged quay wall, and didn't mind losing my first command after less than twenty-four hours nearly as much as I thought I might have.

By the time I had regained the quay, the blunt, battered and scarred bow of the tanker had interposed itself between me and the *Nissos*, so I couldn't see how

Rex was faring beyond observing the top third of the mast. Since it was still vertical, and not getting any shorter, I concluded that we had, in our unorthodox little way, managed to get her clear in time. To judge by the dented, bruised and gashed plating of the tanker's bow, it was a good thing that we had, because all the evidence indicated that she had no particular objection to physical contact.

A rope came snaking through the air, and I stepped in to catch it. Simultaneously came a shout of warning and a loud clang, then something rock-hard tapped me painfully on the ankle-bone; the rope I had just tried to catch had a damn great eight-tonne shackle on the end of it! I shackled the line to a ring on the corner of the quay, watched impassively by two shadowy heads poking over the bow-apron. Then I retreated in horror to watch from a safer distance as the captain used this line as a spring to lever himself alongside. The engine appeared to operate only on full revs, either ahead or astern, which at times subjected the rope to appalling, tooth-tingling tensions that would have sent me digging for cover like an aardvark on adrenaline had I been on that fo'c'sle. The two shadows were of stoical mould, however, and stood contentedly behind the glowing tips of their cigarettes. I never did see them move, until they abruptly disappeared as the engine died, apparently of tuberculosis. All the lights went out at the same time, and the tanker commenced a most convincing impression of the *Marie Celeste*. I hopped on board, called Rex, and he simply backed *Nissos* up to the tanker.

I had been going to move out to anchor, inspired by a distinct and healthy lack of inclination to remain in the vicinity of a tanker-crew given to smoking on deck, but as I crossed her decks there was no smell of an oil-cargo and an open tank-lid proved to be full right into the coaming with a very neutral liquid. Identifying our neighbour as a water-tanker, and judging that further nocturnal disturbance was unlikely given the volume of snoring already issuing from a port-hole under her bridge, we simply tied the back-end of *Nissos* to the tanker's rail, re-tensioned the anchor-cable and went back to bed.

It wouldn't be fair to say that Malcolm had not even stirred during all this. He had, in fact, rolled over.

***

I wish I could say, as most sailing stories do, that I was gently brought to wakefulness the following morning by the lapping of the water on the hull and the gentle tap of a halyard on the mast, or the creak of the warps and the chatter of jovial fishermen. Alas, my slumbers were more prosaically broken by the sound of a body forcing itself into the 'Iron Maiden'... or 'Iron Midden', as Malcolm had taken to calling it. Suddenly starkly aware of what was about to happen only inches from my head the other side of a thin piece of plywood, I egressed swiftly onto the foredeck via the fore-hatch.

Seen for the first time in full daylight, Perdika was a welcome sight. It would have been welcome for its own sake, even without comparison with the atrocities being committed below, because it is a very picturesque little harbour. Situated in a triangular bay which opens westward onto Moni Island, the pretty little white-painted community fills the hillside which slopes down to the water on the north side. The village nestles around a traditional church, and is colourfully fringed by the awnings of the restaurants along the top of the sea-wall. Brightly-painted fishing boats ring the quay, whilst the stark, rearing rock of Moni Island catches the bright light of the morning sun, gleaming impossibly white. The south side of the harbour is a promontory covered with scrub, towards the western end of which was a single object sticking up out of the undergrowth... a Doric column at least, by my reckoning. That, I decided, would definitely bear investigation later in the day, despite the 'No Entry' signs which hung in dereliction around the promontory from a dilapidated wire fence.

In the cockpit, Malcolm had emerged blearily to sit, blinking and scratching in a most un-alluring manner. He was the hands-down winner of the 'Least Lovely Thing in Perdika This Morning' competition, and when I complemented him on the achievement, he muttered something about me being too kind by far, and offered me the use of his shaving-mirror. He continued to scratch in an abstract, somewhat simian manner, and fixed his eye on the other yacht in the harbour. This was anchored off. It flew a German flag at the crosstrees, and four veritable Teutons were healthily cleaving the water, jumping in and doing back-flips off the stern. Malcolm shuddered with distaste, and averted his gaze. Exercise is obscenity to Malcolm ... his idea of a video-nasty is watching the Olympics ... and he diverted his eyes towards the tanker, which still lay silent. If it occurred to Malcolm to wonder where it had come from, he kept his puzzlement to himself.

I think it was in order to attempt to shock him further that I announced my intention of going for a swim, but he just gave me his bloodhound-with-a-hangover look and went back to contemplating the world through his jaundiced eye. I dived over the bow.

Even here in the harbour the water was clear and just cool enough to be invigorating. It was a new man who emerged from the water to drip without due care and attention onto the morose figure in the cockpit; a man glowing with virtue and moral superiority. Malcolm was immune to moral superiority as well, it appeared.

Rex appeared in the open at last and proposed that we repair to Stavros' for breakfast, and at last Malcolm showed signs of animation. We dressed hurriedly and clambered over the tanker. Malcolm nearly broke into a trot along the quay.

Stavros was just as obliging as I remembered him from the night before. We asked for a traditional Greek breakfast, and were told that we could have an English one or a continental one. The latter was bread and jam, and the former, which we elected to try, turned out to be bread and jam with two eggs.

Greeks, Stavros explained, rarely breakfast. They have a *koulouri,* a ring of crisp bread, with coffee; then they have an ouzo with a mezé mid-morning. "Greeks have very good things for breakfast," announced Stavros, "yoghurt, honey, nuts. But they don't eat. Only tourists eats breakfast, so now is everywhere only English breakfast. Zassolze!" An English breakfast, he told us, went by the name of a 'full' in Greece.

The bill came. I nearly choked… a quick calculation brought it to nearly twelve pounds a head! I was drawing breath to dispute this vigorously when Rex pointed out that the bill included the meal of the night before… and there can't be much wrong with that! I suppose that if one cannot remember major events such as getting home, then such minor affairs settling the score are liable to be a trifle hazy as well. We parted company with Stavros well satisfied, with fond protestations of undying friendship, and set off to have a look at the ancient ruin that my beady eye had spotted.

A few minutes' walk brought us to the south side of the harbour, past some 'No Entry' signs in various languages, and then past a sign which showed a picture of a man with outstretched arms and legs standing on an irregular five-pointed star, which made no sense to us. We hiked on, undeterred by the sign, but definitely wary of some large, unfriendly turkeys which seemed to have the run of the place. At the top of the slight rise, we came face to face with the column, and with the history of Greece.

The column rose from a shallow dip in the ground. It was ribbed in what I believe is the Ionian style, although I am remarkably open to guidance on this, knowing as I do about as much about classical architecture as a cannibal knows about Nutella. The column reached a height of approximately four feet above ground level and had a flat top, in which was set a bronze plate inscribed with runic characters. Rex hazarded a guess that we were looking at the defence-works of one of the warrior tribes that had over-run Greece in days gone by, and close inspection of the writing on the plate proved it. It said 'Krupp. Kiel. 1940'. Further investigation revealed a load of post-classical reinforced ferro-concrete pits and bunkers in the Todt-style, so popular in coastal areas across Europe a few decades ago.

As we walked, giggling, back towards the village, we came again across the picture of the man standing on the star, which now that we knew the origin of the ruins made awful sense at last. It was a warning notice for a minefield! It was admittedly ancient, but it stopped us in our tracks no less effectively for all that. Rex indicated some of the large birds passing a few yards away.

"There can't be any mines still here, surely. They'd have been set off. There's some pretty hefty turkeys running around here."

Malcolm looked hard at him and nodded.

"Three, to be precise."

We strolled nonchalantly back to the beach at the head of the bay, staying very casually to the precise centre of the dirt path.

As we headed back to the boat, we met Stavros one last time, revving the engine of his little Honda step-through like a jet-turbine as he prepared to attempt the hill out of the village. We told him about mistaking the old gun-emplacements for ancient ruins, which he thought was pretty priceless. He thoughtfully made sure that most of the rest of the village enjoyed it too.

"Zassolze!" he said, slapping his thigh.

Remembering that this word was one he had used a lot the night before, I realised that it might be one of those really useful, multi-functional words like 'wunderbar!' or 'mañana'. I asked him what the word meant. He didn't appear to know it for a moment, then enlightenment dawned on him.

" 'S not Greeks, 'S English!" he grinned, "…Is assholes!"

I hung back for a moment, having suddenly remembered that the six-thirty forecast had passed by without a hiccup in my snores. When The Motley were out of earshot, I asked Stavros if he knew what the weather would be like today. He looked around, glanced upwards at the sky and said, "'S okay."

Lowering my voice still further, I asked him where the hell we should go today, to get around not having access to the pilot book.

"Poros," he replied without hesitation, "…'S nice place." When I asked him what the harbour was like, he shrugged. "Don' know. I never been."

Armed with meteorological and pilotage advice of this quality, I strode manfully down to the dock to take my ship to sea.

***

The significance of the fishing-line stretched tautly across the stern, which I confess had eluded me the night before, became rapidly more apparent as we attempted to depart. With the engine as close to idling as its shuddering clamour could approximate, we cast off the stern and Rex heaved mightily on the handle of the ageing anchor windlass until the hook broke surface. I gave our friends at Stavros' taverna a parting wave as we cleared the water-tanker's bow, put the engine into gear, and heard it stall. They heard me curse, loud and clear across the quiet bay. I quickly found that the engine started OK, but stalled when put into gear. We drifted slowly with the light, northerly air towards the rocks on the south side of the harbour, punctuating the peace of the morning with the churning of the starter-motor, the grinding of gears and the expectoration of obscenity and blasphemy which I heaped upon the engine. Eventually I told Rex to drop the anchor again, but too late. By the time we were brought-up, the boat was gently aground on the lee side of the bay.

The previous night's turn before parking — most yachts do it, like dogs settling down for the night — had, of course, wound Malcolm's fish-dredging line around the keel. Subsequent manoeuvring had enticed it into the environs of the propeller, which welcomed it with open blades and clasped the nylon firmly to its phosphor-bronze bosom.

As much as I like a swim this was the third one of the day, and it was still only mid-morning. Assisted by a crustily decomposing mask excavated from one of the lockers, and wielding the bread-knife (an indispensable propeller-maintenance tool which small-craft omit from their inventories at their peril), I hacked and sawed at the mat of tightly-wound line. Cut followed thrust, slash, stab, hack... Errol Flynn himself would have applauded. Rarely was a swash so buckled! I nearly changed target altogether when, during an air-break, Malcolm requested me not to cut the line any more than necessary, and I might indeed have done so had Rex not wisely pulled up the bathing-ladder.

There comes a moment in the clearing of propellers by this method where, just as exhaustion begins to tilt the mind into a state of abject surrender, a large lump of the obstruction floats free, giving fresh hope and inspiring the flagging worker on to redoubled endeavour. This process repeats itself until the entanglement finally disappears completely, just as the diver expires from exhaustion. It is a process carefully calculated by some higher power to extract the very last ounce of effort, ensuring that there can be no sweetness in the final victory. I dragged myself back on board, feeling like an orange that has just contributed substantially to a screwdriver.

We motored out of the bay under the silent gaze of a hundred pairs of eyes, none of whom had taken the slightest bit of interest in our departure until something had gone wrong. I reflected upon this; upon the lack of spectators for our mooring the previous evening; and upon the attention we had enjoyed during our departure from Kalamaki Marina the previous day. It was at that moment that I formulated what will I hope become recognised as Blatchley's First Law of Nautical Recreation: "The competence of the manoeuvre is in inverse proportion to the number of people watching it." It was corroborated within moments of its conception as we glided around the headland and set sail flawlessly and efficiently... just out of the line of sight of the people in the harbour.

***

The sail south to the island of Poros was largely uneventful. The navigation was not such as to tax me overmuch, and I was able to devote most of my attention to making Malcolm feel guilty about his part in causing the morning's embarrassment. I might as well have saved my breath; Malcolm would as soon admit to guilt as an airline pilot would to vertigo. I did find one chink in his armour, however. He regards himself as a sportsman with regard to his fishing, projecting an image of man locked in skilful battle against a cunning adversary, using minimal tackle to put all advantage with the quarry. When I commented that a line of the diameter of the stuff I had sawn free of the prop-shaft would have held anything short of a moderately fit nuclear submarine, he went into transports of rage. For the rest of the holiday, he could be reduced to a fit of sullen, baleful glaring for a good five minutes at a time simply by referring to his trolling line as his 'trawl-warp'.

From Perdika, the course to Poros heads exactly south along the East shore of the Methana peninsular. Moni Island drops away astern to reveal the island of Angistri and the craggy, towering north end of volcanic Methana. Between these two, if your day is clear, is framed the blue-ish outline of the distant hills of the north-east Peloponnese around Epidaurus. Ahead, the peak of Poros is, at first, slightly difficult to pick out against the mainland hills close behind it. By the time the town of Methana is abeam, however, the island is easily distinguished from the backdrop. Poros lies very close to the mainland and forms an almost land-locked bay, the entrance to which was quite clearly in view by the time Malcolm had recovered from his sulk and recommenced his trolling over the stern. The wind held north-easterly for us again, a nice, therapeutic force three, and we rolled along quite pleasantly, sipping beer and absently noshing cheese and paté. Discussion of various subjects, all of them uncharacteristically non-controversial, proceeded in what can only be described as languor. If there were any nautical disasters or outbreaks of maritime mayhem, I for one must have been looking the other way. It was in fact the longest single spell of tranquillity, even temper and aquatic competence of the trip, and as such is of absolutely no interest to the reader whatsoever. The First Law of Nautical Recreation held good. There were one or two fishing boats in sight, far away, and a couple of day-cruise ships carted late season tourists from island to island. One other sail was to be seen well out to sea in the direction of Athens, but otherwise the October sea was ours alone. By midday, shirts were off, and the holiday was proceeding entirely as planned. This, naturally, caused us to become restive. One needs a little spice in life, and our cynical senses of humour needed some grit in the Vaseline, some impediment, some imperfection to coalesce upon. It was a feeling of… well, not quite boredom, more a feeling that the situation had more to offer.

Just such a feeling, in fact, as that which, some years previously, had sparked off the Affair of the Great Big Bouncing Wheel. I digress...

***

When I was a cadet on a general cargo ship, we once discharged a cargo at a small island in the Adriatic. This island was a customs pound from which the importer could ship goods to the mainland only after paying the import duty, and as such it was treated as a bonded area and guarded by the army. Ships crews were not permitted to go to the mainland, and, apart from a pretty lousy little cantina, there was nothing to do on the island other than wandering around, poking around the piles of goods. These were waiting, mostly in vain it seemed, for the luckless importer to produce the readies before they rusted, rotted or otherwise decomposed. The ships berthed on the seaward side of the island, and on the inshore side lay the guard-post and gate, the cantina and a small coaster-wharf from which duty-paid pieces of merchandise were shipped to the mainland. A great variety of items lay haphazardly around on the spine of the island, and, at the top of this slope one fine night, a party of four of us, driven abroad by tedium, found a large wheel about seven feet in diameter, and complete with an inflated knobbly tyre, propped up against a container. Now, a wheel left lying around on top of a hill in this manner simply cries out to be shown the path of duty, not to say gravity, and I am convinced that much less red-blooded chaps than ourselves would have done the same. It was the work of an instant to wheel the thing to the metalled roadway which ran over the crest of the island and let it go down the side away from the ship.

It was shortly after sunset as I remember, and the light had faded quite a bit, but we could see that at the end of the curving road lay the gateway and a small guard-hut, apparently abandoned. The wheel set off almost reluctantly, scrunching on the gravelled road and wobbling so much that at first we thought it would simply fall over. It soon steadied as it gathered a bit of speed, however, and trundled off down the road, seemingly overjoyed to have at last found its true purpose in life. Before long, it started to make little hops clear of the ground, seemed to like the idea of this exciting new dimension opening before it, and was soon bounding along splendidly. It bounced every few seconds with a strange mixture of sounds in which the 'crunch' of impacted gravel mingled with an odd, hollow, rubbery and jaunty 'boing' noise.

It was undoubtedly this sound which alerted a young soldier, whose presence was hitherto unsuspected. He emerged from the sentry-box with what, even in the failing light, could not be anything other than a sub-machine gun slung under his right arm. We were horrified, but the wheel continued to accelerate in cavalier disregard for the new development.

There comes a time in these affairs when one knows that the act of a sane, rational mind would be to instruct the legs to initiate a hasty retrograde motion, and maintain it until sanctuary of the impermeable variety is reached. It is an act of the utmost foolhardiness to wait and see the outcome of one's intemperate deeds, but one is none-the-less strangely compelled to do so. We took cover, and from my vantage point behind a large packing-case I saw the soldier stop in the middle of the open gateway and peer down the road towards the cantina, gun half at the ready as he tried to work out the source of the gravelly 'boing' noise. Behind him, the Great Big Bouncing Wheel loped on, very much the wheel in form, looking as if it would impact with a mass of tangled metal junk by the fence to the left of the hut with what promised to be a most satisfying noise. As luck would have it though, the road at the crucial point had a slight kerb, and the wheel was deflected slightly and adopted a new course... straight for the gate!

I think that it was at about this moment that the sentry realised that whatever was going on was going on behind him, and he swung towards us. Too late! The wheel just clipped the three-foot high fence and struck the sentry-hut at mid-height, demolishing the roof and one wall with a great splintering crash. It knocked the opposite wall flat and continued over the wreckage to bounce on the quay. Because of the way he had turned, the sentry had his back to the hut at the moment of apocalypse; at the sound of rending wood, he spun round to see his refuge of a moment before in pieces on the ground. At this moment, the wheel left terra firma and hit the water with a wonderful splash. The sentry, who I don't think ever saw what it was that had Hiroshima'ed his hut, apparently lost his nerve at this point (not, perhaps, unreasonably) because he brought up his gun in a smooth sweep and let what appeared to be the whole magazine go in a wild and generous arc. The incredibly fast burp of the weapon split the night, and it was sufficiently dark that the muzzle-flash was most impressive.

It may be that the sentry's aim was as impressive as his speed of reaction, and that he hit his assailant, or it may be that the weight of the not inconsiderable hub of the wheel was enough to overcome the buoyancy of the tyre; whether it sank, or he sank it, or it simply vanished in the dusk is immaterial, for it was seen no more. The unfortunate sentry was left with an embarrassing lack of exhibit 'A' with which to explain why he had machine-gunned his hut to a pulp to the shambling knot of soldiery rapidly emerging from the cantina.

Giggling hysterically despite our fear of the consequences of the evening's entertainment, we legged it back to the ship before young Rambo could put another magazine in his perforator. We spent a dreadful hour in the bar, huddled together concocting alibis with a lookout posted at the window to warn of the jack-boots of Nemesis. We shied instinctively away from imagining what sort of sentence we would receive for a crime of this nature in a country that let young lads wander around after dark with loaded sub-machine guns. A jeep did, in fact, drive slowly along the quay at one point, but incredibly we heard no more about the affair. There's probably a file on the incident somewhere... it would be worth learning Serbo-Croat to read it.

***

The west entrance to Poros is a narrow-ish little strait, marked by a most professional-looking lighthouse. We were halfway through this gap when we heard a strange hum which swelled to a rumble we could almost feel, then grew to a tremendous roaring sound. Seconds later, round the headland we were lazily approaching, came the sort of creature which I had previously thought was only seen by people who take LSD. It looked for all the world like a massive cockroach in a Leeds Rugby League strip of blue and yellow. It poised precariously above the ocean on a multitude of stilt-like legs, and had curved windows at the front which leered down at us like the eyes of a huge and ill-disposed fly. The shape of the thing was composed of the sort of curves I have always associated with 'Fifties radio-sets and table-lamps. Down its spine ran a fin like that of an American car of similar vintage, and right on top was a small cabin. This, one could only hope, contained a driver who could A) steer the incredible machine clear of us, and B) wanted to. Assuming the former to be the case, its current course left us in some doubt about the latter.

It hurled itself into the corner, leaned over rather unsteadily and turned until we had a face-on view as it raced towards us. I had a sudden feeling that I now knew how a two-inch nail feels when it is first introduced to a three-pound claw hammer.

Discussing the event afterwards, I explained to Malcolm and Rex that I had taken no evasive action because I was under sail and therefore had right of way, and because any action on my part would possibly have confused the driver of the Martian war-machine. In truth, I couldn't have got out of his way by any means, even if I hadn't been absolutely rigid with shock. The monstrous insect held his course for a moment longer than I felt was really amusing, then swayed fractionally to one side and crashed past us in an explosion of noise and flying curtains of water. Through this roaring maelstrom of engines and tortured sea, the creature incongruously tooted a jaunty little horn... one felt such a vessel should have possessed a bellowing klaxon as ugly and bizarre as itself... and a cheery, blue-uniformed arm waved from the cockpit. For all the sheets of water it hurled around with such wanton ferocity, the wash was quite small, and the surreal machine thundered away in the direction of Athens, leaving a wide foaming wake and a trail of diesel smoke. We sat and watched it go in awed silence. The boat rocked, the sails slatted unattended, and Rex broke the silence. "Special effects by Stephen Spielberg, from an idea by H.G. Wells," he muttered to no-one in particular.

"What, in your professional opinion, the hell was that, Bligh?" Demanded Malcolm, ever the man for the pertinent question.

"That," I replied, recalling the logo on the tailfin, "was a Flying Dolphin, apparently."

"Dear God! It can read!" he muttered. "...And in your educated opinion, are we likely to encounter many more of these intriguing beasts?"

"Why don't you look them up in your clever little book," I retorted. "You never know, this may be their mating-season."

Rex chipped in at this moment to point out that if target-practice could be deferred for a moment, there was a corner to be negotiated. And a most rewarding corner it was.

***

Entering the bay of Poros by the west entrance, one turns left at the, 'Welcome to Poros and have you thought of fitting a solar water-heater?' sign around a low, rocky point. In an instant, the vista of the bay appears, a little inland sea stretching east to the gleaming white town two miles away. To the south, the high ridge of Dharditsa soars up over two thousand feet, whilst on the northern side, the sharp-peaked main island completes the encirclement of this delightful backwater. The striking point of the whole is the richly forested slopes of both the island and the adjacent mainland, Poros and the mountain being almost totally covered with green pines, whilst the lower-lying Peloponnese shore is fertile ground with great expanses of citrus orchards. There is a heady scent of pine ever in the air. From the west, the town of Poros is perceived in the fork of two green inclines as a charmingly irregular agglomeration of largely white houses with terracotta-tiled roofs. Here and there are just enough buildings in sandy natural stone to break the snowy uniformity we had found in Perdika. Crowning the whole, at the south-western tip of the town, a crag rises from the houses, upon which stands a stately, white clock-tower looking over the strait to the mainland town of Galatas.

The approach to the town, which we made by tacking into the gentle wind that was bent easterly by the shape of the bay, passed a chain of attractive anchorages on the south side of the island. The town opened further as we approached to reveal the lovely ochre-and-white buildings of the old naval arsenal and the intriguing silhouette of an ageing warship. That sail down the bay of Poros, in a lazy sailing breeze and on a warm, brilliantly clear autumnal day, is one of the three or four memories which spring to my mind whenever sailing is the subject of the moment. Nor was I the only person who thought it was a bit of a spell-caster because Rex was moved to open one of his good bottles of white wine in honour of the occasion. Even Malcolm had little cynical to say apart from wondering in a general sort of way whether the old warship burned NATO-standard nutty-slack. He was soon busily engaged with his camera, clicking and whirring most professionally, bemoaning the detrimental effect upon art of the tacking and muttering seditiously about F-this and F-that. Eventually, he retired to the foredeck to practice his muse, where he could be heard abusing the genoa and sheets as Rex and I tacked in idle moments between civilised sips of Vin Plonk Luxuriouso, or whatever it was. By the time we reached the town,

Rex and I were far too relaxed to contemplate anything as boorish or energetic as dousing sails or mooring, and in any case, the bottle was not yet empty. It was the decision of an instant to run downwind back to the mouth of the bay, and do the whole approach again!

CHAPTER FOUR

DALIANCE AND DECADENCE

*In which we assess Poros...The anatomy of a debauch...Aspects of amour...Of fish
and fishers...The fracas at Tselevinia...More fish...A night visitor...A fishy tail.*

The waterfront of Poros is quaint, traditional and overwhelmingly nautical in
flavour. Crisply white houses with terracotta tiles are stacked steeply up the
rocky slope, providing a classical counterpoise for the cosmopolitan
waterfront which rings the town with life. Brightly-painted fishing boats, large
and small, commercial and therapeutic, nuzzle the dockside. Interspersed
amongst these are the pleasure boats; sailing-yachts of all sizes, the ubiquitous
small motorboats loved by the Greeks, and the towering, gleaming and usually
whited mega-yachts of the super-rich. Boats of all sizes nod and sway like late-
night dancers in the constant wakes of the water-taxi boats which ply to the
beaches and the mainland town of Galatas. At frequent intervals, the growling
hydrofoils pass through at an ill-tempered crawl, and sometimes a large ferry
throbs past, hooting imperiously at the lesser craft. The scene is impeccably
Greek. Fishermen throng the wharf, mending nets and selling fish. The market
writhes with trade, delivery-men bustle, restaurants churn. The intermingled
throng of soberly dressed locals and kaleidoscope tourists is scattered with
naval uniforms from the naval training school, and everywhere the tavernas
and kafeneions bubble and boil with contention. The impression is picture-
postcard Greece, very traditional and, notwithstanding the numbers of
tourists and yachties, there is no doubt that this is a live, vital, working town
and port.

The First Law of Nautical Recreation let us off relatively lightly as we
moored. We went stern-to the south quay fairly close to the east end, next to

a most inviting little clutch of tavernas and bars, fortunately finding a rare space just between the high bows of two large fishing caiques. Only a couple of tobacco-tranquilised fishermen and half a dozen or so perambulating townsfolk saw Rex nearly lose the boat-hook, his balance and possibly his life trying to retrieve a fender upon which Malcolm had demonstrated his ineptitude in macramé. The mooring was in all other respects workmanlike, and the fender was shortly thereafter recovered from an enterprising young lad for a modest sum.

The short October day lost heat fairly quickly again, and whilst Rex headed off with his towel and matched set of 'Chauvinist for Men' toiletries, Malcolm did his greased-pig-in-a-cupboard act in the Iron Midden again and I took my manly shower on the foredeck. Learning from the previous night, I surreptitiously used warm water this time and kept out of the cockpit in order to have somewhere dry to sit and enjoy my G and T afterwards. By the time the others were eligible for arrest on a charge of fragrancy, I was comfortably ensconced in the corner next to the tiller with the first holiday-sized G and T already history and enjoying a memorable sunset.

Poros has a magical quality at the end of the day. To the west of the town are the hills of the north-east Peloponnese which, viewed from the Poros Strait, look exactly like a sleeping lady. She lies on her back, one knee raised, her hair flowing back from patrician frontal lobes, and has a full, shapely bosom. After sunset, the light is quickly excluded from the town by the high crest of Dharditsa to the south of the strait, so you look past the early lights of the dusky town to the sleeping lady, backlit in red by the dying glow of the sun. I would have quite enjoyed the scene, had it not been for the enthusiastic cavortings of Malcolm trying to catch it all on camera. In his search for the artistically perfect composition, he sprang to and fro across the scene like Cecil B. DeMented.

We noticed later as we walked up the main street that there was less of the touting for business which we had experienced in Perdika. Here the season had obviously not yet quietened down quite so much, and most of the restaurants we passed were already fairly well patronised. Waiters would wave vaguely towards the menu-boards and sometimes call out a half-hearted "Fresh fish! Hello!", but it lacked conviction, and did not aggravate our bigotry glands. We ambled on, emulating the local populace in strolling casually down the centre of the road, weaving amongst the motorists and moped-riders. The continual wasp-like buzzing of their engines and horns as they picked a way through the crowds drove us into a kafeneion set away from the road at the back of a small square next to the museum. Here we collapsed happily into wrought-iron chairs on the front doorstep and drank in the very Greek atmosphere. Kafeneion 'I Plateia', or The Square Cafe, was evidently the gambling den of the town.

Inside the cafe there were three round, green-baize tables, each one packed with earnest card-players sandwiched around its rim. Wherever the shape of the tables left a triangle of space, there was a smaller table shoehorned in supporting an acrimonious backgammon game. A television offering a muted version of a musical show stood totally disregarded in the corner, all attention being focused on the cards. It must have taken some concentration to see them too, because the whole room was virtually obliterated by tobacco smoke. They were either very honest, or else they were all cheating at a uniform level, but it seemed to work.

After a brief wait, the owner wandered out to see what we wanted. He was a lean, saturnine chap in a bland shirt and a lack-lustre cardigan, who didn't at first seem too gratified by our custom. He had a disconcerting habit of gazing absently away as he talked (in accented but excellent English) and then looking straight into your eyes as he waited for your reply. He made me feel like an inattentive school-boy singled out for a difficult question. His manner was initially a little off-putting, but I'm glad I didn't walk away because Petros very swiftly proved to be a man of character, humour and skill.

"What you like to drink?" His eyes panned disinterestedly around the square as he spoke, then gimleted into mine as he waited for the answer.

"Erm," I muttered, so un-nerved by the stare that I was momentarily unable to think of the name of a single alcoholic beverage, "Erm, what do you have?"

He considered this question at length, his eyes tracking away, and suddenly became fond as they passed over a disreputable black spaniel which was approaching from what appeared to have been a highly successful dustbin raid.

"How 'bout a Pina Colada?"

Now, the idea of an ethnic gambling and drinking den such as this yielding anything as exotic as a Pina Colada was so incongruous that it took me moment to get my mouth closed again. By the time I managed it, the spaniel had sat down firmly on my foot and the eyes were again spearing into mine.

"Fine, Pina Colada then!" I muttered with as much conviction as I could muster. Rex gave me a startled look, and then he got the eyes and ordered one too. Malcolm, however, was made of sterner stuff.

"Do you have a really dry Martini?" he challenged. Petros turned the Basilisk loose again, and then gave a hint of a smile.

"Sure. Shaken or stirred, Mister Bond?" Petros ambled away at the speed of an arthritic slug, gazing around his fume-filled domain with evident approval. The spaniel started to scratch vigorously close by, then came up for a stroke, but he brought with him a smell to match his foul appearance, a rich, semi-sweet stench of decay that could be physically felt in the throat. Despite my almost indiscriminate fondness for dogs, I felt no compunction in shooing him away.

When the drinks arrived, they were superb. I don't drink Pina Coladas as a general rule, but that is probably because, after Petros's, they would only be a let-down. Malcolm was impressed with his Martini as well. Petros came back after a while with a bowl of peanuts to find all three glasses empty. He raised his eyebrows, rocked the table experimentally, and said, "I gotta fix that table. Too many drinks gettin' spilt." He refilled the glasses without being asked.

When he came out with the second round, he bent to beckon the spaniel from its place under an orange tree. The dog put its head down and approached happily, wagging its tail. Petros spoke fondly to the dog for a moment, although he wisely refrained from touching it, and then pointed across the square. When the dog seemed reluctant to move, Petros straightened and savagely swung his boot in a theatrical kick which just missed the dog's rear end. The dog slunk away to the café on the corner of the square, and disappeared under the table of a group of flashily-dressed tourists. Petros smiled evilly.

"I always do that when he dirty," he announced. "...Make him go sit in the other cafe. When he smell bad, 's like a ferret, you know?"

"A skunk, you mean?" corrected Rex. Petros frowned.

"No, a ferret. You no scare rabbits with a skunk!" Even as he spoke, we could see patrons of the other café becoming unsettled and starting to look around for the source of the smell. Petros walked away wearing a grin which Machiavelli would have been leery of.

We sat in Petros's for some time. I can't remember another occasion when I have begun an evening with three liver-puckering Pina Coladas, but it certainly set the mood for a memorable night. By the time we rolled jauntily out of the small square in search of dinner, we were in just the mood for a spot of Greek dancing. Well, it just so happened that providence had provided, in the alleyway next to Petros's cafe, a well patronised taverna at which the clients were being entertained by that very muse. Three waiters in black trousers and matching T-shirts were stepping and high-kicking gravely to the measured clapping of their clients, clicking their fingers and slapping their heels to a sonorous bouzouki recording. They didn't flicker so much as an eyelid as Rex did an elephantine pirouette between them and their audience before disappearing up the alley. Malcolm followed with a can-can which accomplished in enthusiasm what it never had a chance of achieving in grace. The audience loved it! They were creased with laughter even before I attempted what I believe is known in terpsichorean circles as a 'jete'. I felt that it went rather well, right up to the last second when I descended onto a previously unseen step in the alleyway and measured my length on the stone flags. We retreated from the braying laughter, lucky, I thought, not to be pursued by irate waiters. I suppose they get fairly used to that sort of thing in the course of a season.

To describe the backstreets of Poros (or, indeed, any Greek island town) as 'serpentine' scarcely does them justice. If, like Shakespeare, I were accorded the convenience of inventing the language to suit my needs as I went along, I could here bequeath the word 'octopuscene' to the nation's literary heritage. Alternately brightly lit and swathed in stygian blackness, these stone-girt lanes wound in tortured curves, now flat, now more or less steeply stepped. The sides of the steps were un-guarded... I suspect that there is no word in the Greek language for 'banister'. Only the housewives' habit of whitewashing the sides of the paths and steps preserved us from broken bones. They generally paint the entire step except for the actual stepping-place, and one steps on the darker patch. It is a touch unnerving not knowing whether one is about to tread on the un-whitewashed step, or plunge fatally down a hole in the ground.

By the simple expedient of turning right at every opportunity, we arrived first in someone's back yard, then in a church, and finally back on the main waterfront road. I don't know how long we were in the maze, but we emerged again about three doors from Petros's cafe. I suppose a reader of the classics would have had a ball of string handy.

One would not reasonably have expected to equal the bonhomie of our meal in Perdika two nights running, but nevertheless we were again serendipitously delivered to an entertaining taverna. Sotiris, our flamboyantly moustachioed host of the evening, performed with dash. He kept us amused throughout the meal, conducting his restaurant by means of threats, imprecations and theatrical blows. The long-suffering waiter bore it stoically, and the whole experience was as much a Fawlty Towers re-run as a meal. I recall that we dined royally well on *kleftiko*, which is lamb and potatoes slowly cooked in spices and cheese in greaseproof paper and is sinfully rich and juicy. Rex insisted on trying the bottled white wines this time, and his cynical asides faded somewhat as he sipped and grudgingly approved of Greek viticulture. He eventually pronounced himself surprised but satisfied with several of the common-or-garden table-wines, which he decided were a very fair quality at the price. For myself, I followed my own taste and tried the red wines, and not being overly impressed with my first acquaintance with the bottled ones I shifted to barrel wine. This I found fruity, light, and eminently quaffable.

***

It was well into the last hour of the day by the time we emerged from the restaurant. What with Petros's Pina Coladas, an in-depth investigation of Greek wines red, white and rosé and latterly a stiff metaxa apiece, I doubt if we were at our most receptive; and yet we hadn't gone far along the road before it became evident to all three of us that a subtle transformation had taken place whilst we dined.

It took a moment or two to work out what had changed. Outwardly the town seemed the same, except that now the bar lights were all on. There was still the backwash of music along the front, but instead of the strumming of bouzouki-strings and the plaintive ululations of evergreen Greek love-songs, there now pervaded a primeval rhythm which imparted an unconscious pulse in the pelvic region. Greeks still promenaded the streets, conversing and clicking their beads as they walked off to dine, but the evening now seemed to belong to the young and the glitzily-dressed. The night was taking over, and whereas a couple of hours earlier Poros had appeared to be just closing down, now another incarnation seemed to be just opening up. This Jekyll and Hyde municipality, so solidly Greek by day, now metamorphosed into a multi-national melting-pot as slickly as a Far Eastern night-market rises, phoenix-like, from the ashes of the day-market. The waterfront of Poros is by night a 'strip', a necklace of cosmopolitan bacchanalia girding a citadel of Greek respectability. By day, there is little hint of the toper's paradise within; the parrot, umbrella and sunglass-gilded cocktail lists and the chalk-boards bearing the tidings of "Tonight's Special! A Naked Death Warrant, only 500 drax!" are decently cloaked in the shade of the sun-awnings covering the fronts of more ethnic emporia, the tavernas, kafeneions and leather-ware shops. Only after the alchemy of dusk, when the sun-awnings are drawn back, and the moon rises, does Mr. Hyde emerge from the shadows, his whiskers a-tremble and loins oscillating to a rhythm as primordial as it is synthesised. This hedonistic periphery makes no inroads past the first row of houses, however, and there seems to be a comfortable co-existence with the town proper. Our views on the desirability of the two faces of Poros were characteristically hypocritical... wholeheartedly approving of the cultural conservatism and tradition of the inner town, we ignored it and flung ourselves gleefully into the parted thighs of the whore that was the waterfront.

The fascination of Poros by night or day lies to a great degree in people-watching. Even at this late stage of the season there were sufficient revellers about to make sitting in the lazy chairs outside various cafés and watching the road a most rewarding and entertaining experience. Some locals took their post-prandial stroll and some tourist couples meandered, but the night now mainly belonged to the single, bar-and-party set. These included a few men, mostly be-jewelled iron-pumping hunks in shirts too small to button-up, but the female of the species predominated by a very unusual proportion. Women circulated in packs, of all ages from late-teens to middle-age, dressed to the nines and gleefully infused with the joys of the night. Despite the slight autumnal chill in the air, a wonderful array of outrageously short skirts and plunging necklines, tight jeans and party dresses paraded the catwalk of the main road. A miasma of perfumes mingled with the scent of grilling souvlakis, jasmine and orange-trees, and the tinkle of feminine laughter dulled the rasping of the cicadas. Jewellery, teeth and eyes sparkled in the lamp-light and hair swirled in the air. Soft and shrill their English, French, German, Dutch, Italian and Scandinavian voices fell upon the ear. In summary, a perfect sisterhood of Aphrodite flowed around us for the delight of our chauvinistic gaze, leaving us blessed but also bewildered by the apparent lack of men desirous of sharing this sensual banquet. Since most of the bars operated a waitress service it was not until a call of nature prompted a visit to facilities inside a bar that I became aware that the missing half of the puzzle was within.

Ranked two-deep at the bar were the local young bloods. Occasionally conversing in pairs, more often singly contemplating a long drawn-out drink, they flexed their bodies and posed sub-consciously. They stared in manful detachment into nothingness behind the bar, where mirrors allowed them to furtively check their coiffure. Their necks were adorned with chunky jewellery which failed to outshine the glorious confections of their Hawaiian shirts; they stood with one leg raised on a stool-rung or foot rail, creating alarming tensions in their tight jeans. Scattered around the bar, at the various tables or in secluded nooks, those who had already made contact with like-minded tourist ladies paid court with much rolling of smouldering, dark eyes and what sounded like an unbelievable amount of what I shall politely term 'romantic endearments' (Malcolm preferred the term 'knee-deep bullshit'). I will not conceal the fact that the three of us were impressed to the point of silence by the success-rate of these Lotharios, and not a little peeved by the number of fine, upright young British lasses who were being snared in this foul, foreign manner. Then the even more uncomfortable thought occurred… who was pursuing whom?

During my early days at sea, I served with a cargo-ship company which loaded in continental ports for the islands of the South Pacific. High on the list of European ports visited were Hamburg and Antwerp. Now, both of these fine cities, in addition to their being justly famed as cultural and architectural centres, boast red-light districts of international renown, the Reeperbahn, the Herbertstrasse, or the Havenkwartier, where sailors, naughty businessmen, devout lechers and (if the Tabloids are to be believed) an unreasonable number of clergymen flock into the sin-sodden streets to see the disdainful, hard-faced ladies who sit in the red-lit windows. Suitably attired in fish-net stockings, leather Basques, high-heeled knee boots and even guide-dog harnesses, the Sirens ignore the browsers at the window, quietly reading their books or toying with their whips. I don't suggest for a second that Poros is a knocking-shop, but I couldn't ignore some similarity with the great sea-ports. In both, Mankind's oldest need was being serviced, but in Poros it seemed to be the girls who were window-shopping and the boys were wearing the fish-net stockings.

Initially we just watched and commented on this circus. Rex described the array of womanhood before us as a Banquet of Beauty, to which Malcolm added "Sort of a Smorgas-Broad". We continued our commentary in this vein, but eventually it was inevitable that manly confidence should wax parallel with national pride under the influence of alcohol. Observation metamorphosed into obsession and we decided forthwith to try to save at least three of the young wantons from the vile clutches of lustful Levantines. Hitching up our sagging waistbands, and drawing in our sagging waistlines, we entered the fray.

Firstly we cheerfully accosted girls in groups of three at a time. It appears in retrospect (that most precise of sciences) to be a fraction optimistic to expect three boys to meet three girls, instantly strike up three mutually compatible relationships, and then come to an amicable agreement about who is going where with whom. This is especially so when the three girls are living in a single rented apartment room, and the three boys inhabit a small boat where any action of an intimate nature is effectively performed in very close confines and under acoustic conditions which would be the envy of classical soloists. The mathematics of decency dictate that one pair is going to have to emulate Captain Oates and 'just step outside for some time', quite a sacrifice when you consider that the cinema in Poros is open-air, the hillsides are rock and scrub, and Greek beaches are mainly pebbles and boulders. Nevertheless, we bought drinks for several trios of ladies without any intimacy developing at all beyond Rex determining that he had once lived in the same county as a girl called (if memory serves) Trixy.

Malcolm advocated the broader view. Tackle larger groups, was his recommendation, there is a higher percentage chance of finding three visually-defective wantons in a larger group, and the expenditure in alcohol will, in the long term, prove cheaper. We hurled ourselves into this scheme enthusiastically, only to see several considerable investments in parrot – and sparkler – bedecked, multi-hued drinks evaporate as a couple of macho-men marched past.

"Ta for the drinks, ducks!" seemed paltry recompense for the outpouring of wit and intoxicants we produced.

Subterfuge in these matters is, I regret to say, frequently all. I recalled a visit to the port of Lae, on the north-west coast of New Guinea, which required more guile and stratagems than most.

We had arrived in the port from Panama, a voyage reckoned in weeks rather than days, with only brief stops at Tahiti and New Caledonia en route. These latter two ports were so prohibitively expensive that we had effectively had no social life outside the ship for about six weeks. Fortunately, there was at that time in New Guinea a reasonable selection of the fair, single ladies of predominantly Australian and New Zealand origin who worked as teachers, nurses and secretaries, and who lived in a similar social vacuum as ourselves. They were mostly as glad to see us as we were to see them. The normal approach was to let the matron at the hospital and a very active Dutch lady at the port offices know that on the night of arrival, there would be a 'reception' in the officer's bar onboard the ship. It was unnecessary to say more, the time and required dress being tolerably public knowledge amongst the ladies of the town. Indeed, it frequently occurred that the first news many a belle received of the arrival of the ship was a phone-call from a taxi-driver or a boutique-owner soliciting custom for the party. Anything new in the fashion line was, if possible, the first thing we offloaded, and some ladies even managed to attend wearing our cargo.

On the occasion in question, however, we arrived at about five o'clock on a Saturday afternoon to be told that everyone would be attending a fancy dress ball at the Aero Club that night. This was a drinking establishment whose sole aerial connection was a faded photograph of a Lancaster bomber over the bar. In the early evening, therefore, everyone not on duty taxied up to the club. Here we found a 'Romans and Slaves' night in full swing, and the few bachelors of the expat community were not going to sit back and watch us troop off with the ladies yet again, so they declined us admittance because we were not in fancy dress.

Following a muttered conference of war in the car-park of the club, we all leapt back into the taxis and scooted back to the ship. On board, over several large drinks and in an atmosphere of great hilarity, we used a vast amount of cardboard and silver cargo tape to convert ourselves into Roman soldiers. Safety-hats reversed and covered with tin-foil, with brush-heads screwed to the top for plumes, made admirable helmets. The handles of the brushes became spears, work-belts held the armour in place over khaki uniform shorts, leather sandals were donned and cabin door curtains made fine matching cloaks. More cardboard made the shields, and a black marker pen made short work of the insignia.

The taxi-drivers had unwisely been induced to wait by issuing them a ration of hard liquor, and were in something of a condition when we returned to them. To the sound of their hysterical mirth, we eased and wedged ourselves back into the cars and our return to the party was accomplished erratically, but without serious casualties beyond an odd spear up the nostril. In the car park, we formed up in two ranks and marched straight past the doormen to a burst of triumphal applause... from expulsion to return had taken about an hour and a half. We soon settled in, extricating ladies we wished to talk to from other company by the simple expedient of forming up, marching across the bar to cries of, "Leftus, Rightus, Leftus, Rightus, Legionarius, Stoppus!" We then arrested the lady in question on suspicion of Christianity.

It would have been unreasonable, in retrospect, not to have experienced some hostility from the unattached gentlemen of the community, who had after all worked very hard to set up a very fine 'do', complete with barbeque, live music and decorations. However, with a certain urgency brought on by a prolonged period at sea, we were all for the party moving back to the ship... apart from anything else, we had our comrades on duty to consider. We were therefore incensed to hear that the harbour-master had been prevailed upon to instruct the dock gatekeepers to permit access to the ship only to ships staff and genuine guests of the Master.

I recall that I left the party sometime after midnight, and that I had in my company a veritable tigress of a woman, a gloriously drunk, voluptuous creature of Polish and Swedish ancestry. Her costume, never substantial, was by the end of the night positively indecent, and required careful placement of my cloak to make her taxi-transportable... such a bounty of flesh would have tempted fate beyond all reason in a country which not only has a healthy libido, but has not yet entirely eradicated cannibalism!

We were delivered to the chicken-wired gate of the main dock, and my Machiavellian plot was prepared. I announced loftily to the gate-man that I was the Master of the ship, and instructed him to allow me access to the ship with my guest. He apologised profusely, but said that (and here he produced his carefully kept record book in evidence), he had already admitted SIX Masters and their guests to the vessel, and he just couldn't believe that such an ordinary-sized ship could have seven captains! He was an honourable, decent, trustworthy chap with a sense of duty to his employers, so the bribe didn't work either, and a poor night it would have developed into if the enterprising senior cadet had not taken to running the offshore life-boat round to the beach for the token consideration of a case of beer a time.

I recall that when woken for work the next morning, my head was the worse for wear, and that I came to on my couch. The Polish/Swedish mountain of bounty was sprawled across my bed, with a half-finished pint of lager wedged in the corner by the mattress. In sleep as in waking, she was larger than life, snoring contentedly. By the time I came off watch again at midday, she was drinking pint-for-pint with the Mate and wolfing down a dustbin-full of curry. With a sigh, I let her go... some creatures are too magnificent to cage, and far too dangerous to have running loose around the house.

***

Back in Poros, I recalled the ruses of that far-off South Pacific debauch, and decided that our current situation called for some similar dissimulation. Rex (admittedly somewhat hazed by the cocktails) had adopted a policy of discussing Greek mythology with one not-quite-so-young lady, who unfortunately appeared to connect only clean bathrooms with the name of mighty Ajax. Malcolm's strategy was sounder at first appraisal, based as it was on his encyclopaedic knowledge of pop-music. On closer scrutiny, however, his tendency to laud the less known groups whilst scorning the half-shaved, leather-clad sex-symbol currently selling millions seemed doomed to failure. He might well have done better discussing some of the weightier issues in his *Angling Times* in my humble opinion. No time this, I thought, for showing one's true colours: I am personally unable to name a single footballer since Sir Alf Ramsey and tend to be of the opinion that music ceased to be written upon the death of Sir Edward Elgar. I therefore wandered off on my own, complacently leaving The Motley with a bill that would have funded a town by-pass project, and strayed into an establishment by the name of The Jungle Bar.

Inside these palm-leafed premises music attained levels just short of physically painful, which was a pleasant relief from some bars I had stuck my nose into. It was loud enough to make conversation difficult, however, and close-packed crowds made semaphore impractical, and probably immoral to boot. Unless you and your interlocutor were familiar with sign-language, there was no better way of communicating than by postcard. These the bar thoughtfully provided. Waitresses conveyed them around the room, frequently to the wrong person, which added a certain piquancy to the proceedings. All this was performed under the manic eye of the tall, magnificently moustachioed, wild-haired proprietor whose teeth flashed like an enamelled bear-trap. His arms rarely descended below the level of his shoulders, his shoulders never ceased to rotate, and I would guess that his feet had only a passing acquaintance with the floor. Anyone who was fortunate, or unfortunate, enough to make direct eye-contact with him was instantly required to drink something called a 'slammer', which was small, highly colourful and looked infinitely evil. He periodically emerged from the bar onto the floor where he elbowed clear just enough room to dance, and kept it free with wild and erratic explosions of gangling limbs. He was the life and soul of the party and ran it with a frenzy of glee that Lucretia Borgia let loose in Porton Down would have found hard to match. Several attractive and apparently foreign waitresses galloped around the premises, controlled by a lady who sat at the end of the counter with a serene manner and a Buddhistic economy of movement. She had a captivating face dominated by huge dark eyes, piles of hair roiled up on top of her head, and extravagant silver earrings. She looked positively Egyptian, which just shows how wrong you can be, because it transpired that she came from Reading. This partnership of opposites was Stathis and Mary, and fine, original hosts they were.

My roving eye detected at the other end of the bar a woman apparently sitting alone. She was moderately dressed by the standards of the evening in jeans and a white blouse and she appeared none too pleased with life in general, gazing at the bar-top and toying with her glass. Her sandy-brown hair was pulled severely back into a ponytail, and she wore no cosmetics that I could see. I sent her a card asking if I could buy her a drink.

Her reply, damp from its passage down the bar, said simply, 'I warn you, I'm a lesbian'. Thinking subterfuge, I replied 'That's all right, I'm gay'. She looked at me, shook her head with a smile, and sent me a further note. 'Fine. Metaxa and Coke. Don't bother if you are an accountant'. We were getting on famously! I bought her drink from Stathis in one of his less enervated moments and joined her.

After 1.00 a.m., the music level was reduced following an acrimonious exchange between Stathis and two policemen, and with conversation now a viable option, my companion heaved a sigh.

"Oh, God. That was going very nicely, and now we've got to talk!"

Asked if that was so terrible, she replied, "Probably. You are going to ask my name, how long I have been here, when am I going home and where am I staying. We will then discuss the best beach, bar and restaurant. You will tell me that you name is Dave; that you work in…" Here she picked up my hand and examined the palm and nails; "…Light engineering, which is at least better than accountancy, and you will tell me about your Ford Escort called 'Flash'. Finally you will attempt to lure me into your bed or mine with the mind-bogglingly contemptible bait of a cup of coffee. Right?"

"Remarkably perspicacious, my dear!" I replied. "Except that I am well aware that your real name is Ulrika Strumpf, here on behalf of the People's Popular Movement for the Liberation of Multi-pedal Invertebrates to blow up the winner of the All-Greek octopus-splatting championships to be held here tomorrow. I, of course, am the dreaded amateur vasectomiser, Heinz Beenz, Count von Zehn. I cannot drive, am a leading member of the Movement for the Abolition of Caffeine Containing Refreshment, and am currently taking a cruise for tax purposes."

She clutched my arm in mock terror. "You won't give me away, will you? The rostrum's already mined!"

"Not so long as you promise to speak not a word of sense for the rest of the evening!" I declared.

We listened to a very long, involved story from Stathis concerning his father and a slammer, which involved everyone having to drink one, and then my octopus-liberator leapt off her stool, saying; "Come on, let's get out of here before the Wally I was waiting for turns up!"

"Why?" I asked. "Has he got a Ford Escort?"

"Worse. He's Greek, and he's got a Honda 50. Come on."

We next found The Gorilla Bar. A much quieter one, this, with good Sixties music, and another Anglo-Greek partnership, Michaeli and Maggie. The former was a nuclear-powered, muscled, square-set little chap who seemed to exist for the sole purpose of transporting an impossibly large smile around the place, and the latter was a sweet-faced, baroque temptress with amazing mobility of feature and a wicked, mischievous sense of humour. Whilst Michaeli hurtled around the bar uttering cries of, "Okee Dokee!" Maggie ruled behind the bar, and had a most disturbing habit of up-ending a bottle over one's glass, and then abstractedly answering the phone or having a chat with another customer before eventually re-corking the bottle when there was hardly any room in the glass for a splash of mixer.

I noticed in a fleeting glimpse of reality that Malcolm had gravitated to this hostelry as well, and was sat in the corner under a most apposite caricature of a monkey doing a little courting of his own. Now, my companion had perhaps eaten just one steak-and-kidney pud too many in her time and possibly wouldn't have got a job as a model for Dior, but that was fine by me because artists don't queue up in front of me with their easels either. Malcolm, however, appeared to have taken the name of the bar too literally. He seemed to be doing a bit of voluntary social-work for a home for inebriate major primates. When his muse embraced him, it was only one step short of a mugging. I decently averted my eyes.

"A sad case," I said, when 'Ulrika' (we were still avoiding real names) asked if I was acquainted with him.

"Ford Escort?"

"With spoilers and fluffy dice," I lied. (Malcolm is a stout supporter of the local bus-company.) She shook her head sadly, and we moved on again, partly to avoid looking on at a man in adversity, and partly to avoid another one of Maggie's horse tranquilisers.

In a quieter bar, by now more early morning than late night, an important break-through was made: 'Ulrika' was unmasked as Jill, an air-hostess with an

Arabian airline on a two-night stopover. There was no Greek on a Honda 50. I declared my identity, and Jill proposed a move back to the Gorilla Bar, explaining that she did not want to spoil an excellent night by throwing an amorous me off her balcony, so another one of Maggie's cocktails should make it impossible for me to get onto the balcony in the first place. It did not, in fact, work. We ended up sitting in the cockpit of *Nissos* after the bars closed, watching the revellers going home and sipping Metaxa. We welcomed Rex home at a late hour and politely did not comment on his fat lip or single status. We shuddered in unison when we considered the awful significance of the continued absence of Malcolm. Finally, after all the night-life had drifted away, and as the very first glimmer of dawn lightened the sky, Jill and I rolled, fully clothed, into the V-berth... and slept.

Jill awoke first in the morning, about tenn-ish I suppose. She conducted a swift self-examination, found herself un-ravished, and thanked me profusely. Whether these thanks were for a pleasant evening or for restraint I was unsure, and thought it best not to ask. Then Jill said that if we were fated never to meet again that she wished me a nice life, commented that she had to be on the twelve-twenty hydrofoil, and climbed out of the fore hatch and my life. Jill, you witty, vivacious creature: If you ever read this, I am now a successful author and, amazingly, still free. Be an angel, give the publisher a ring and make an ageing lecher very happy...

***

Upon arising, I found an unshaven and dishevelled Malcolm asleep in the cabin. He claimed that, even in alcohol, he had been unable to accede to the demands of Clyde, as his paramour became known to the expedition. He had panicked and fled, only to find himself in a pine forest. (He produced some pine needles from his pocket in verification.) Here, lost, he had slept for a while until the early light of dawn showed him the blessed clock-tower, and the way home. He had learned a considerable amount about Greek gardening on the way. That was his story at any rate, and I for one accepted it wholeheartedly. And ignored the lone pine tree in the corner of the adjacent square.

Rex awoke with a fat lip, obtained in an affair of honour. Observing a bit of a fracas between an English girl and her Greek boyfriend, Rex had mounted his moral white charger (twenty-two hands high at least) and galloped to the rescue of this maiden beset by foreign cads. Thus his injuries were gloriously sustained, but the fact that they had been inflicted by the maiden herself vexed him sorely. A slap in the kisser and a nasty stiletto heel to the shin, accompanied by the screeched demand that he "Leave my Adonis alone!" left him a sorrier and wiser man.

Whilst tut-tut-ting sympathetically with my crew, I did nothing whatever to confirm or deny reports of my own prowess, but I did take care to ostentatiously deposit six empty condom packets in the garbage bag just before Malcolm took it ashore, to establish the immoral superiority of the captain.

Having had a full day of watching me squirm over the issue of the pilot book, Malcolm now handed it over. It was the excellent 'Greek Waters Pilot' by Rod Heikell, and it served us superbly until the end of the trip. The similarity of the author's name to an infamous German bomber, however, led us into the habit of always referring to the book by names connected with Teutonic military aviation.

"Let's see what Messerschmidt says," would come the cry, or "Junkers says there's no bank there," and it amused us to try to use a different reference to the Luftwaffe and it's antecedents at every reference. Given our cantankerous dispositions, planning meetings often became quite heated and abusive and the pilot-book was frequently referred to, which eventually strained our stock of Teutonic flying references. Running out of aircraft types, we progressed to the names of German flying aces of increasing obscurity. Eventually, Malcolm, in support of one of his more unreasonable proposals, proclaimed, "That's not what Boelke says."

"Who?" we asked.

"Boelke!" muttered Malcolm, leaving those of us with a lesser knowledge of First World War aviation history to assume that he had become abusive over the matter.

***

I don't suppose that many of the charter-boats leaving Poros heading southward do so without making Hydra their next stop, and initially our intention was the same: However, the previous two nights (and more particularly the subsequent early mornings) had sapped our stamina a touch. Feeling that a quiet night in a little bay was called for, we identified a suitable refuge just south of the Tselevinia peninsula about half way to Hydra. Then, having of course missed the Oh-Christ-hundred weather forecast on the radio, I set off to get a weather report.

During our session at Petros's café the previous day, he had informed me that the Port Police office would always have a weather forecast, but that they rarely spoke any English. Mulling this over during the evening, I had taken the matter up with a barman during my peregrinations with Jill, and had spent twenty hilarious minutes learning the correct way to ask for a weather report in Greek. I had also written this down phonetically on a bar mat, to allow me to recap in the morning. By the sober light of day the scheme appeared to stand up to the fleeting scrutiny it received, and so, Malcolm and Rex's scorn for the plan notwithstanding, I strode confidently into the Port Police office to obtain the forecast. Confronting a charming young chap, I confidently demanded '*mipos echete toh prognostika kairou, se parakalo*'. Yes, yes, I know what you are thinking, but the barman had not been evil, and I didn't end up in the slammer for telling the port policemen that his mother was an incontinent gerbil; I have since learned that this is, indeed, a very polite way of asking for the weather forecast. Unfortunately, possibly due to my fragile condition, I had failed to think the scheme all the way through to the point of the reply. This, not unreasonably, came back at me in a flood of rapid Greek no doubt as fluent as my own. I might as well have tried to understand the back end of a flatulent rhinoceros. I only knew one other word of the language, *Efcharisto,* or thank you, so I promptly used it and got the hell out. This probably left the Port Policeman thinking, 'What beautiful Greek for a foreigner. And *such* nice manners!' and it left me knowing no more about the weather than I could divine by peering at the sky. But Malcolm was waiting outside, and admitting failure was not to be countenanced, so I cast a leery eye at the bright, blue, benevolent heavens and decided to wing it. I gave him a cheery thumbs-up before dispatching him to buy the makings of a solid peasant lunch, some ice for the beer and wine, and a large portion of frozen prawns, with which he promised to produce fine things along the line of a prawn curry for dinner. I then wandered round the docks and noted that most of the little fishing boats were going out. As a weather oracle, I decided that that was good enough for me!

I passed a few minutes investing about ten quids-worth of drachmae from the common fund in a small spear-gun. These preparations complete, we breakfasted at George's cafe in the main square. Poros, it seems, is not the sort of place where a full breakfast ordered at one-thirty in the afternoon raises any eyebrows, and by two-thirty we were en-route in the afternoon sun for our bay.

***

We had a gentle easterly, which gave us a five mile leg close-hauled on the port tack to start with. I got Rex steering reasonably and started playing with tracks, halyards, sheets and what have you to try to improve *Nissos's* less-than-sparkling up-wind performance. Malcolm, who was beginning to convey quite clearly that his unsuitability for the sport of wind-induced nautical peregrination was exceeded only by his indifference to the science, engaged himself diligently with his new fishing rig. Using a reel attached to the pushpit, he trolled astern of us a succession of garish, wickedly be-hooked lures. Whilst tending this contraption, he kept up a steady stream of disparagement regarding our speed. When I announced that my adjustments had resulted in an increase in speed of about half a knot, he expressed great enthusiasm and asked rather cuttingly what that might translate to in miles per hour. By way of a riposte, I gave it as my considered opinion that it was a poor intellectual triumph to catch a creature so abysmally dim-witted as to put one of his lures in its mouth. Rex waxed lyrical on the subject of viticulture, prompted by the information in the pilot book that the adjacent coast was noted for its vineyards. In the higher flights of his enthusiasm, his steering became noticeably less reliable, so to avoid unscheduled departures from the course (and, on one occasion, from the sea entirely), I took the helm.

Sailing to Hydra from Poros, one passes out of a widening funnel of high, forested land formed by the east end of the island and the mainland. Keeping close in with the latter on your starboard side, the track lies roughly south east to a sharp point called Tselevinia, which is tipped by two small islands. Here it is normal to pass through the channel formed between the outer island and the inner one; it is *most* unrewarding to try the passage between the inner island and the shore, due to a disappointing lack of aqueous profundity. One then turns fully ninety degrees onto a south westerly heading for the town of Hydra. Our bay, lurking behind an islet close in to the shore, lay about a mile around this corner. I intended to pass through the navigable channel, which I discretely checked several times on the chart to ensure I had the right one. I had just taken the tiller after a last check of chart and echo-sounder (the latter being mounted at the chart-table) and was happily steering into the gap when Malcolm let out a purely animal grunt of satisfaction and began to wind in on the trawl-winch.

Looking astern, I saw the satisfying splash of my dinner on the surface some way behind. Winding his line in furiously, Malcolm issued a staccato succession of orders to Rex for the receiving and subduing of Leviathan. A bread board and a sharp knife from the galley, together with a vicious bludgeon and an odorous landing-net from Malcolm's unsavoury and decrepit B.O.A.C. bag, were prepared for the ritual slaughter. The two valiant warriors stood in the back of the cockpit, Malcolm winding furiously and Rex struggling inelegantly to assemble the landing-net. They were distributed one either side of the tiller, considerably restricting its motion, and also my view aft. By concentrating through a tangle of erratic limbs, I could catch an occasional glimpse of the splashing getting closer to the frying-pan.

It may perhaps have been that I spent a fraction too long looking astern, but my attention was shortly drawn back to the direction of progress by the urgent flapping of the sails. For a moment, I thought that I had wandered off course, but quickly I realized that the wind had shifted in the passage to come dead against us. I put the tiller up as far as it would go against Rex's legs, and bore off to starboard to come back on the wind. The sails had just nicely filled again, and *Nissos* was accelerating recklessly through the one-knot barrier when a booming roar announced the arrival in the south end of the passage of a behemoth of a power-cruiser. With great, elaborate, chrome-trimmed bows cocked ludicrously high, and out of the water for half of it's length, it curved into sight round the rocks at the other side of the passage, throwing a monumental curling 'Vee' of water from it's bows. It steadied on a course which would intersect ours with highly regrettable consequences in what looked like about thirty seconds.

That was half of the bad news.

The other half was that close on the shoulder of this gleaming specimen of maritime modesty came a hard-charging hydrofoil in the now familiar blue-gold livery, evidently intent on overtaking the gin-palace in the passage. As a premeditated attempt at maritime destruction, this situation appeared to rival unrestricted submarine warfare for destructive potential. Technically, I had the right of way, but I had no desire to let lawyers become fat on the academic question of whether I had legally or illegally become the strawberry jam in this sandwich. Rule Two of the Collision Regulations permits: "...a departure from these rules in order to avoid immediate danger." Feeling that the wild-card effect of my good self moving obliquely across the nautical equivalent of the Grand National turning Chair Corner might not resolve the affair for the best, I turned hard to starboard to run directly away from them. This was calculated to remove the crossing aspect of the situation, whilst making myself the smallest target possible. I will not swear that the decision making process was quite as ordered or logical as it is here recorded, but it came to me fairly swiftly. And indeed, had Rex not been standing where he was, stopping the tiller from going over more than ten degrees, there is little doubt that it would have worked. As it was, however, we merely wallowed around and paid off into the path of the behemoth.

Noise always seems to me to increase proportionally to the cube of the actual threat factor involved. Minor mooring scrapes produce an awesome cacophony of raised voices, revved engines, clattering windlasses and, naturally, the barrage of utterly useless but well-meant advice which these ruckuses invariably attract. The swell of noise helps further unnerve anyone hewn of less than granite, giving rise to a touch of panic, which increases the noise still further, and so on. These contributory factors multiply and create something really spectacular and entertaining... as long as you are not embroiled in it... out of a minor event. Several people I have met have commented on the stupendous volumes attained in small-boat collisions, for example. Only the truly major, hugely gargantuan cock-ups are achieved in stupefied, awed, reverent silence. A chap who was on the bridge of a container-ship berthing in a New Zealand port told me of the unholy hush that engulfed all assembled when it became evident that the flare of the ship's bow was about to scythe down a brand-new, towering container crane. During the dignified collapse of the crane, which I believe was at the time the largest single insurance loss in the Southern Hemisphere, silence reigned apart from the distant crumpling of folding steel. Only as the last girder shuddered into immobility was the pilot heard to mutter, "Oh my gosh!"

Our current situation, not being quite of this magnitude, was naturally a very noisy affair indeed. On a good foundation of four thundering engines at high speed, add the sudden, frantic braying of some impressive air-horns on the power-boat and a friendly, sympathetic toot or two from the hydrofoil. Mix in Rex, screaming blue murder as I tried with every fibre in my body to push the tiller through his kneecaps and into the cockpit coaming, and a frantically gibbering Malcolm who, oblivious to the Armageddon unfolding around him, was solely concerned with not losing his fish. Garnish with a flapping sail, as I let the main go to bring her around more easily, and serve piping hot... a clamour in which it would have been very difficult for the steadiest, most self- assured of captains to formulate clear plans of action. Far from formulating a plan of action, I was unable to summon up any thought at all, beyond an abstract and not strictly constructive mental image of how well a large bloodstain would stand out on the gleaming white bow of the power-boat.

The first hint that the crisis might yet be happily resolved came when the bow of the power-boat first dipped dramatically as the throttles were chopped, and then swung fast to starboard to come around our stern. The hydrofoil leaned drunkenly the same way, obligingly making room, and both of them thundered on their way with friendly waves. The only acrimony arising out of the affair, I regret to record, came from a blue-faced Malcolm, who roared invective at the gin-palace until it cleared the end of the fishing-line. Engines receded; the noise-level dropped to almost nothing. There was just the slosh of the power- boats' wake and Malcolm muttering, "I think it's still on... Damn, I've lost it... No! It's still there!" I set about getting the boat back on course, and Rex massaged his knee in stoical and righteous silence.

The end of the affair saw Malcolm, previously tensed for combat like a spaniel on a game-moor, suddenly wilt in stature and stand very still for a moment. He then heaved his quarry on board... a splendid, twenty-gram plastic shopping bag. He unhooked it in tragic silence and dropped it on the deck. We all stared at it for a moment, then Rex picked it up by the handles and hopefully peered into it, but it contained nothing more nutritious than a portion of Aegean Sea. He shook his head mournfully. Malcolm, pausing only to comment that breeding and manners were not consistent with malicious, hysterical laughter, withdrew with damaged dignity to the foredeck to sort out his tackle.

The time — all thirty minutes of it — that we took to sail the remainder of the distance to our bay for the night was spent in tacking through the gap with our ears cocked keenly for the first hint of an engine, and in enjoyable acrimony, slander and mutual deprecation. Rex, embittered, I suppose, by my attempt to prune him at knee-level, was delightfully sarcastic about my handling of the 'Channel Dash', as he called the afternoon's incident. I scored a point or two back when, securing the boom after stowing the mainsail, he pulled the topping-lift tight and then let go of it without checking to see that the rope-clutch was holding. The effect of this was that he had deliberately lifted a large metal object some three feet up in the air, and dropped it on his own skull. This cheered even Malcolm up for a minute.

We dropped anchor in Soupia without incident, naturally; no-one lives there, and there were no other boats to watch. Rex, on the bow, said that he didn't think that the anchor was properly dug in, with which opinion I disagreed in a lofty and patronising manner. "It's in like Flynn," was the term I used, I believe.

"Fine by me," agreed Rex. "And I'm sure an honourable man like yourself couldn't be unjust enough to ask me to get out of bed in the middle of the night if the contrary should prove to be the case!"

***

The sun was, by now, dropping fast down the western sky, highlighting the island of Dhokos and the hills of Ermioni. Malcolm was preparing what he called a nightline, which judging by the number of hooks he put on it seemed to be an infernal device intended to entirely denude the Aegean Sea of fish at one foul stroke. Rex monopolised the foredeck with book and chilled wine to hand, liberally smeared with sun-protection cream. Even in the late, watery sun, his skin was an interesting shade of salmon-pink. I decided to go into competition with Malcolm, and slipped into my swimming-shorts and T-shirt for a spot of spear-fishing.

Malcolm stopped work, watching with close attention and a sardonic smile as I spat in my mask, donned fins and gloves, and optimistically tied a mesh shopping bag around my waist for the catch. He cocked his head in an attitude of intelligent fascination as I rinsed the mask, fitted it, and put the snorkel in my mouth. As I stood up on the transom and executed a stylish straddle-jump into the water, my un-cocked spear gun clasped harmlessly across my chest, he nodded approvingly. When I surfaced, still holding my mask in place because the rotten strap had parted, and having lost my right fin, he smirked openly. And when, having changed the mask and recovered the fin, I commenced loading the gun, he ostentatiously took cover with just the top of his head protruding above the coaming. I doubled up in the water with the butt of the spear gun on my right thigh and pulled mightily on the rubbers to cock the gun. Sadly, every action has an equal and opposite reaction, unless I have been unreliably informed, and the butt slipped. Propelled by the impressive tension I had imparted to the rubber slings, the rather uncomfortably-shaped pistol-grip shot between my legs, lacerated my inner thigh and came within a millimetre of qualifying me for a responsible post in a harem. Malcolm snorted in pure delight and called out to Rex, "Oy! Come and meet Jacques Clouseau!"

By the time I had loaded my weapon and swum away, the pair of them were on the top of the coachroof nasally approximating an excerpt from The Pearlfisher's duet.

Finning towards a hopefully fishy-looking sort of rock, I had a sly look at the anchor. True to Rex's dire prognostications, it had no hold on the seabed at all and was kipping peacefully on its back. Only the weight of the chain was holding the boat, so I dipped down and (in a manoeuvre which is glaringly absent from most of the authoritative manuals of seamanship) physically picked the anchor up and rammed its point into the bottom.

The fishing proved to be a disappointment, as even the magnification caused by the mask could not produce any form of marine life larger than my finger. However, when you have a powerful weapon in your hand for the first time, it is incredibly tempting to use it on something. I have to hand it to all the nations with multi-megaton nuclear weapons at their disposal; I am sure that I would NEVER have found the self-restraint not to let off at least a little one somewhere. Even France, that most devil-may-care of nations, has restricted itself to an occasional indulgence in atomic mining in the South Pacific. Stronger they in self-denial than I, it must be recorded. Just because I could, I let fly at a blameless and rather pretty little stripy fish, who ambled innocently in front of me committing the capital crime of appearing to be a full half-ounce larger than anything else I had seen.

The shot, probably due to the surge of bloodlust I experienced at the moment of firing (much the same as elephant-hunters of old, I should imagine) was spectacularly inaccurate. So much so, in fact, that the fish went peacefully on its way totally unaware of the titanic missile launched at its person. The impact of the spear was absorbed by a large rock of the durable looking sort that is in much demand whenever there is a re-make of Wuthering Heights. Retrieving it by the string, I found that my puissant trident had become a mangled monodent with which Annie Oakley herself would have been lucky to hit a whale in a Jacuzzi. Fishing over for the day, I emerged plesiosaur-like onto a small beach, and set off up the hill to investigate a small monument I had noticed on the way into the bay.

In many countries, small shrines are set up where fatal accidents have occurred. In the main, these are found on roads within one mile of a public house next to an appalling hairpin bend or resilient tree, but in a seafaring country such as Greece, there are no small number of them on equally prominent features of the coastline. This one, set about thirty feet up from the sea on the rocky east side of the bay, was fairly typical, a nicely-built, mortared-stone cairn topped by an ornate miniature church. A glass case contained a photograph nearly unrecognisable through damp, a small wine bottle with some dried flowers in it, a night-light type of candle and a box of matches. It was evidently a memorial to a lost fisherman or sailor, which prompted a few minutes of contemplation. I gazed around, mentally trying to construct from the peaceful seascape before me such desperate events as may have occurred here... a sobering exercise if one's calling or inclination is the sea, because there is no shortage of them.

Finally, getting cold in the early twilight, I decided to head back to the boat, but on impulse, and because there appeared to be no habitation for miles from which anyone else could come to do it, I lit the shrine's stump of candle for the night.

I have no idea where she came from, but half way down the path to the beach I met a young girl on her way up to the shrine. She was reserved in reply to my greeting, and I hurried on thinking that I would have done better to leave well alone. The girl caught me up just as I was getting back into the water, and approached me diffidently, speaking Greek and obviously wanting to confirm that it was I who had lit the candle. When I nodded, she thanked me gravely (*Efcharisto*, or thank you, I could at least understand by now) and trotted off again to God knows where.

On the boat, a most civilised evening ensued. Malcolm proved a prawn-curry maker of some competence, and a quiet glass of wine or two in the cockpit under the starry sky provoked deep discussion, silent contemplation of good things, and early, deep and wonderful sleep. In the middle of my dreamless slumbers, I became vaguely aware of a muted, pulsing engine sound at some point, and again jack-in-the-boxed out of my hatch to find a badly-lit fishing boat heading away from us out of the bay. It rounded the headland, and soon the lapping of the water and the whooping of a Scops owl ruled the night again. I slid back into oblivion.

***

I was first up the next morning, with the idea of a swim. But despite the bright early sun there was a distinct chill in the air, so I reconsidered and elected to wake myself up with coffee instead. Turning to go below again, I noticed on the side-deck two glorious, pinky-red fish laid carefully together on a white plastic bag. In the cerebral stupor common to me between the body awakening and the mind receiving a jolt of caffeine, it took me an unconscionably long time to connect the engine-noise in the night with the little girl the night before, and realise that the family had left the fish as a thank you for lighting the candle in the shrine. Things like this leave a very pleasant, warm feeling inside, and prompted me to a moment of contemplation in which I reflected that the Greeks I had so far met by no means conformed to the vaguely mediocre stereotype I had conceived before my arrival. I was beginning to very much enjoy this country, with its variety of sleepy villages, vibrant towns and deserted coves, its humour, hospitality and generosity. In contradiction of all my expectations, I was developing a very warm, good feeling about Greece and the Greeks.

Naturally, such feelings of affection for mankind in general did not for one second deter me from taking this heaven-sent opportunity to score a point over Malcolm. Before going below to make coffee, I pulled out the boat's very rudimentary fishing kit, which was no more than an agglomeration of incompetently-knotted and badly degraded nylon wrapped round a chipped plastic hand-reel. In a moment of inspired evil, I replaced the rusty hook with a small safety-pin. On the pin, I put a piece of white-ish string, and then I left the line half uncoiled next to the fish, which I put on a plate. The plastic bag went into the bin, and then I put the kettle on and set about gutting the fish.

The double-take which Malcolm performed upon emerging from his blanket was worth a case of beer. It was all I could do to keep a straight face and go on gutting the fish, whose stunned, open-mouthed expressions mirrored that of the ship's fishing expert to a 'T'.

"Magic!" I greeted him. "We used to get them the same way in the Red Sea, when I was a cadet. Just a simple hook and a bit of string for bait, and jiggle it up and down on the bottom."

The jaw dropped another inch on seeing the safety pin, and then disbelief set in.

"You got them off my bloody night-line!" he accused, and straight away, still wearing a strange, unhygienic-looking green-and-white-striped Arab galibeya in which he slept, Malcolm started heaving in the multi-hooked line he had left out overnight. And let no man say that he failed in his quest. He had baited his hooks with a nasty-looking paste made up from, if I recall it aright, sardines, bread and old cheese-rind, and this it swiftly became evident was the preferred bedtime nibble of an utterly evil-looking species of starfish. Malcolm soon had five red, wriggling and irritated examples in the cockpit.

This was fine stuff, and I, joined by the newly arisen Rex, applauded the bountiful harvest loudly from the safety of the companion-way. Barefoot, Malcolm stepped gingerly around the bench-seats trying to avoid writhing starfish and naked hooks. In fact, he was so preoccupied with preserving the watertight integrity of his tootsies that when the eel came over the rail, it quite surprised him.

Now, it wasn't by any means a large eel, and indeed, it never got any bigger; but by the time it met its premature end, perhaps three minutes after coming face-to-face with a totally unprepared Malcolm it had wrought such havoc as has rarely been wrought by eel-kind. To begin with, writhing around on the bottom, it had enmeshed itself in the fishing line so that, attached to its side for all the world like Ahab on the flank of Moby Dick, was yet another starfish, and sprouting from all over the eel were more hooks. Malcolm dumped the thing unceremoniously on the port bench and leapt for the starboard one, but not before the eel had bequeathed him a generous dollop of slime in the lower-leg area. This caused an uncontrolled descent of our Mr. Crabtree into the cockpit well, with legs akimbo. Believing whole-heartedly in the strategy of forward-defence, the eel jumped in on top of him.

At this point, Malcolm was probably spared the loss of the facility of reproduction by his unsightly nightshirt. Spread tightly between his parted knees, it formed a trampoline above his genitals on which the eel, bristling with hooks and starfish, writhed in manic abandon and liberally dispensed slime from an apparently inexhaustible source. If Stephen Spielberg were to apply his incredible talents to hardcore, science-fantasy pornography, (and I would like to assure his lawyers that it is emphatically not my belief that he would, should, has, does or will!) it is unlikely that he would create anything as bizarre as the sight of a gibbering, night gowned and slime-daubed figure, lying on a bed of live starfish, with a demonically-possessed, multi-articulated phallus tied up in nylon and apparently doing the samba in his groin. Any assistance Rex or I may have been capable of was unforthcoming, firstly due to debilitating hysterics and secondly to a very reasonable desire to have nothing whatever to do with the slime.

Eventually a Mexican stand-off was reached with Malcolm, wild-eyed and indescribably unkempt, standing on the side-deck whilst the eel appeared willing to take on all comers in the cockpit sole. We were not without a sense of sporting justice, and for such a gallant defence, we felt that the eel deserved life, but it wasn't on to let him go covered in hooks. Malcolm was handed a winch handle, the longest one we had, and the eel was decently dispatched. Rex asked Malcolm if he would like to have his photo taken with his foot on the beast's chest, following which *bon mot* Rex and I hid in the cabin whilst the Gladiator Piscatorial washed down the cockpit and disposed of his menagerie. By the time he was done, and had had a swim to clean himself up, we had cooked 'my' fish, which mollified him slightly. He still did not believe that I had caught them, but could not think how else it had been contrived. In fact, only now is the truth revealed…

After the events of the morning, almost any subsequent occurrence would have been a total anti-climax. Almost any occurrence, that is, apart from our day in Hydra harbour. Suffice it to say that the six-mile trip to Hydra was so lacking in incident that the only recollection I have of it is that it was achieved in a flat-calm under motor. Mind you, with our motor, that was a notable achievement in its own little way, of course.

CHAPTER FIVE

THE NOBLE ART OF PARKING

Reflections upon the sailing press... The problems of staying still... A grand entry into Hydra... We meet a man among men... and Alf... Mooring enjoyed vicariously... We assist at a traffic accident... Musing upon the muse... The German breakout... The gregariousness of ground-tackle... Malcolm emasculated.

Our arrival in Hydra (pronounced 'ee-dra') brought us face-to-face with an aspect of sailing which, common as it is, rarely enjoys the focus of attention in the sailing press that it truly deserves.

The effect upon trees of Agent Orange pale into utter insignificance compared with the de-forestation caused by the publishing industry in its quest to bring to the armchair-sailor the heroic feats, daring deeds and superlative physical and literary stamina of the world-girdlers. Knox-Johnston, Jones, Francis, Moitessier and the like have been round it. Blyth did it the other way. Chichester and Rose apparently valued the solitude. Arthaud, Tabarlay, Jeantot and their ilk did it, or bits of it, faster. Street did it without an engine. Adlard-Coles and Novak did it in places and conditions that most of us shiver watching documentaries about. No small number failed to do it, and very thought-provoking their stories about the vulnerability of life-rafts and the inattention of ships' lookouts are, too. And all of the successful ones, plus the more fortunate of the unsuccessful ones, have burst emphatically into print to share their hard-won triumphs, trials and experiences with the rest of us. Thus, we may exalt and tremble vicariously in their achievements, and they, on the proceeds, can do it again (all but the unsuccessful ones, that is; they may care to use the royalties to set up a nice stable yak farm in, say, Ulan Bator).

Now, I would be the last man in the world to denigrate in any way these truly splendid achievements. Civic receptions, water-firing tugs, naval escorts, the freedom of Plymouth and the enmity of the tabloid press for the lot of them, say I. Lob 'em each an O.B.E. as they pass through the Thames Barrier. But no-one, to my knowledge, has written a book which deals with how to leave your boat in a busy tourist harbour for long enough to assimilate half a kilo of spaghetti Carbonara and a thousand calories of muscle-relaxant and return to find your boat still where you left it. What most of these chappies are writing about is the sailing equivalent of motoring across the Nullabor Plain, whereas those of us who sail for alleged 'relaxation' do so upon an aquatic parody of the M25. How many useful tips can a weekend or holiday yachtsman pick up from *Sailing Across Thirteen Oceans*, by Hugh Mungous-Wave, I wonder? Obtaining drinking water from the bladders of fish, whilst vital to some, is unlikely to be strictly necessary when one's voyage will at no time take one out of sight of the saloon bar of the 'Admiral Nelson'. And you just try streaming a warp astern to check your speed in heavy stern seas in the Solent… you'll slow down all right; and probably end up going backwards, with some monstrous great hydrofoil wrapped up in the end of it. No, what the holiday yachtie needs is a book which tells him how to get a berth in Yarmouth, I.o.W., on a bank-holiday weekend. (A thirty-foot shoehorn and a pail or two of Vaseline comes in handy!) And it's all very well avoiding a tabular iceberg in the immensity of the Southern Ocean, but what about a supertanker off Fawley? More to the point for today's yachties, how do you afford the blasted harbour when you DO miraculously get into it? Without selling the kids for vivisection, that is? ('Go to France' is the snappy answer to that one.) None of this bothers our intrepid ocean author, of course. He rarely stops anywhere, and even if he does, he gets towed in, a special berth at the opera-house, a car laid on for him and the bill is obligingly picked up by 'Gnash-Flash Toothpaste', or whoever else has managed to get a bill-poster up his spinnaker.

He will earnestly tell us how to survive after a knock-down; his boat will right itself, and off he will go again having made a new mast out of some sticky-backed plastic and two squeezee-bottles. We, on the other hand, will be stuck upside-down with our mast-top imprisoned in top quality Hamble mud. What we WOULD appreciate would be a word or two on how to avoid getting knocked-down in the first place. Most of these chaps have now done it so often you would think that they would be starting to find out what is causing it. (Personally, I suspect that prudent use of the reefing arrangements may be found to be of service, but then I always over-simplify things.) Hands up everyone who would subscribe to *The Amateurs' Guide to Managing Holiday Harbour Hell-spots*? Right, pass me the typewriter, chop down a Matto Grosso or two, and get the pulp-mill greased up; my fortune is assured!

I shall now descend with dignity from my soap-box and continue my story.

***

Hydra Harbour is one of the most picturesque ports anywhere. A natural bowl in the craggy, mountainous island sweeps down steeply and evenly to form three sides of a small bay. The north side is enclosed by a substantial stone mole, and the main town of the island is piled up the fringing hillsides. The mouth of the port is guarded by battlements east and west of the mole, from which sprout numerous cannon of substantial calibre. Here, one feels, is a community which believes passionately in the adage about strong fences and good neighbours. High above the town, several gleaming white monasteries perch perilously on the heights.

The town itself is superb. The natural and military defences of the place brought, in days gone by, security and massively successful commerce to the island, and this is reflected by the impressive merchants' mansions that rear amongst the humbler houses. Dressed natural stone (much of it rifled from the local antiquities such as the Temple of Poseidon at Poros) alternate with mock-classical facades and traditional plastered construction. Painted buildings are gently faded by the sun to comfortable pastel shades of umber and ochre, and the waterfront is canopied by the softly contrasting colours of the awnings of the kafenieons and restaurants. Behind the town is the landscape of the island, barren rock rearing majestically two thousand feet with a small clump of pine here and there and scattered areas of agricultural terracing. Its barren rock and scrub are a total contrast to the pine-wooded Poros, the cultivated Aegina and the fertile Peloponnese.

As the town of Hydra is contained in its natural rock amphitheatre, the full breathtaking vista does not open out until the seaborne visitor rounds the point to enter the harbour, and the abruptness and closeness of the revelation stuns the unwary. The practical upshot of this on the yachtsman is, therefore, to awe and astonish the crew at a crucial moment. Skippers are looking anywhere but at the entrance, crew are fumbling with cameras instead of fenders, and this is a dreadful shame, because wandering into Hydra Harbour in a distracted state of mind is about the same as materialising in the middle of Spaghetti Junction in a pedal-car at rush hour. At any time, Hydra is an aquatic loony-bin. Fast yellow or red taxi-boats swarm like bees; slower caiques, doubling as cargo and passenger transport, mill in genial, bovine confusion, and irate fishing-boats curse and jostle through the melee with long-suffering impatience. Both inside the mole and out, there will be a Red-Indian circle of yachts either 'stacking' or performing the mooring-dance. Naturally, in addition to the normal groundswell of activity, when I attempted to enter for the first time the entrance was half-blocked by a cruise-ship lying half in, half out of the harbour on the east quay. It was named *City of Poros*, which was appropriate because in the confines of Hydra, it looked about the same size as its namesake.

My first attempt to use what remained of the entrance was aborted hurriedly in the face – or rather, the arse – of yet another hydrofoil. This was peacefully engaged in reversing out of the reduced gap with only marginally less enthusiasm than it displayed when going forwards in open water. As I circled to avoid it the stern swung towards me, and for a moment or two we had a merry game of chase, in which I sportingly pitted my greater manoeuvrability and amusingly asthmatic engine against the hydrofoil's superior speed and total indifference. Finally, tiring of this, the hydrofoil revved its impressive engines, waddled unsteadily onto its legs and thundered out of my life in the direction of Poros. Malcolm suggested that we should get a time-table for the damn things. Rex pointed out that as they managed to catch us at every narrow point they already seemed to have *our* timetable... an observation which, while not strictly helpful, did appear to be true.

On our second attempt, we got into the harbour with only a brief skirmish with a water-taxi. Now, we had studied the plan of the port in the pilot-book, seen a photo of it on a post-card, and looked at it carefully from the outside. But nothing quite prepares one for the actual size of the place. It really is minute!

The east side of the harbour is reserved for ferries and hydrofoils. The west is occupied by a stone jetty used for unloading construction materials and mooring the small wooden fishing-boats which every male Greek seems to own. The south quay and the inside of the mole on the north side are used in roughly equal proportion by yachts and local commercial boats. Even at this late stage of the season, I could only see one clear place, against the quay on the north mole. Staking my claim to it before a large green charter boat which had followed us in, I had Rex hurriedly dump the anchor in the middle of the harbour and backed towards the alarmingly small gap. The skippers of the yachts on either side of it emerged on their respective foredecks and peered suspiciously at me, but they waited until I was almost into the space before telling me how to do it.

My own plan had been simple to the point of imbecility. I intended to reverse in until I could grab hold of both boats and manhandle *Nissos* back to the quay. This was evidently not the way to do it, however. I was the unwilling recipient of a large amount of gratuitous advice, in strongly accented English, which may well have been selected from the finest available in the donor's native tongue. Most of it seemed to lose coherence, relevance and touch with reality in translation, however, and in any case my two instructors were quoting conflicting authorities. Stalwartly applying the principle of 'One Boat, One Captain', I ignored them, and whilst Malcolm and I walked *Nissos* back from either side of the cockpit, Rex slacked the anchor chain. Hands from the neighbours implored us for ropes, hands, fenders... and the more I ignored them, the harder they bellowed to overcome my apparent deafness.

The noise factor was growing again, and I really couldn't see any reason for it; but since few of our manoeuvres so far had been elegant, the evident distress of the neighbours began to undermine my self-confidence. I started to look surreptitiously around for the unseen pitfall, and when I couldn't find one it only made me look the harder. Whilst I was thus preoccupied, Malcolm was diverted from the path of righteousness by the Italian to starboard and induced into messing around with a totally irrelevant fender. I, meanwhile, came under well-meaning attack from the Austrian to port, who had armed himself with a telescopic boat-hook. Rex, trying to let a bit more chain out whilst his attention was half on the deteriorating situation at the blunt end of the boat, got an careless finger-end in the gypsy and added a creditable number of decibels of his own to the acoustic pot-pourri. I managed an outraged bellow myself when, half way through remonstrating with Malcolm for listening to bloody foreigners, I received a brisk rap on the backside from the Austrian's wayward boathook.

The noise had started to attract a few spectators, who gathered ghoulishly at the edge of the quay. This enraged me, especially since the wind was so light that if everyone concerned had dropped dead at that precise moment (and I confess that I believe I recommended that very course of action to several people during the affair) the boats would have stayed exactly where they were with never a blemish on their respective gel-coats.

In raising my own voice to re-assert my own authority on the proceedings, I merely increased the noise and irrationality factors. I threw a rope to the quay, which was grabbed at by so many willing hands that it inevitably fell back into the water. It was at this instant that I put the engine astern to bring us to the quay, but fortunately we were saved another propeller-clearing debacle by Malcolm, who accidentally kicked the engine out of gear again during one of his otherwise fruitless migrations up and down the side of the cockpit. I threw a second rope, which was helpfully put through a ringbolt and thrown back so accurately that it landed on the Italian boat. I also caught a sidelong glimpse of the Austrian, who now had his boathook inexplicably thrust through our toilet window.

At this moment of high farce, the crowd on the quay parted like the waters of the Red Sea, and to the edge of the parapet strode an unbelievable figure. A barrel-shaped individual, the new arrival wore baseball boots, odd socks, knee-length Bermuda shorts of badly faded and stained lime green, and a light-blue vest emblazoned with the words 'Charter Flights are a Plane in the Ass'. Of his face, only a bulbous, sun-savaged nose and sapphire-blue eyes wreathed in wrinkles could be discerned; the rest was hidden behind a massive, greying spade-beard and a gaudy red handkerchief, tied pirate-style around his head. From under the latter cascaded a leonine mane of grey-brown, shoulder-length hair which combined with the beard to entirely conceal his neck. His body was round, with barely a trace of a waist. However, any thought that he was merely fond of his food was still-born because his whole body displayed, through tangles of wiry hair, the sort of musculature normally created on film stars in Incredible Hulk re-makes with the aid of bicycle pumps. The word 'Colossus' came irresistibly to mind and it took some moments of looking at him to realize that he was, in fact, below average height. His voice, when it came, was no disappointment. A deep, commanding bass silenced most of the noise, leaving only the Italian still in opposition.

"Gimme the rope!" roared an aperture in the beard, and then, to the Italian, "Hey, you! One boat, one captain! You hush up, eh!"

I was momentarily delighted by this re-enforcement of my position, but before I could open my mouth to take charge again, it became obvious that I was not the captain the newcomer had immediately in mind. He swiftly had Rex letting out chain, Malcolm heaving on a rope, and me reversing the engine. Having no further use for my mouth, I closed it to stop flies getting in and did as I was told.

The boat slid easily into position and we had her tied up in a trice.

"Perfect!" enthused our saviour, and then he bent close to me and, with a genial grin, confided to me in a conspiratorial rumble which only carried a hundred yards or so, "You don' needa mess widda rope, y'know. Jus' pull y'self in widda hands!" He gave me a wink reminiscent of a lethargic giant clam closing and ambled off up the quay, with his legs bowed and his arms held clear of his sides to stop his muscles fighting each other.

Stunned by the injustice of the whole thing, I turned to have a look at the fendering and found that the Austrian had lost marginally more face than myself. Having extricated his boathook from the toilet window, he had placed it on our coachroof grab rail and, for reasons probably amply clear in the *Alpine Sailing Manual* but obscure to me, leaned heavily on it. Being telescopic, it collapsed slowly, and he subsided to end up hung like a sack over our two guard-rails. I helped to extricate him without his falling between the two boats, gave him his boathook back, and thanked him kindly in my schoolboy German for whatever service he thought he had rendered. He was at least grateful, which is more than could be said for the Italian. He carried on chuntering discontentedly until I finally divined that he was concerned that my anchor chain was on top of his. I said I didn't think so, but in any case, as he was not leaving until morning, we could sort it out then. This failed to console him, and he continued to pace operatically up and down his side decks, muttering things like "Vesuvio!" "Molto Porco!" "Mio Dio!" and the like. They didn't teach Italian at my school, so I left him to it.

The affair had inevitably resulted in my style of captaincy coming under Malcolm's caustic scrutiny again, with myself (under the pseudonym of Captain Chaos) being found inferior in all respects to the Man-Mountain. I wasn't going to win this argument verbally, so I contented myself with rigging the gangplank precariously high up on the top rail of the pushpit. Malcolm is no gazelle in these matters.

We were well into the early afternoon beer when Mr. Colossus reappeared and asked us if we needed water. It transpired this was his official function, and with the massive hose coiled over his shoulder he resembled nothing so much as a psychedelic Michelin Man. I decided that we could do with a bit of water, so whilst Rex battled with the obstreperous filling pipe, I invited the water-man on board for a beer.

Anyone who has been in Hydra will undoubtedly have recognised Pandelis from the earlier description. The official water-man, semi-official berthing-master, unchallenged world-champion anchor untangler and intimate of all waterfront confidences, Pan is a man with a past that has involved sponge-diving, emigration to the U.S., various dark rumours about a military career, and numerous business ventures. He is as much a part of the Hydra waterfront as the clock-tower on the monastery. He will drink one coffee with anyone, two coffees with virtually no-one. His hyper-active mind springs from subject to subject like an antelope on amphetamines, leaving his interlocutor about four unrelated statements behind. His wit is sharp and penetrating, his insight keen and his powers of observation disconcertingly acute. He is humorous, friendly, and speaks a fluent New York-American-English. He is the unpretentious yachtsman's friend, although sometimes rather a rough diamond. The slightly macho veneer melts in an instant at the sight of children, and he is, despite his desperate piratical dress (which is the same day and night, summer and winter) a polished courtier in the presence of the ladies.

During his stay, Pan was accosted by our disgruntled Italian neighbour, who evidently believed he was appealing to a higher authority, and told that our anchor was over his. Pan embraced the whole harbour with one magnificent, proprietorial sweep of his muscular arm and snorted, "Mistah, *everyone's* anchor is over yours!" And indeed, in such a small harbour with boats pointing every which way, there must on sober consideration be an awesome lattice of anchors and chains on the bottom. The Italian stumped off, and Pan resumed his seat and his beer. "Anyway," he added with a knowing grin, "...there's two flotillas coming this afternoon.' 'Nother thirty anchors. He's gonna go crazy!"

The harbour was already full, and the green boat which had followed us in had started to form a second row out from the quay. Pan told us that, in high summer, there were often four rows of boats on the north side of the harbour and another two on the south. He advised us to be on our boat by four P.M., to protect our own investment from the depredations of the aquatically insane, and to enjoy the fun.

"Some of dese guys, you call 'em 'Captain' one time, dey go power-crazy!" He announced as he left. At this, Malcolm gave one of his nastiest smiles, and Rex added sagely, "Detached from all reality, poor souls," with an exaggerated sidelong glance in my direction.

***

We lunched well on kalamari and a juicy roast of lamb at a restaurant next to the Merchant Marine Academy on the east side of the harbour. Then we wandered in leisurely fashion back around the busy front. It was only when we were hooted at to move by a garbage lorry that I suddenly realised that it was the first vehicle of any kind we had seen, and it later transpired that all forms of automotive transport are banned on Hydra. There are a couple of corporation light trucks and a garbage wagon, and that is it. Anything else that requires moving goes either by water-taxi or, more commonly, by quadruped. The muleteers are to be seen everywhere, loading strings of mules or donkeys, guiding them through the crowded narrow alleyways, and tidily sweeping up the droppings. There is a mule-rank... quite a rank mule rank... in the south-eastern corner of the quay.

We retired into a cafe in the other corner of the port, right next to a statue of a magnificently-moustachioed gentleman in a naval uniform, whose chest we could admire; his head poked forlornly through the cafe canopy. Here, from a shady base admirably well connected to a friendly and efficient source of cold refreshment, we conducted several short sorties of the shopping and money-changing variety. In between these bursts of energy, we enjoyed the panoramic view of Hydra, a-bustle with artisans, muleteers, water-men and visitors. Then we settled the somewhat pricey bill and, dumping our purchases on the boat, made a preliminary safari into the back-streets of the town. This foray was prompted partly by a commendable interest in the local architecture and customs, and partly by the realisation that we were in the Greek equivalent of San Tropez. The cafes on the waterfront charged, in Rex's descriptive words, like wounded wildebeest.

In the winding alleys of the town, it became tolerably evident why motorised transport had been legislated off the island. Alleyways with average widths of perhaps seven feet, liberally strewn with chicanes, steps and porches were less than ideal country for the infernal destruction engine. That is not to say that the Greeks wouldn't have given it their best shot, of course, which is no doubt why the Iron Horse is banned.

Back in the heady days of the Greek revolution, in the 1820's, the population of Hydra was swelled dramatically by refugees from islands more vulnerable to official expressions of Turkish displeasure. Perhaps the subsequent overcrowding has left a lasting impression on the Hydriots, because they have developed a taste for high-walled gardens around their houses, which exclude the street commerce entirely. Tantalising glimpses can be had of shady, private and well-kept little courtyards, but otherwise the private lives of the people of Hydra are as safe from the eyes of the tourists now as they once were from those of the refugees. We wandered in silent, deserted, walled lanes, with a shop, a church or an ornate bell-tower here and there to break the mould. The siesta tradition is strong in Greece, and apart from the odd mule-string and a tourist or two, we saw little life. Away from the bustle of the harbour the silence was incredible, and only the occasional contented snore from an open window stopped us making noises just to make sure that our ears still worked.

Some of the walled gardens have been converted into very attractive-looking restaurants and bars, and although we marked a couple down for investigation later, they were all closed for the afternoon. It was only after a lengthy traipse around the lanes that we found a small ouzeri open in a narrow alley. We quickly settled around the rickety tin table and shamelessly woke the proprietor, who was snoring irregularly through a walrus moustache in the doorway.

The ouzeri is distinct from the kafeneion in Greece in that it has a narrower selection of drinks and no sweets. The kafeneion will generally have some form of easy seating, whilst in the ouzeri one's buttocks are commonly at the mercy of the appalling wooden, rush-seated upright chairs already mentioned. I can only suppose that these instruments of torture were designed for less well-nourished people of a more Spartan age, and that the carpenters are still using the same jigs passed down to them by their forebears. In most ouzeries, a well-proportioned gentleman like me is well advised to sit on the wall, or ask for a cushion.

Greeks rarely drink alcohol without some morsel of food to accompany it, and these varied snacks go by the name of a *mezé*. With ouzo, octopus cooked on a charcoal grill is a traditional favourite, and other *mezes* may include hard cheese, olives, cucumber, various sorts of spicy local sausage, meat-balls, anchovies and tomatoes. In good ouzeries a different *mezé* is served with every drink ordered, often taxing the originality of mine host severely by the end of a convivial session. A healthy lunch notwithstanding, we had fallen to an enthusiastic study of this agreeable local custom when a major traffic accident occurred right under our noses.

The alleyway we were in was quite close to the harbour, and slightly downhill from the ouzeri were a number of tourist shops; boutiques, gift-shops, a *croissanterie*, and the like. Opposite our ouzeri there appeared an old lady carrying an enormous pot of whitewash and a long-handled brush. The latter had seen better days, and appeared to possess considerably fewer bristles than the old lady herself. She began to whitewash the wall of her house with commendable energy.

Into the alley from the bottom end to our left came a string of five mules, quite heavily laden with construction materials. The front three had square wooden saddles roped about with bags of cement. The last two, on longer reins, had respectively long lengths of timber and concrete reinforcing steel rods lashed to their saddles, so that the loads passed each side of their heads and protruded some way ahead and astern of each beast. The mules evidently knew whither they were bound, as the muleteer was walking about halfway down along the string, rolling a cigarette, paying little attention and letting the lead-mule find the way. All went well until, about five yards short of us as we sampled our second ouzo-mezé, the lead-mule passed the old lady, who at that instant was whitewashing the underside of a small balcony. I think the beast must have nudged her, because she let out a little cry, and the brush went wildly astray. By one of those thousands-to-one chances which tend to occur more often than not, the brush struck an elaborate plant in a large hanging-basket and detached it from its hook under the balcony. The basket and pot plunged to the cobbles next to the old lady and exploded like a bomb right between the first and second mules. The old lady let out a scream.

It would be difficult to say which mule was the most startled by this; the second, who was actually lashed across the face by the flailing tendrils of the falling plant, or the lead mule which did not have the un-nerving visual experience of the plummeting rockery, but was totally un-prepared for the eruption in the vicinity of it's privy parts. The piercing shriek of the old lady didn't help, either. The second mule shied back onto its haunches and effectively sat down, whilst the lead-mule scrabbled wildly on the cobbles, giving an impressive display of hoof-spin. After an instant, the tatty rein tethering him to number two broke and he galloped past us up the lane. Eyes wide and nostrils flaring, he laid hoof all the way to the corner, lost his back-end in the turn, sideswiped a fire-hydrant, which spectacularly burst one of the cement bags, and made his getaway behind a choking cloud of cement-dust.

Meanwhile, back at the pile-up, number three ran into the back of number two and bucked backwards. Number four, on his longer lead, overshot number three, was sandwiched by number five, and jack-knifed across the road. This had the effect of squashing the muleteer to the wall on our side of the road and squeezing the old lady into a doorway on the other. She screamed; the sitting mule brayed deafeningly, and scrabbled frantically to regain its footing; the pail of whitewash went flying on the end of an inevitable hoof. The muleteer, squashed against the wall, thrashed wildly at the rump of number three and the head of number four, roaring all the time in pain and rage. This caused number four to reverse, neatly inserting the trailing end of the bundle of timber on his back through a boutique window. Starting forward at the sound of breaking glass, the front end of his load became involved with a resilient sort of climbing-plant on the opposite wall, and number five, going full astern, used this as a fulcrum to pull number four's back end round and complete an impressive swathe of destruction in the boutique display.

The old lady, like most Greek mothers, could give any self-respecting banshee a run for its money. She now set up an eldritch screech of

"Vangelleeeeeeeee!", no doubt for assistance from a loving husband or offspring. This had the effect of sending the melee in our direction, so abandoning the drinks we shot for cover inside the ouzeri. We were followed through the door first by the proprietor and then by a table, unerringly hoofed by a maddened moke.

The table, being tin, made such a clatter that it drowned all other noise for a second and seemed to stun the mules. This gave the muleteer chance to escape from the amorous clinch he had been enjoying with his number three beast and retreat to hug his bruised ribcage. In the lull, the AWOL mule could be heard braying hysterically somewhere in the distance in an incredible parody of a police-siren, which had us choking with suppressed laughter.

The mules started to skitter again, and the whitewash lady renewed her appeals to Vangelis, but Vangelis had evidently found something more rewarding to do than extricating ageing relatives from the clutches of berserk quadrupeds. Shutters on balconies started to slam open as the rudely awakened burghers of Hydra emerged to stare in disbelief at the shambles of mules, boutique wreckage and whitewash at their feet. The buzz of conversations between the balconies began to mount and sharp, recriminatory tones from the far side of the debris indicated that the boutique owner had arrived and was energetically taking the matter up with the muleteer.

The second mule was on its feet again as we emerged cautiously from the ouzeri, scattering more cement dust from its leaking load, looking like the leading lady in a Hitchcock film drawing breath for the Oscar-clinching scream of the year. I really couldn't bear to see the mayhem start all over again, so I approached the animal slowly and started to pat it nervously, whispering sweet nothings into its neurotically twitching ear'ole. The ouzeri owner slipped out with a knife and separated my mule from number three so that I could lead it quietly away.

Rex approached number three with the same aim, but backed swiftly away on receiving what he later described as a look of unbalanced, venomous ill-intent. This was undoubtedly wise, as the beast then flattened its ears, peeled back prehensile lips from a set of horrific, yellowing teeth, and sank then briefly but whole-heartedly into the shoulder of number four. This ill-used creature merely gave one last, half-hearted lunge, which brought down a rack of glittering ladies dress belts in the boutique, and effectively proved to be the swan-song of the embroilment.

Number three was finally calmed by Malcolm, in whom it probably recognised a fellow jaundiced misanthrope. Rex grabbed a green canvas bag from a patient number five, and hooked it over number three's nose and mouth to prevent further chomping of the innocent. Rex and Malcolm then led it off to be tied up to the fire-hydrant with number two and as they passed me, I heard Malcolm whispering in the brute's ear, "Who's a good little psychopath, then?" In retrospect, I wonder that an animal of such spirit did not wreak a terrible vengeance on all concerned for the final indignity we subjected it to; it turned out that the bag we had put over its nose, which Rex had assumed to be a feed bag full of scrumptious fodder, was in fact the muleteer's dung-bag.

We were quite willing to assist in the freeing of the fourth equine anarchist from the joint clutches of the boutique and the rampant jasmine, but by the time we got back to the scene every amateur donkey-extraction specialist in Hydra had gathered there so, seeking out the owner of the ouzeri, we thanked him for the cabaret, paid him and trotted off back to the harbour to see if the arrival of the two flotillas could manage to out-do the mayhem that the Hydra Highways Department had to offer.

***

It would be unjust to suggest that the arrival of the flotillas was in any way as Wagnerian as the pile-up. Never the less, we were pleasantly entertained (and occasionally involved) for an hour and a half or so. By the time we arrived back on board, the two lead-boats were in, and the two skippers were whizzing about in inflatables, directing their respective charges into the best places remaining. One flotilla consisted of twelve yachts with mainly British clients, in uniform boats about thirty feet long and smart matching logos. The other was an agglomeration of much larger boats, which were of differing designs and hues between thirty-five and fifty-odd feet. Their clientele could be identified beyond doubt as American, even without referring to the stars-and-stripes that fluttered at every yard-arm. Both nationalities displayed a debonair disregard for hallowed practice in parking their boats, but before I come to them, let me introduce you to Alf.

As I returned to the boat, I noticed our Austrian and Italian neighbours once again pacing their decks in agitation. The cause was a small, dark-green sailing boat with an incredibly faded red ensign, which was performing the circling stage of the berthing-dance just in front of us. We had just got down our gangplank when the newcomer, whose boat, her spray-dodgers informed us, was called *Idleswyne*, committed himself to what appeared to be a stern-first approach. A very elegant lady on the fore-deck dropped the anchor instantly on the skipper's casual wave, and the boat gathered sternway smoothly. The anchor was efficiently run and snubbed, and *Idleswyne* reversed true as an arrow for the space between *Nissos* and the Austrian. The latter was again wielding his boathook on his foredeck. Just when it appeared that *Idleswyne* could no longer miss her designated space by anything short of spectacular divine intervention, the skipper shouted out to his anchor-lady,

"Daph, old thing! Hold the pick, the gearbox has gone tits-up again!"

"Righty-ho!" came the reply, and a second later *Idleswyne* was brought up sharp with a jarring crash by a casual flick of the windlass pawl. With her engine still running astern, she swung broadside-on to her original track and started to progress backwards across our bows.

Neither the skipper of *Idleswyne*, who was cheerfully whistling and hammering violently at some unfortunate object in the sole of his cockpit, nor his anchor-lady, seemed in the least put out by events. I managed to slack my anchor-chain down a bit before they caught their keel on it. *Idleswyne* reversed blithely over our anchor and that of the once-more operatic Italian, whilst on our port side the Austrian made several unsolicited, diabolical swipes at their front end with his Ninja-stick. With the last one, he caught their forestay at full stretch, which at least had the beneficial effect of disarming him; he was left with only the handle end of the telescopic boathook in his hand, and at this point becomes un-interesting and fades from the story.

Having apparently exorcised the demons in his gear-box and stopped his propeller, the skipper of *Idleswyne* took stock of the situation, and if he felt any dismay at finding himself laterally displaced by two boat's lengths from where he had intended to be, he displayed it only as a toothy grin. Calling for the chain to be slacked, he stuck the tiller to port and neatly put his boat bows-in between us and the Italian. He was now bows-too, anchored by the bow and with his mooring ropes all uselessly lying on the stern, in a berth he had not aimed for and the wrong way round. As a mere footnote to this, his anchor-chain was draped in a great, extravagant loop around most of the north-west corner of the harbour!

"Hold the anchor, Daph!" he called. "You'll have to get the ropes from down here." He then considered for a moment before fishing his anchor-chain up to his stern with a boathook and tying it with a piece of string... 'line' would be far too grand a title for the straggly remnant he used... to his stern-light bracket. The chain led off in an interesting direction which suggested that it went over the Italian's cable, hinged around his anchor, zigzagged sharply back across my chain and eventually met up with his anchor somewhere the far side of the Austrian's. The latter was mollified enough by the return of the errant half of his boathook, but the poor Italian was almost in tears.

"Eet ees not right!" He howled at the complacent new arrival, who considered the demented Latin sympathetically as he lit his pipe.

"Couldn't agree more, old chap. Someone'll be summonsed, like as not." He turned to me, "Sorry about that, old chap. Bit of a cock-up on finals. Sort the anchors out in the mornin', if that's all right with you?" With that, he exhaled a luxurious gout of smoke and disappeared into the cabin.

I helped his wife tidy up the fenders and mooring-lines.

"Quite nicely done, at the end of the day," I ventured, just a touch caustically.

She took it at face value, and beamed back at me, "Oh, yes. Alf's VERY good. He used to race for the R.A.F., you know."

"Well, he certainly takes things very calmly," put in Rex.

"Oh, he never gets rattled," was the intriguing reply. "Not even when he crashed the Vulcan!"

By comparison, the berthing of the flotilla-crews was appallingly unimaginative, but we enjoyed them. Alf re-emerged, and this was obviously his most treasured moment of the day. Every manoeuvre was subjected to lengthy, hyper-critical analysis (and I hasten to record that few of them deserved any adverse comment at all, least of all from a practitioner of Alf's standard).

"Good lord, look at that!" he would mutter, and, "Well, I never, where *do* they learn this stuff?" as yet another boat made a tricky, restricted berthing without major incident. Alf was a man in paradise at these moments.

"Ha! Good old Pan! He'll sort 'em out!" he crowed jovially as Pan, thrashing from side to side of the harbour in his little red boat, went from berthing to berthing like a midwife nine months after a power-cut.

There were two note-worthy arrivals. The first involved a large boat full of Americans, who elected to come in bows-to between ourselves and the Austrian. They approached nicely, and appeared to be well under control. We heard crisp orders given for the anchor to be dropped, noted the gentle braking when nearly in position and the quiet, collected manner of the skipper. The Austrian was desperately trying to reassemble his boathook for a valedictory lunge or two, but he didn't look like making it in time. With the boat nearly in position, I called to the stocky, capable-looking lass in the bows,

"Throw me a line." A second later, I received forcefully in the teeth a neatly coiled and lashed length of rope attached to nothing at all.

A few minutes later we had got the Americans all tied up, to the accompaniment of strangled, horse-like laughter from Alf. I was about to go back to my G and T when the scarlet-faced American skipper said that he would have to go out again, as his anchor-man had dropped their stern-anchor into their dinghy.

The other berthing of note was achieved by one of the smaller British-crewed yachts. It had been lucky enough to acquire a place right on the dock by dint of a fishing-boat going out at the crucial moment, and the evident husband-and-wife team came in bows-to against the high stone quay. (It certainly looked a lot easier than reversing in, and I determined to try it myself at the next opportunity.) The skipper got his anchor down in good time, and as he approached the quay at a nice, steady, low speed, his lady wife perched herself precariously on the outside of the pulpit with a mooring-line in one hand. The skipper of the flotilla at this point came running down the quay, and when the boat was about a length off he called out in broad, reassuring Australian, "That's great. Put her astern, now... Check the anchor-line... put her astern, please... PLEASE! SIR! Put her astern! ASTERN! Oh, Christ!"

In reply to this, he received a beatific smile from the lady, and a ferocious stare of concentration from the man. The boat, unaffected by any attempt to slacken its speed whatsoever, struck the stone mole with a good, solid, noisy 'Crunch!' The lady shot off the front and measured her length on the quay, got up after a short contretemps with a piled fishing net (from which she evicted by her impact an unusual number of cats) and 'secured' the rope by winding it industriously around an old, disused fisherman's engine. She did not seem to have noticed anything out of the ordinary in this performance, so I supposed that was how they always did it. This theory was confirmed by the reaction of the flotilla-skipper. The lady faced him, sprung to exaggerated attention, made a theatrical salute and cheerfully demanded, "How was that, then, Skip?"

"Oh, fine! Marvellous! Magic!" muttered the skipper, and was led away by the flotilla-hostess, clenching his fists, and shaking his head at the ground.

I should point out at this juncture (otherwise someone will do it for me) that I have been involved in some fairly un-orthodox moorings myself from time to time. There was an embarrassing moment years ago when I dropped a four-tonne anchor from a cargo ship which, by some trifling oversight, did not actually have a chain attached to it. I was also present at an incident where, berthing a ship on a large old colonial-style wharf without assistance during a tug-strike, the master got it *nearly* right. Unfortunately, at the last moment, we hit the quay with such a shrewd blow that about twenty yards of warehouse, which stood along the centre of the pier, collapsed on top of our cargo. Fortunately there was no-one inside and it was only baled cotton, and so not damaged, but it took them two days to dig it out with a mechanical shovel. This the master represented in the log-book as, "Vessel rests lightly on wharf."

On another occasion, we encountered a rather stiff anchor-brake. On being told to let the anchor go when coming alongside the wharf, it took so long to release that by the time we managed to free it, the flare of the vessel's bow was over-hanging the dock. The five-tonne anchor shattered the concrete, and a serpentine nest of water-mains, and disappeared through the concrete in an impressive geyser of water. You have never seen wharfies run so fast in your life.

Perhaps one of the classics is the story of a master trading in the South Pacific. Possibly apocryphal but widely attested to, the story goes that he sent a telex to the company's London office reading, "Hit wharf Yandina, demolished same. ETA Rabaul 0600/23rd. Regards Master." I did not have anything to do with that one even if it did happen.

One I did have something to do with — in fact, I perpetrated it — was a little gem of a mooring performed on the Norfolk Broads. A sea-going friend called Dave and I were sailing down from Yarmouth to Reedham, and intended to quaff a foaming stoup or two at the legendary Berney Arms en route. The wind was favourable, but the tide was stronger against us than we had realised, and it became apparent that it was going to be touch-and-go in those days of afternoon closing. Arriving within moments of time, desperate measures were called for, so we ran the boat straight into the soft bank with her sails still up and legged it for the bar. By way of a mooring, I took with me the hefty mud-weight used for anchoring, which I threw into the telephone box outside the pub door. Pausing only to slam the door closed on the rope, I followed my companion into the hostelry and sank a swift brace, much enjoying the expressions of more traditional yachtsmen who stalked the banks, puffing in righteous indignation at their meerschaums.

To return to Hydra, that about concluded the daylight program of entertainment. There was a bit of shouting at the end of the mole at one stage, but we couldn't see what it was about from our berth, and I felt it was a touch ghoulish to actually go and have a look. Alf had no such inhibitions, though; he was off like a champion hurdler, ignoring my gangplank in favour of a flying leap to the quay in his eagerness not to miss any of the fun. He returned snorting mightily with amusement.

"You know the problem with boats?" he asked me. "Same as parachuting. Any bloody idiot can fall out of the aircraft. It's the last two inches where the professionalism is important."

I don't quite know where that leaves Sir Francis Chichester, but I can't help thinking that he had a point. It is like yachting qualifications; the world over, the less qualified we are, the closer we have to stay to the rocks. Imagine saying to a newly-qualified airline pilot, "Now look here, old bean. You are pretty new at this, so we don't want you to take your Jumbo Jet more than ten feet off the ground until you have got the hang of it." It is no part of the purpose of this story to examine the structure of sail-training, but I have an enquiring mind, and I can't help wondering... certainly most of *my* nautical disappointments have occurred in attempting to reconcile the sea/land interface. I can candidly admit that to myself, however, which is more than could have been said for Alf, who seemed blithely oblivious to the fact that his own petard was jammed firmly into his rectum with the fuse fizzing merrily.

Later in the evening, whilst enjoying a sun-downer at the cafe, I got talking to a chap who had a yacht moored on the south quay, and who told me a bit about Alf and Daphne. Alf was a retired R.A.F. pilot who lived on his boat. A top-class racing helmsman in his day, he had apparently never quite got the hang of parking. It was said of Alf that his idea of a successful mooring was to 'T-bone' your boat, lob his anchor through your fore-hatch and put the kettle on. In the opinion of my new acquaintance, the practice of R.A.F. personnel retiring onto the sea was an admirable one which kept a useful number of lunatics off the roads and out of the asylums. However, since it later transpired that this opinion was that of a retired Army officer, I am prepared to admit that there might have been just a soupcon of inter-service rivalry behind it.

***

We dined that night in one of the little courtyards that our explorations had unearthed during the afternoon. We had not got as far as admitting it out loud as yet, but the concrete convictions we had held on the insubstantial, un-hygienic and horribly foreign nature of Greek food had so far turned out to be about as far wrong as only spectacular bigotry could make them. In fact, we had not yet had a meal that was anything less than substantial, tasty and remarkably good value. I would not go so far as to suggest that Greece is a gastronomic destination, the food is more workman-like than epicurean, but it appeared to be varied and (no inconsiderable factor to three trenchermen such as composed our company) there was plenty of it. If, deep within our breasts, there lurked an unworthy wish that we should encounter a thoroughly lousy restaurant to vindicate our prejudices (and I fear that there probably did) we found no solace in Hydra. The restaurant *O Kipos* was a gem.

O Kipos means 'The Garden'. Whatever other fine qualities we were beginning to find in the Greek people, they were never in any danger of being accused of rampant originality when it came to naming things. If a place has deep enough water to get a ship into, it is called *Vathi*, meaning 'Deep'. If it is at the bottom of a path leading up to a higher place, then *Skala*, meaning 'Stairs', springs inevitably to the Hellenic cartographer's mind. A small, enclosed harbour is almost invariably *Mandraki*, or 'Sheepfold', a flat area, *Plaka*. A cape is *Akrotiri*. Any sniff of old fortification and you must be in *Kastro*, and if the fortification appears to be in good repair and standing in a field of herbs, why, I suppose that would be 'Neokastron upon Thyme!' (Sorry. Can't resist appalling puns. Never could.)

Any place failing to fit conveniently to the above formula is named after a saint; but even here, with seemingly thousands to choose from in the Orthodox faith, it appears to be Nikolaos, Georgios and Maria who take the brunt, with the Prophet Elijah putting in some sterling work on the higher peaks.

What a let-down this lack of originality is after some of the places I have been! Take Ascension Island, in the South Atlantic, for instance. Names to delight the romantic mind abound... Green Mountain, Comfortless Cove, English Bay, Two Boats and the Devils Riding School; Robert Louis Stevenson, eat yer bloody heart out! How this story could wax in stature with the inclusion of a few lines like, 'We sank Cape Desolation at Noon, and stood westward into the offing...' It does not have quite the same effect to come across 'We weathered Akrotiri' something like twenty times in a single chapter.

In an aside here, it must be admitted that not all British explorers were quite so ingenious in this respect either. Captain James Cook, for example, was so at a loss for creative names that he clutched at any association, however tenuous, to christen a place. Therefore, whenever he was somewhere new for Christmas, we have a Christmas Island. Whitsunday, Easter and even humble Thursday are duly commemorated. He evidently found a lizard on one island, and presumably had sausages and rum-butter on his mind when he named the Cumberland Group. He sorted out what must have been a dilemma of considerable lack of inspiration by dedicating two entire archipelagos to the Percys, Earls of Northumberland. When at a total loss, he named new finds after his ship (which we may safely presume someone else named for him) and occasionally, in desperation, himself. King George the Third and the Duke of Clarence filled a useful gap or two, and Australians and convicts alike can be grateful that Sir Joseph Banks was a botanist rather than a brain-surgeon; otherwise they would be bound for Lobotomy Bay. In a final stroke of genius, Cook named the Hawaiian Islands the Sandwich Islands. He did this to honour his patron, Lord Sandwich, but the name later became shockingly apposite; it was in the Sandwich Islands that Cook himself became one... or the filling in one, at any rate. Possibly the first recorded instance in history of an American short-order Cook?

Cook passed into memory leaving many a colonial administrator greatly relieved that he never discovered an island on his Great Aunt Nelly's birthday. You could hardly have asked the Paras and Marines to yomp eighty miles across the bogs to liberate the Great Aunt Nelly Islands, now, could you? But I digress; let me return to a restaurant on Hydra.

So far, our Greek gourmandising had encompassed seafood, the *meze*, and *mageireftika*, the long-cooked, taverna style food. *O Kipos* proved our introduction to that delight of the Hellenophile carnivore, the charcoal grill.

The magical phrase to look for on the menu-board is *Sta Karvouna*, meaning 'on charcoal', and while many restaurants will have a smaller grill on which they will swiftly knock you up a juicy pork chop or a fish to order, the true glory of charcoal cooking in Greece is the spit-roast. There are a fair variety of spitted foods you may be offered, and *O Kipos* seemed to have most of them. (Confirmed vegetarians may care to flip forward a page or so at this point.)

Kondosouvli was my particular favourite; pork marinated in herbs and slowly spit-roasted. *Kokoretsi*, a sort of haggis-like sausage made up of liver, kidney and other tasty offals, is juicy and very rich. And often a good grill-restaurant (known as a *Psitopoleion*) will have a lamb-roast, the whole extravagant animal revolving sedately on a spit. *Exohiko* is another favourite, being a foil, or grease-proof paper, wrapped parcel of pork or, occasionally, lamb. Also in the parcel are vegetables, and the whole is slow-cooked until the meat disintegrates at the mere sight of your fork. The wrapping keeps the juices in so well that one ends up eating what amounts to stew out of newspaper! There is a friend of mine, whom we will refer to simply as 'Pit-bull', who, like a good little Cumbrian, condemns all Greek food out of hand because he maintains that the nation is incapable of making gravy. One day I am going to buy him an *exohiko* and see how much non-existent Greek gravy he manages to get down the front of his Pierre Sangan finery!

Finally on the Greek grill, normally relegated to the back spit by the sound business practice of not upsetting the delicate tum-tums of the golden-egg laying tourist-bird, are the lambs' heads. Greatly prized by the Greeks, they leave a certain something to be desired in the field of presentation, with their staring eyes, lolling tongues, and bared teeth. These delicacies, like sheep's eyeballs and monkey-brains, have rather the same effect upon me as stories about survivors in lifeboats who (from necessity rather than rancour, one hopes) eat one another; initially there is a certain fascination, but on brief consideration, one doesn't really want to know. We eschewed the sheep's heads, but apart from that we went through most of the menu.

***

After the restaurant, we ended up in the cafes on the waterfront again. We did peer briefly into several of the bars around the town, but the bar-trade in Hydra seems to suffer from a Catch 22 situation; anyone who has lived so long as to have earned enough to be able to afford to drink in one has long ago lost the urge to do so. Music pounded, lights flashed, and the public stayed away in droves. In any case, Hydra is a place to see and be seen, and the social and fashion show cannot be enjoyed from inside a bar. The late evening must be experienced from the terraces of the harbour cafes, where the locals, the artists, the fashionable of many nations and the tourists mingle in the low, easy cane chairs and maintain a cicada-like buzz of conversation right round the waterfront. Colour is everywhere; a Van Gogh Montmartre scene where bright clothing flares and faded awnings glow in the yellow light spilling from the doors of the restaurants. The port is a bowl of radiance contained in the blue-black, star-pecked canopy of the sky. Very little music is played. The bass-line of the distant discos bumping gently in the background does not diminish the chatter of voices, the clatter of plates and the tinkle of laughter, which carry clearly across this picturesque little amphitheatre of a port in the still evening air. We found seats in a good central spot at Tasso's cafe, and absorbed in equal proportions the sights, the sounds and Metaxa brandies with cappuccino chasers.

There was something to interest everyone, male, female or adaptable; young, old or deceptive. We sipped our drinks and enjoyed the parade of elegant, immaculate womanhood passing before us.

One unbelievably pneumatic blond had Malcolm rolling in his seat in a transport of lustful delight, muttering, "Oh! I could do something to that!"

"No you couldn't, he wouldn't let you!" replied Rex, pointing out a rather proprietorial and decidedly physical-looking specimen walking a couple of yards behind the lady, apparently for the express purpose of enjoying the sensation she was causing. Malcolm howled mournfully.

"Just get rid of it for me, would you, Skipper?"

"And just how, precisely, do you suggest I manage that?" I enquired.

"Oh, use your initiative. Put Paraquat in its bananas or something." Malcolm shook his head sadly as the vision undulated out of sight.

There was one wonderful comment overheard that night which lived with us for the rest of the holiday and beyond. On the next table, and closest to Rex, a lanky chap dressed like a cricketer and a sequined lady who had been energetically trying to hold back the march of time with a wall of facial mortar were having a *sotto-voce* but bitter argument which ended when the man left abruptly. Affecting a magnificently theatrical air of disdain, in which a long, black cigarette holder played a central role, the lady turned to Rex and confided to him in a heavily accented aside

"You moost excuse my hosband. He has bad mood. Today, on thee sweeming rocks, he was bitten on thee balls by a scorpio!"

"Oh, dear! How terrible," empathised Rex sincerely. "But it can't have been our skipper. He's a Taurus."

We were tucked up in bed at the reasonable hour of one in the morning and dozed off swiftly to the sounds of cups and glasses clinking and the murmur of conversations.

***

When I awoke, there was no trace of the night-sounds of Hydra, just a loud, unmelodious bellowing close by. As I lay cursing and trying to make out a syllable or two of this unlovely voice, the boat heeled sharply and the rigging tinkled and clattered in annoyance. A hefty footfall resounded through the hull. With thoughts of dire emergency and a brief, horrible vision of the consequences of a boat on fire in the middle of the mass of craft jammed in the harbour, I erupted from the fore-hatch as far as the waist this time. Rotating and wildly looking around for the source of the noise, I came face-to-knee with a man hanging from our shrouds. He was evidently very drunk and calling in a cracked voice for someone by the name of Olaf. From this, I assumed him to be a Scandinavian of some elk.

After a moment or two, he became aware of my portly and naked form, apparently cut off at the waist, and he made a massive effort to focus on me.

As he shuddered, swinging gently from the cap-shroud, I could imagine Nordic folklore combining with booze in his mind to produce the very worst explanation for the bizarre, truncated troll he suddenly found at his feet. He jabbered something which I will bet good money that even his own mother could not have understood.

"What the hell are you trying to do?" I enquired, quite reasonably under the circumstances, I thought.

"I go to my boat!"

"Well, this isn't it. Which one is yours?"

He drew himself almost erect, gazing sadly round at the mass of boats packed tightly into the little port. "It is a white one!" he announced. With that, he uttered a blood-curdling scream and leapt over the life-lines, landing with both feet square in the middle of the Italian's foredeck. Then, like a hurdler whose joints are all coming unscrewed, the Scandahooligan bounded away across the raft of yachts. By the time the incensed Italian had jack-in-the-boxed out of his fore hatch, I had ducked for cover and the Nordic nightingale was out of sight. As I rolled back into my bed, I heard the now familiar Italian screech of, "Eet ees not RIIIIIGHT!"

***

A breakfast session of the planning committee the next morning developed into a rather warm affair. Rex had become distressed by the Greek method of presentation of his breakfast eggs in the cafes. Whilst thoroughly fresh and wholesome, they arrived at our table like culinary parodies of a major ecological disaster, surrounded by immense slicks of thick oil. Greek bacon is also lacking in English eyes, being so thinly sliced as to make one suppose that it may be removed from the pig without killing or even seriously inconveniencing the animal. Rex is a great practitioner of the traditional English breakfast, as anyone who has broken their fast at his inn will confirm. A beautifully presented collation of sausage, bacon, ham, mushrooms, beans and a brace of aesthetically perfect pre-packed, pre-natal chickens, together with piles of crisp toast, cereals, a teapot the size of a moderate septic tank and a choice of newspapers on a bright gingham tablecloth is the standard he provides for his guests. He furnishes in one fell swoop a whole week's overdose of all those delicious dietary elements upon which mankind has existed for seven millennia or so, but which medical science now insists will cause metabolic breakdown, internal combustion, proportional representation and lingering death if he so much as shares the same room.

Feeling strongly that, at breakfast at least, he was being foully done-to by the Greek cuisine. Rex prevailed upon Malcolm to don the mantle of *Chef de Grill* and put together a selection of calories and E-numbers more to the English taste. This Malcolm set about gracelessly, but lavishly.

Less alluring sights than Malcolm in his bubonic galibeya, sporting four days stubble and wielding a frying pan encrusted with the earthly remains of sausages long organically recycled are, fortunately, rarely encountered. The smells he started producing were of a much more appetizing nature, however, and by occupying one's eyes entirely with the pilot-book and sensing only with the olfactory, a pleasant state of anticipation could be achieved by the willing mind.

The planning discussion was carried out at considerable volume, in order to let Malcolm (deafened by the sizzle of his cauldron) and Rex (doggedly attempting to shave in the Iron Midden) participate. The debate centred upon getting us as far as the island of Spetsae. It was another of those confounded democratic affairs, degenerating into the usual cynical sniping-match between Malcolm and myself. Rex enjoyed these affairs hugely, keeping quiet himself unless some maliciously barbed comment or wilfully evil red herring was required to keep the fires stoked. Malcolm wanted to go to the mainland port of Ermioni, on the very excellent grounds that I did not. Eventually, Malcolm attempted to force a decision by proposing a vote, which would have effectively ended the debate, but Rex hadn't had anything like his fill of rancorous diatribe yet and scotched that by abstaining. I then created something of a constitutional crisis by (quite reasonably, I thought) according myself the privilege of a casting vote in my capacity as captain. Malcolm countered by moving that the captain should have no vote at all, on grounds of evident diminished responsibility. Gerrymandering of this nature drew forth joyous and oratorical flights of lavish abuse and castigation, which were only silenced by a quite extra-ordinarily spectacular occurrence.

Malcolm, attention more upon some juicy calumniation of his captain than his cooking, rather negligently added some more cooking oil to the frying-pan. It later transpired that, in his preoccupied state, his groping hand had lit erroneously on the methylated spirit bottle used for priming the oil-lamp. His harangue ended abruptly in an irate exclamation as his right arm and head were engulfed in a startlingly large fireball.

In my haste to extinguish Malcolm and save the breakfast, it appears that I stood on the squeezy plastic bottle of meths which he had dropped on the floor. Since the end of the cap was nicely alight, this meant that the jet of meths propelled out of the bottle by my ample weight became a jet of liquid fire. The miniature flamethrower spurted the full length of the cabin, driving Rex back into the minute toilet and setting a good blaze going at the foot of the bulkhead and along the cabin sole.

The descent from debating society to Dantean inferno was meteoric, and not a little unsettling, coming as it did before breakfast. In hindsight it seems there is something in the British psyche which responds better to stress and crisis *after* a good, solid, calorific start to the day, and our attempts to put out the Great Fire of Hydra, successful as they were, lacked something in the line of traditional British stoicism. They involved the stripping naked of Malcolm under the public gaze in the cockpit, some wild flailing with a towel, and the rather cavalier lobbing of a couple of buckets of water down the main hatchway. One feels that, as Britons, we should have managed it all with more dignity, somehow.

Whenever imperturbability is the subject of the moment, it brings to my mind a chief mate I sailed with when I was a cadet. We were on the Chilean coast, discharging some massive plant machinery with a fifty-ton derrick. Having had a morning walk around his domain, the mate was sitting opposite me in the duty-mess, enjoying his breakfast. Suddenly, the whole ship began to vibrate and a horrendous screaming sound began outside. This crescendoed rapidly, accompanied by howls of fear and alarm, and the whole ship was shuddering back and forth as if she had just struck a heavy sea head-on. Realising that a winch had run away and the derrick was coming down, I leapt out of my chair and was halfway out of the door before I realised that the mate was continuing his breakfast. With the shouting of men and the screaming of wires getting louder still, he neatly speared his last piece of bacon and looked thoughtfully at me as he masticated it thoroughly. As I gibbered, and he carefully wiped up the last of his egg with a roll, the climax came with a great, shuddering crash which shook the ship violently. Several loud after-shocks reverberated through the superstructure as he drained his tea-mug, and then, as shocked silence fell, he dabbed his lips briefly, folded his serviette, and finally stood up.

"My boy," he said as he ambled past me to go and survey the damage, "when you have been at sea as long as I have, you will instantly realise that noises like that do not happen on ships without something MOST undesirable being the cause!"

The Great Fire of Hydra left remarkably little damage. Only the meths had been alight. No fabric was involved, fortunately, with the exception of the towel used to extinguish Malcolm, the sleeve of his galibeya and an eyebrow or two. The varnish had already suffered too many indignities for a couple of scorch-marks to be apparent, and thankfully none of us had been so appallingly lacking in originality as to use one of the fire-extinguishers; being dry powder, they would have made a worse mess than the EC farming policy. Judging by the remains of some suds at the forward end of the cabin, it appeared for a moment that Rex had found and used a foam extinguisher, but it transpired that he had put out the fire on the forward bulkhead with his shaving water.

Embers quenched and Malcolm re-dressed, we took stock of breakfast. Rex peered carefully into the frying-pan, shook his head mournfully, and poured himself some cornflakes, which he carried into the cockpit. Alf had obviously enjoyed himself enormously at our expense.

"Sounded like a splendid argument you chaps were having over there," he commented to Rex.

"Oh, just a discussion," replied Rex, airily, "but it did get a bit heated."

I then repaired to the Port Police, in their stone casemate overlooking the harbour, to pay the harbour dues and enquire again after the weather. On this occasion, however, I declined to try in Greek, and adopted a new strategy. Puffing my cheeks and blowing hard to indicate wind, I simultaneously shrugged my shoulders and looked questioningly. The Port Policeman grasped this instantly, and gave me the finger. Then he gave me *three* fingers. Ah! Southerly wind, force 3! I gave him the thumbs up and off I went, happy as Larry.

***

So many sea-faring texts treat the act of leaving harbour with remarkable brevity. "We won our anchor, and stood into the offing…" is the sort of thing one comes across in the older chronicles, or, "*Saucy Sue* got underway just on the slack, and dropped down river on the strengthening ebb." Can it really be that other people never encounter the same problems leaving a harbour that I do? I have seen innumerable horrible tangles... either this never happen to the people who subsequently burst into print, or else their memories are selective. Someone is putting it about that this 'dropping down river on the ebb' business is somewhat easier than it really is. We read little about the blundering great rhino of a ferry which has decided to leave at the same time, a manoeuvre that it performs at an alarming speed. Nothing about the tangles of anchor and chain, nothing about ground-tackle that lives up to the maker's claims so well that it cannot by the sinew of man be coaxed from it's comfortable niche in the estuarine ooze, and, particularly, nothing about the fact that what appears to you to be a logical time to leave harbour is likely to be just as logical to everyone else. Naturally, in a restricted port like Hydra, the sort of organised chap who makes it his business to arrive nice and early in order to secure a berth next to the quay is also the sort of organised chap who decides to make his departure nice and early in order to secure the same sort of berth in the next port. Here beginneth the lesson...

The debris so well known to even the most efficient of fire brigades had hardly been cleared up when the ball was set firmly in motion by an unbelievably optimistic German, whose boat was stern-to the quay just the other side of our Austrian neighbour. After a spot of authoritarian organisation on his part, which was listened to with polite disbelief by the two British boats outside him, and with sleepy incredulity by the American and Swedish boats outside *them*, the German gave a series of very Teutonic orders which appeared to end with "Ready or not, here I come". He then slipped his stern-ropes and, by casually flicking a switch in the cockpit, he activated a monstrous, gleaming chrome chain-gobbling machine on the foredeck. Like a pasta enthusiast sucking up a single strand of spaghetti, his boat squeezed between the British boats. Almost impossibly, in the pack of boats, he actually started to part them. With his crew frantically dashing up and down the side decks, trying vainly to reposition fenders squashed almost flat against the other boats, our Houdini helped to deliver his boat from its tight womb with judicious little touches on his engine. These delicate nudges caused his stern to drop about six inches, while black smoke erupted from his exhaust and the water under his counter turned to froth. The tighter he jammed himself into the gap, the more frequent these 'touches' became, until the bow-lines of the two British boats hummed like harp strings. Finally, with the contractions coming about every thirty seconds, the widest point of the German boat passed those of the two British boats, and he was delivered with a sudden rush into the gap between the second and third rows.

Having already commented on the volume of noise which these shenanigans generate, I will leave the reader to form his or her own mental impression of the revving and howling that accompanied this manoeuvre. I will limit myself to cataloguing the reactions only of our immediate neighbours and friends. The Italian, finally driven beyond the bounds of sanity during the night by the nocturnal visitation of our Nordic friend, was racing up and down the length of his boat like an enraged gibbon in a zoo-cage. Alf was guffawing loudly and occasionally choking on his pipe-stem. He was laughing so loud, in fact, that he was attracting venomous looks from the German, who could hear him despite the amount of noise closer to home. Malcolm adopted an attitude of watchful attentiveness, his head cocked to one side like a spaniel, whilst Rex sat transfixed with a spoonful of cereal half way to his open mouth. The Austrian had emerged in a state of *dishabille*, and his irrelevant efforts with his boathook were sadly hampered by the necessity of keeping one hand on the towel around his waist which preserved his modesty.

By the time he arrived at the third and outer row of boats, the German was standing on determinedly, but taking heavy fire from all sides. I couldn't decipher what the Swedes were saying, but the American invective was largely concerned with copulation, parentage and a cavity in a donkey. Not one whit discouraged by this, the German breakout took the outer rank of boats by storm, heaving his way through the less tightly packed row by means of the windlass alone. At last, in the middle of the harbour, he stopped, swung to the light northerly wind, and wandered up forward to watch benevolently as his rattling chain-muncher devoured yard after yard of cable. After a moment or two, it started to slow down, then the chain started to jump noisily on the gypsy, and finally the windlass stopped all together. With a curse, the German and a hefty Brunhilde from his crew started to work the windlass manually by means of a large lever. They had no easy time of it, and about ten minutes later, the reason became apparent. An enormous ball of chain broke the surface, with anchors sticking out of it in all directions. All stopped whilst the Germans inflated their dinghy to get at their Gordian knot.

As far as I could see, our anchor was not directly involved with the collection acquired by the Swine from the Rhine, as Alf christened him. The Austrian was, however, as was evidenced by the fact that he was peering myopically over his bow and making tentative jabs at the water with his boathook, and since I was fairly sure that Alf's anchor was over the Austrian's, and definitely over mine and the Italian's, I had a strong presentiment that we were ultimately part of the equation. In order not to be caught napping when the trumpet called our tune, I set about making the boat ready for sea and singled up to one slip-line onto the quay.

Whilst we were doing this, Pan had appeared like magic at the first hint of trouble. With his hair tied back in a bushy pony-tail and sporting a tattered baseball cap, his eccentric figure ploughed across the harbour in a solid little red dinghy, standing in the stern and leaning forward on his oars like a gondolier. Once he had arrived at the scene, there began a titanic battle of wills between him and the German over whose method was to be employed in clearing the tangle. Nobody who knows Pan, however, will be in any doubt as to the outcome of this, and in any case, once the sturdy little dinghy was in place under the bow of the German's boat, no-one else could even see what was going on, never mind interfere. The only thing that could meddle was the weather, and it did. The fitful light northerly flicked round to the south, and gently started to waft the boat back towards the others on the quay. As her stern swung past us, I noticed that her name was *Serendipity*, which seemed not entirely appropriate in the circumstances.

Pan directed the untangling operation like an orchestra conductor, summoning slack chain from various boats with sweeping gestures of his arms and dismissing those whose anchors had been liberated from the snarl-up, and who were free to re-tension their cables. Most of these said the hell with it and left anyway, which eased the congestion of the pack of hulls. This allowed the remaining boats room to move, and the light southerly air began to blow round the bows of those boats which had slacked their chains for untangling. Eventually boats were lying at all angles, their crews adopting some very odd positions as they tried to hold themselves clear of their neighbours.

I suppose Pan had extricated about half of the anchors from the cowslip-ball of meshed ironmongery when Alf's bit of string, which was holding his anchor-chain up to his stern, parted under the strain. At the same time, a low moan of despair came from the Italian's boat as his cable started to grate. Alf let go his bow-lines, backed out, and then, heaving on his windlass he made his way towards the untangling operation. En route, he paused for a moment as he excavated the Italian's light plough anchor. This he casually lobbed back into the water where he had dragged it... about five yards the other side of the Austrian! Alf's anchor finally came up with just the Austrian's across it and, deftly hooking this clear with his boathook, he gave us a cheery wave and motored off smelling of roses. By the time Pan had found and freed the Austrian's anchor, he had drifted with the German boat across MY anchor...

From a final choice of three, the German selected one anchor that he liked the look of, and set off out of the harbour. It became evident, however, that he had omitted to recompense Pan for his time and effort, because Pan held firmly onto the side of the yacht as it gathered way. Quite a heated argument got going. The German played what he thought to be his trump card, revving his engine to shake Pan off. Pan was made of stern stuff, however. The last we saw of him, he was disappearing out of the harbour mouth at about five knots, hanging on grimly whilst his sturdy little dinghy did the yacht's topsides no enduring amount of good.

No time like the present, I thought, so we slipped and Rex began to heave the windlass. I have already touched upon our windlass. It was an immense, ancient, galvanised contraption which required the cherishing caress of a three-pound hammer to engage or release the brake. This hammer head was welded to the end of a mighty iron bar about three feet long, which, when reversed so that the hammer-head made a 'T' shape at the top, became the operating handle. The gearing was so slow that hitherto we had largely ignored the windlass, pulling the chain in by hand. It was no angel, this geriatric contrivance, being ever ready and willing to mangle a stray finger-end and penalising any inaccuracy with the hammer by an agonisingly bruised shinbone, but by God, it could lift some weight! If you are contemplating a sailing holiday in the Med, your anchor-windlass is probably the most vital piece of equipment on the boat, closely followed by the fridge.

We recovered the Italian's anchor about ten yards out, the windlass plucking it effortlessly to the surface from whence I tossed it nonchalantly in the general direction of it's unhappy owner. The Austrian's Danforth was hoisted contemptuously, and treated in the same cavalier manner, and then a small grapnel, which appeared to come from the starboard side and was attached to God knows what, was disposed of. Then the windlass started to slow down. Rex laboured harder and harder at the lever, and as blood-vessels started to bulge ominously on his forehead, I lent a hand. There was an incredible weight on the end of the chain, and I soon discarded the theory that we were breaking the anchor out of the bottom; the links continued to come in, but agonisingly slowly. There was a creak or two from the windlass bed and the bow of the boat was noticeably down. Then, suddenly, there was a slight jump on the chain, after which it began to come in a fraction easier. Eventually, as I began to feel that I was in imminent danger of a heart-attack, Malcolm, who was looking over the bow to tell us when the anchor came into sight, announced that he could see our problem. The gist of this announcement was that we had managed to lift an anchor of surprising proportions given the size of vessels to be found in the port. I will here record only the substance of the statement he made; the actual phraseology Malcolm employed would not further this story and would considerably distress his parents, who are gentle folk. Intrigued by the vehemence of this pronouncement, I had a butchers myself, and was disagreeably surprised by its accuracy. If anything, Malcolm had erred on the side of understatement. We had hooked the head of our anchor around the crown of a stocked anchor about five feet long. I hazarded a guess that it probably weighed well over a hundred kilos, not including the damn great chain attached to it.

I believe that I spent a moment or two railing at the irresponsibility of the sort of people who go around negligently hurling such extravagant items of ironmongery into busy and congested harbours. H.M.S. *Victory* not being in port at the time, I could only suppose that the beast of a thing belonged to a large caique which was loading crates of empty beer-bottles on the opposite quay. This being so, it seemed a bit bloody much to have dumped the thing on OUR side of the harbour! It was a wonder that the windlass deck-bolts held.

Having got the thing just breaking surface, we had a brief conference about how to get rid of it. An odd sight we must have been, having our usual spirited chuntering session on the bow of a boat inclined downwards at about fifteen degrees. Eventually, galvanised into action by the realisation that the windlass was probably going to part company with the deck at the next ferry-wake, I passed a stout rope under the fluke of the anchor with a boathook, and made it fast on the forward cleats so that it could later be let go, even though under tension. With the brute thus supported, I hoped to let our anchor down, guide it clear with the boathook, then recover it onboard and finally let go of one end of the rope to rid ourselves of the monster from the deep. All went well until I came to the bit about lowering our anchor.

With the strain on the chain, it was an act of some courage to release the pawl and brake. Heaving back on the lever, I took the load off the pawl so that Rex could flip it clear of the gypsy. Then I ordered Rex and Malcolm to get back to the mast for safety. Once they were out of the way, I reversed the lever, took up a safe but awkward stance clear of the chain, and took an enthusiastic swing at the brake-lug. My first shot missed, and the momentum of the hammer took it over my shoulder, past my left ear, and left me tottering for balance on the toe-rail. Rex grabbed me just before I went over the side, to Malcolm's evident disappointment. My second swing was even more spectacular. It just clipped the brake-lug, releasing it successfully, and carried on as before… only this time, the hammer grazed my shin and then slipped from my fingers and shot along the deck in the general direction of Rex. He leaped to avoid it, but at that second the load coming onto the rope as our anchor dropped ripped one of our mooring-cleats clean off the deck. Freed of the massive weight of the caique-anchor, *Nissos* bounded upwards, leaving me again wind-milling my arms desperately to stay on the boat. I was luckier than Malcolm however. He, unbalanced by the movement, took an involuntary step backwards and inserted his right foot down the open fore hatch. His rapid descent into my boudoir ended abruptly an instant later, when those parts of his anatomy associated in the world of classical sculpture with the strategic positioning of a fig-leaf came into violent contact with the hatch-lip. Rex, already tottering, chose this moment to glissade down the sloping front of the coachroof as *Nissos* lurched forward again. He landed heavily on the hatch-lid, slamming it closed across Malcolm's right thigh, which was effectively the same as putting him in a pair of nutcrackers no matter how one looks at it.

I personally find public demonstrations of uncontrolled emotion both unseemly and distasteful. A return to the traditional British virtue of uncomplaining stoicism is long overdue in my book, and how any Man could regard himself as such after having emitted, in public and in front of foreigners, a noise such as that which Malcolm now produced, I am at a loss to explain. His agonised cry, a ragged, ululating scream of piercing intensity which brought to my mind an unnatural (not to say unlikely) congress between a half-slaughtered pig, a circular saw and a Stuka dive-bomber, stopped all activity in the port of Hydra and even the mules looked round in horror. In embarrassment, Rex and I unceremoniously stuck Malcolm's left leg into the hatch as well, and heaved him gracelessly into the forepeak berth. Then we shut the hatch to muffle the howling and set about recovering our anchor, rather self-consciously trying to ignore the noise, which now changed dramatically. A deeper note of rage began to make itself heard from the fore-cabin, and solid thumps indicated that our casualty was taking revenge for a succession of maritime grievances on the largely blameless toilet door.

Poseidon, who so far in his capacity of god of the sea had revealed himself as being the possessor of a rather mean and perverted sense of humour, must have momentarily looked the other way. Almost impossibly, the descending caique anchor had not landed smack on top of our own, which we were now able to hoick effortlessly out of the water with only one extraneous light chain still attached. This we discarded, then recovered the line with our errant cleat still made fast to the end, and turned to leave the harbour. As we approached the entrance, we met Pan returning in his dinghy, rowing standing up again. He had evidently not had a wasted trip; his teeth were bared in a wolfish grin, from which protruded a five-thousand drachmae note.

I hailed him as we passed, telling him about our damaged cleat, and asking whether it was possible to buy stainless steel bolts in Hydra. His grin became instantly and impossibly wider. With a sweep of his arm, he indicated the host of gold and jewellery shops around the harbour-front.

"Eighteen carat gold, twen'y four carat gold and silver we got. Stainless, you gotta go to Athens!"

We exchanged farewells, a whey-faced Malcolm making a late and cautious appearance at the hatchway.

As we passed the ferry quay, a uniformed Port Policeman hailed us to ask if we had paid for using the port for the night. We were able to assure him with entirely clear consciences that we had paid in more ways than one, and motored out of the picturesque little place. In the bright morning sunlight, it basked serenely at peace with itself and the world and only the rather odd angle of the booms and masts over the mole showed anything out of the ordinary had ever occurred.

Perhaps, on reflection, it hadn't.

We had a light beat to the island of Dhokos about five miles to the west, where we had decided to swim and finally make the decision, adjourned during the fire, about our evening destination. Ghosting along at about two knots, we were distracted by watching Malcolm who, with the assistance of a shaving mirror taped to the handle of a soup-ladle and a powerful torch, was engaged in examining the less savoury portions of his anatomy for lasting damage. This depraved contortionism brought forth a flood of unhelpful advice and insensitive ribaldry from Rex and myself, seated comfortably just out of ladle-reach. Malcolm took it all with restraint up until the point when Rex and I vetoed the eating of soup onboard until a new ladle could be obtained. At that point he commented quite mildly, without interrupting his scrutiny, "Bligh, you are the sort of man who would take a bus-load of vegans on an outing to an abattoir. And as for you, Rex, I would not be in the least surprised to find you having a barbeque in the grounds of a crematorium."

CHAPTER SIX

ABROAD ON THE MAIN

In which marine biology features... A whale of a time... Sharkasm... Spetsae unveiled... A carriage to the cabaret... A court of inquiry... A bit of a ruckus... The lemmings of Kiparissi... Some historical character... The moles of Kiparissi... The art of navigation... Gerakas... Cats... Ruins... Malcolm's first solo.

Progress was slow that day, and a bit of late morning cloud meant that the vote to postpone the swim at Dhokos was one of the few unanimous ones of the voyage. As we cleared the west end of Hydra, we found that the wind went southerly a bit. We were almost able to lay a course to the Spetsae channel on one tack, so we trickled happily onwards. The towering cliffs of the south coast of Dhokos slid past to starboard, the jagged cone of Trikeri to port and eventually, in the late-ish afternoon, we plodded doggedly into the Spetsae channel. There were only three major points of interest.

The first was the complete absence of assault by ferries, hydrofoils, sea-planes or other unidentified floating objects of the obstreperous kind. These all passed at a friendly distance and proceeded about their lawful occasions.

The second was a most charming encounter with a group of dolphins, who lolled and snorted lazily around our bow for twenty minutes or so. This gave rise to a whole host of marvellous subjects for happy ship-board disharmony, ranging from arguments about the correct collective noun for dolphins, through a mild dispute about how many there were in this particular collection, to a sharp little exchange over what species of maritime mammals they were. With regard to the first point, it was finally agreed that, since dolphins appear so much more intelligent than most things coming out of a school these days, the correct term should be 'an institute of higher education of dolphins'. The numbers question was abandoned as unsatisfactory, because attempting to count even slow-moving dolphins in a group is about as pointless an exercise as man can indulge in short of attempting to central-heat Scandinavia*.

The issue of species ran better. Rex though they might be bottle-nose, but I pointed out that they might say the same about him. Malcolm accused me of making defamatory comments on porpoise. I said that I thought they were common dolphins, but Rex opined that this was a bit rich coming from a man with my vocabulary. Rex and I then rounded on Malcolm, asking him what kind of a fisherman was he if he didn't know the name of a thing eight bloody feet long.

"They're large, seagoing mammals. Your field, not mine, Ahab!" he retorted, and then muttered *sotto voce* "...Possibly family, even?"

The possibility of their being pilot whales was discussed, but discounted as we had never seen them in airports. Blue Whales were out, because we had not heard them swear, they were not Finn Whales because they appeared well-fed. We couldn't say they were Right Whales because we didn't know if they were. They could not be Minke Whales... not a fur coat in sight; nor Sperm Whales, because... well, you get the idea. Malcolm got the last word by saying that they were probably just a bunch of silly old belugas.

The third occurrence of note was also of a marine biological nature. Just as we approached the Spetsae channel, we were alerted (by an exclamation of little cultural content from Rex) to the presence of a large fish swimming behind the boat. It was perhaps four feet long, very close to our stern, obviously very interested in a rope's end trailing in the water. Neither Rex nor I needed any assistance from our fisheries expert in identifying this particular maritime garbage-disposal unit; it was a shark!

A word or two may be in order at this point about 'The Dentures in the Deep'. There is probably no subject amongst those whose work place or play-field is the sea which attracts more attention, evokes more emotion or creates more misinformed mythology than good old Nobby Clark. A good shark-yarn session in most ships bars will probably end up with tales of the ravening

---

*More pointless, in fact, since the latter has become a real possibility with EC membership extended to Finland and Sweden, and the discovery of an apparently endless supply of hot air in Brussels.

monsters (never an inch under eighteen feet in length) biting the hands off people on paint-rafts, overturning lifeboats, swimming up sewers and emerging from bidets in the middle of the Gobi desert, and, probably, attending barbeques wrapped in a damp towel. They are credited with the most incredible (and, on sober reflection, unlikely) malevolence and cunning, savagery and greed. Australians are particularly prone to these persecution complexes. Whole inebriated bars-full of them will climb over one another to tell the visiting Pom an even more hideous story than the last. I recall one such occasion in Mackay, a sugar-loading port in Queensland, where, after about an hour of vivid shark-attack stories in which the toothy gentleman in the sharkskin tux was found everywhere except at the drive-in at Macdonald's, our Geordie third engineer suddenly announced that he could never be eaten by sharks. When the incredulous antipodeans asked why not, he told them that he could swim faster through water than a shark could through shit.

Hyperbole aside, I reckon you've got an excellent chance of swimming all your life, even in the Red Sea or Malacca Straits, without feeling the tender tickle of nautical gnashers around your underwater volume. Which is not to say that shark-attacks do not occur, of course; they do, frequently. I have seen hundreds... and the shark hasn't survived any of them!

In Greece, there are no sharks. The Greek Tourist Board is VERY clear on this point. Fine by me, but it does provoke in the enquiring mind some idle speculation on the origins of the large numbers of undeniably fresh small shark one finds on the fish-market in Piraeus. Amidst some mumbling, it will eventually be admitted that, well, yes, perhaps there are some BABY sharks around, but absolutely no big ones. This leads us to two inescapable conclusions. Firstly, tiny, baby sharks occur in Greek waters without the assistance of great big Mummy and Daddy sharks, which seems to be something of an immaculate misconception; and secondly that all the tiny, baby sharks are caught before they grow into great big sharks. One stands in awe of Greek fishermen, who, with casual mien, perpetrate infanticide with such ruthless efficiency. Have no fear bold tourist, I reckon your chance of becoming Sharkies Meaty Chunks are rather less than that of your winning the pools three weeks running. The most dangerous shark you meet in Greece will be sitting in a bar selling timeshares.

It was in the light of the above, knowing full well that there has never been a documented shark attack in Greece, and aware of the undeserved opprobrium heaped on the head of this graceful and much maligned creature, that we decided to kill it.

To this end, I prepared the single-fanged spear and loaded the spear-gun. Rex meanwhile made sure the shark did not swim away by calling seductively, "Here, Sharkie-Sharkie!" and tossing pieces of tuna sandwich into the wake. The shark was obviously not enamoured of tuna sarnies (for which I can only give it credit) but followed us anyway until I was ready for the great shot. Malcolm, of course, would have nothing to do with this unscientific, unskilled and unsporting method of fishing, and ignored the process stonily.

At last, prepared for the shot, I stepped to the stern like Queequeg, took careful aim from a range of about three feet, and fired.

They (being the smarties who tell us all about spear guns and spear fishing) are quite insistent on the fact that one should never load or discharge a spear gun out of the water. I can record here that they have a definite point, and there is a distinct possibility of someone else getting one too. The bloody thing recoiled like a stallion finding a porcupine in his feedbag, nearly breaking my wrist. The spear arched off in a trajectory that endangered only flying fish, easily broke the string, and scored a direct hit on a distant, irrelevant and totally empty piece of the Aegean Sea. The shark peacefully followed us for another fifteen minutes or so, disregarding entirely the lure that Malcolm rather shamefacedly dangled right in front of it, and eventually diverged from our wake and disappeared. It would be nice to think that, if ever I were to be attacked by a shark, it could be capable of a similar farcical incompetence.

***

Spetsae is as different in appearance from Hydra as Hydra is from Poros or Aegina. A much lower, gentler island, Spetsae and the adjacent mainland lose the rugged grandeur of naked rock in favour of wooded, rolling land. The architecture is different too, being, I am told, much more in the Italian style. I will accept that, on the condition that we are talking about some Tuscan village, and not the drab, grey waterfront of earthquake-proof Messina, which is the only form of Italian architecture with which I am acquainted. The chap who designed THAT could well do with having his ruler confiscated.

The main town is a casual, sprawled affair of large-ish white dwellings, all tiled in matching ceramic. The main concentration is around the new port of Dapia, which lies about one third of the way along the north shore from the eastern end. Here some larger buildings, notably the old International School and a few hotels, give the impression of something of a metropolis, but the straggle of bright, white houses on either side form a higgledy-piggledy urban tangle of charm and character.

When it comes to parking your argosy, of course, you are not allowed into the main harbour; that would be far too simple. Yachts have to go to a place called Baltiza Creek, which lies behind a long spit of land at the northeast tip of the island. The setting is very pleasant, with an attractive mess of intermingled houses, restaurants, bars and fragrant pinewoods. On the spit stands a most authentic looking lighthouse, behind which any self-respecting port would be proud to lie.

As you enter the mouth of the creek, there is almost as much to distract your crew as in Hydra, and at least as much reason not to be distracted. In the outer part of the harbour, large yachts lie stern-to on the west side with anchors out ahead and long stern lines to the shore. On the east side are commercial boats... parked ferries, a dredger and a wreck... not very picturesque, but they detract nothing from the impression of a thriving, busy port. The road running around the creek buzzes with motorbikes, and the not-infrequent clang of a horse-bell; like Hydra, Spetsae favours horse power as a means of transportation, but, having rather fewer crags and steps than Hydra, is able to indulge a taste for graceful Phaeton carriages. Drawn not by donkeys but by real horses, a great number of these ornate and carefully-maintained carriages dominate the traffic along the sea-front and into the town, clanging their deep-toned bells to clear their way.

Another traditional pursuit of yester-year pervades Spetsae. All around the creek as we motored in there were splashes of orange-red colour wherever a triangle of land existed between the houses. These on closer inspection proved to be wooden caiques under construction. Crops of ribs, garishly painted in orange primer, apparently sprouted from the earth; frames and half-planked hulls were scattered around, and, over the buzz of the motorbikes and the clop of the horses' hooves, the shriek of circular-saws could be heard. There certainly seemed to be no recession in the boat-building industry. I counted over thirty hulls under construction around the creek, some of them very large indeed.

As we edged further into the creek, we came to an elbow on the east bank where a landing-craft style ferry lay aground at its ramp, and rounding its blunt stern we saw for the first time the whole harbour. But when used with reference to Baltiza Creek, the term 'whole harbour' is blatantly oxymoronic. 'Nothing as small as Baltiza can possibly constitute a whole harbour,' was my first thought, and 'Where the hell do I put my boat?' was the second. It is smaller than Hydra, and being a long, narrow shape, manoeuvring is more difficult. There are two rows of boats permanently moored to the quay, which is on the west side, whilst the east side shoals and is all boatyards, fishing-boat moorings and slipways. There are no ferries or hydrofoils… they use the town harbour… but to make up for that, there are even more fast water-taxis than in Hydra and also a large number of big, caique tour-boats. One look at the number of boats in the little inlet had me giggling in a hysterical, slightly unbalanced sort of way, drawing a sharp look from Rex in my direction.

Boats were everywhere, including half-way or all the way up the beach. If you imagine the sort of pile of cars you see in really big scrap-yards, you begin to get the idea of how boats are parked in Baltiza. And then the dreadful thought came creeping into my mind; every single one of them has an anchor in this ditch somewhere!

I found a spot where we could just squeeze into the second row out from the quay. My intention of using the kedge and going in bows-first was scrapped in an instant. We had no anchor winch on the stern, and if ever we were going to need the old-fashioned brute force of the windlass to get our anchor back, it was here. Even so, when I told Rex to let the anchor go, I don't think either of us really expected ever to see it again.

We backed in with no trouble, and Malcolm reached up to put our stern line onto the bow of a large caique, which I had thought would make an easy bridge to the shore for us. This may have been the case, but we never found out. None of us ever found the courage to try getting past the Rottweiler on the caique's foredeck, and in fact I had to be quite firm with Malcolm before he would even put the stern line around the caique's Samson-post. I couldn't do it myself, as I was busy with… well, something.

The berth was safe and snug, however, and Rex called out cheerfully from the bow, "The anchor's holding really well!" So it bloody should have been. It must have been set in solid steel!

Malcolm set about a bit of fishing for the afternoon, and was soon contentedly annoying whitebait. Rex and I set out to find a canine-free route to shore, which turned out to be something of an effort. Several times we clambered to the inside edge of a boat, only to find ourselves faced with a five-foot jump to the quay. We eventually made it about five boats along from where *Nissos* was moored and arrived on terra firma, feeling akin to the chappies who discovered the source of the Nile.

The first objective of the mission was undoubtedly to take the edge off our ever-present thirsts. Rex and I swiftly dodged out of the sun into a small bar right by the quayside, and promptly found out what a man feels like when he steps into a bus-shelter to avoid a shower, only to find it hosting a convention of violent street-crime methodologists. Approximately eleven seconds later, we were back on the street having consumed minute amounts of beer out of what appeared to be foil-topped ampoules, and with the bulk of our wallets significantly reduced. We staggered a full ten yards to an adjacent taverna, where we took the shamefully un-British step of covertly peeking at the price of a beer in the menu before sitting down. It took us two large bottles apiece to recover from the mugging, and finally the lesson we should have learned from Hydra sank in to our spongified grey matter; in the San Tropez islands of Greece, the difference between a bar and a taverna is about three hundred percent.

A leisurely stroll around the crenulations of the Old Harbour is a definite high point of a visit to Spetsae. Rex and I ambled sluggishly amongst the whitewashed houses in the afternoon sun and browsed in the boat-building yards amidst the skeletal framework of boats unborn, boats deceased or boats in the throes of cataclysmic mid-life crises. We refreshed ourselves periodically in various pleasant establishments whilst pondering where to have dinner, and generally chewed the cultural cud. We soon found the road into the busy town, and, unanimously rejecting that as an avenue of interest, we turned away from the sea and lost ourselves in the back-streets. We were duly impressed by the originality, if not the practicality, of the stepped streets paved with mosaics of pebbles in the form of emblems of the revolution. The monastery overlooking the Old Harbour is rather special. Gleaming white and eerily quiet, with brightly painted flagpoles and surrounded by what seems like a couple of acres of *krokalia*, the pebble mosaic, it nestles in a courtyard almost overgrown with riotous blooms. Facing it across the courtyard is a marble monument to the fighters of the Greek revolution, guarded by cannon and flanked by the fluttering Spetsiot and National flags.

Wandering in the back streets of Spetsae was pleasant but entirely lacking in anything like the mayhem of the previous day in Hydra. Rex and I hoofed for miles, taking a lazy beer here and there, pausing on sun-trap beaches to observe the scantily-clad wildlife and strolling idly down pine tree-lined lanes. After an indefinite time, the cicada's incessant buzz changed to the clop of hooves and we finally ambled from the pinewood tracks back into the town with absolutely no idea where we had been. In a remote suburb, we passed a restaurant in a most idyllic setting, which we marked down for later, and had a good healthy argument about how to pronounce its name from the sign. Both Rex and I fancied ourselves masters of the Greek alphabet already, but rarely came out with anything remotely similar. Malcolm snidely gave it as his opinion that I spoke Modern Greek, whilst Rex spoke the classical tongue. In this instance, we decided that the name of the establishment was 'Climataria', which we pronounced to rhyme with 'primate' and 'area'. I made a mental note of this, and we wandered on down-hill.

After a few dead ends, we found ourselves back in the monastery over-looking Baltiza Creek when we had rather thought we might be somewhere near the International School... a navigational error which was sufficient warning to us that one of the splendid horse-carriage taxis would not only be a stylish way to go for dinner in the evening, it would probably be our only hope of finding 'Climataria' again!

On the subject of the International School of Spetsae, absolutely every printed work which refers to the island points out that John Fowles was teaching at the school when he wrote his famous novel, *The Magus*, and that most of the locations in the book can be identified on the island. In order to lend to this description of Spetsae a touch of individuality, and to establish the independence of mind of the writer, I shall not mention the matter.

On completing the assault course from the dock to the boat, we found a frustrated Malcolm surrounded by tackle, beer cans, an unsavoury assortment of baits... in fact, by everything pertaining to angling except fish. Rex and I rather pointedly peered over both sides of the bow looking for a bulging keep-net, but we got no response from Malcolm. He was as unlikely to bite on our bait as the fish evidently were on his.

Rex busied himself in the galley mixing the evening gins and fixing a few little tab-nabs, and I found myself uncharacteristically in the mood for a little work. Clambering ashore again, I managed to buy some stainless bolts, and spent a happy hour bolting the cleat back onto the fore-deck. Having done this, I briefly contemplated going up the mast to re-reeve the halyard that I had un-reeved on the first day, but as Rex, who would have been the man on the winch at the bottom, was on his third gin, I shelved that idea until the morning. Thus at a loss for something to do, but with restlessness still upon me, I decided to do a bit of fishing too.

During my rummagings of the first day, I had stumbled upon a net on a three foot pole in the cockpit locker. I dug it out, and then tossed some bread scraps into the water. Within moments, a seething mass of small fry were around the rock-hard crusts, pushing each other clear of the water in their frenzy to get at the goodies. One diabolical swipe with the net and I had myself a thrashing, silver mess of small fish. Malcolm, when confronted with this harvest, explained very patiently about the satisfaction he derived from actually *outwitting* his fish. I explained the satisfaction I derived from actually *eating* my fish. I was about to start frying them up as whitebait, but Rex vetoed this on the grounds that he had to sleep next to the galley, so the fish won an eleventh-hour reprieve. I did fill my net twice more by this foul method, but Malcolm contrived to be looking the other way each time.

I suppose that it was about ten minutes later, when I was deep in racontation with Rex over the gin, that Malcolm finally struck pay-dirt. His professional detachment cracked so far as to emit a whoop of delight as his rod tip bent infinitesimally to the weight of a writhing, four-inch sliver that would not, unassisted, have made up a single marketable fish-finger. The luckless creature had swallowed the hook, and so was denied the thumbs-up and dispatched. Malcolm re-baited his hook and resumed. A few moments later, Rex wandered forward with a knife, and started cutting open the head of the small fish.

"What the hell are you doing?" demanded Malcolm.

"Just wanted to see how big this brain is that you've just outwitted," said

Rex. He peered intently into the incision he had made, and added, "I can't seem to find it."

***

"*Estiatorion Climataria, Parakalo!*" I ordered confidently as we climbed into the horse taxi that evening. This statement, carefully prepared with the aid of the phrase-book, was intended to get us back to the obscure restaurant, and the firm manner in which it was said was intended to imply that I knew what I was talking about so that we should so by a speedy and economical route. It was delivered in a grand, oratorical style which Malcolm (who knows little of such things) thought to be rather overdone. Apparently the driver did as well, because he replied rather abruptly, "Pooh!"

There is that in the English character, I confess, which bristles when faced with surly derision in a foreigner, and so I was perhaps a touch peremptory with my second attempt. The driver upped the stakes to, "Pooh! Pooh! Pooh!"

Deadlock in the negotiations now appeared to have been reached. Unable to remonstrate in the driver's tongue, and unwilling to risk a further escalation by presenting my demand a third time, I was at a stand. The driver clucked amiably at his horse, and seemed happy to let things rest as they were. We had reached that stage of the negotiations where the General Secretary of the United Nations is liable to appear gravely in front of the cameras and announce that, following extensive dialogue and full, frank and meaningful discussions, both sides have decided to hammer the living shit out of one another. In line with the dogmatic stance typically taken by parties in this position, we sat firmly down in the taxi.

The intermediaries called in to break the impasse were passers-by, an elegantly dressed chap with a glorious confection of a woman on his arm. When hailed by the driver, they interpreted in near-perfect English.

"We would like to go to the Climataria Restaurant, please," I explained.

"He does not know that restaurant. Can you say where it is?"

I indicated vaguely up the hill to the south of the creek. Comprehension illuminated the face of the driver.

"Ah! Klimahtahreeya! Klimahtahreeya!" His teeth gleamed in the blue light of the bar-sign opposite as he stood on his box and, in the generous manner

143

we had already encountered, shared our discomfiture with everyone in earshot. The interpreter, just barely comprehensible over the driver's rather voluble tale, explained with a wide smile,

"In Greek, you must to be very careful where to put thee stress on a word, otherwise it mean something total different. The restaurant you want is…" he pronounced every syllable very clearly, "…Klim-ah-tah-*rhee*-ya. Is *very* good restaurant."

We thanked him, and sat for a moment whilst the driver finished his side of the story. He closed the account with an imitation of my voice saying 'Climatarea', which made him sound rather pompous, I thought really.

There are four seats in a Spetsiot horse taxi, two facing forr'ad and two facing aft. Malcolm and I sat facing the direction of travel, and Rex was about to sit down opposite us when the driver let us know that there was nothing personal in his amusement at our expense by indicating that Rex should sit up on the box with him. He neatly reversed the horse, jack-knifing the carriage and pulled out onto the road. Then, with a shout and a lazy flick of his long driver's whip, he urged the horse into an easy trot and swung us stylishly off the road into a very narrow alley. The horse settled into what sounded like about fourth gear, and we rattled along splendidly. The hooves and the iron-shod wheels made a splendid, urgent clatter in the confines of the narrow lane, the bell clanged a warning at every junction, and we had an impression of considerable speed. I had a mental picture of Napoleon fleeing the field of Waterloo. The dim oil-lamps cast a yellow, agéd sort of light on the houses as we passed, and the odour of leather, horse, oil and paint mixed with the fragrance of the blossoms which, poking over the garden walls, were exactly at our height. An evening horse-taxi ride through the backstreets of Spetsae is a powerful and evocative experience indeed.

As we passed under the occasional streetlights, I was able to take stock of the carriage itself. It was no latter-day reconstruction, but clearly a venerable chariot. The hood, folded back behind us, was cracked with age and the effects of the sun, its hoops tinged with rust by the effects of the salt air. The gloss-black and gold-leaf paintwork on the carriage was carefully done, but un-even where the many coats had been chipped away in places and over-painted. The steps and handles were polished smooth and shiny with years of use, and all the tack and harness that I could see was black with age and looked as supple as cloth. Three rows of round-headed brass studs on the seats showed where the leather had been renewed, and from the texture and smell of them I suspected that in Spetsae, old coach-horses do not die, they simply graduate from the outside of the coach to the inside.

The driver evidently enjoyed his profession. He encouraged his prime-mover with exuberant cries and occasional cracks of his whip, made use of the bell with a frequency that would have been deplorable had it been a car horn, and from time to time he stood up to see over walls or round corners. Not that he seemed any more likely to yield to other traffic than any other user of a Greek road, mind you. He drove us up the hillside in a series of elegant curves, short, fast, straight dashes and occasional sharp turns, all executed with evident skill and considerable panache. I now have a very good idea of what it would be like to compete in the Monaco Grand National.

The ride to the restaurant probably took ten minutes or so. It seemed to be over in a flash, however, and shortly we were standing in the trellised entrance to Klimata*reeya* watching the taxi nonchalantly reversing back down the hill, having relieved us of a very modest sum for a magical experience.

Fortune, whatever trials she may have laid in our path by sea, had guided our terrestrial meanderings with benevolence up to this point, and she did not desert us now. The random series of turns that had brought Rex and I to Klimatarea during the day had un-earthed a culinary pearl. The restaurant is a traditional tiled house, whose *al-fresco* tables stand on gravel under an extensive vine pergola, pleasantly lit by hanging lanterns. It specialises in the *mezé* style of meal, but in a far more elaborate style than we had hitherto encountered. Yiorgios was an active, personable host, who explained enthusiastically what each dish was. The evening would most probably have been memorable in any case, but was made special by a large Greek family-gathering occupying a long table right down the centre of the restaurant. They were celebrating a *yiourti*, the saint's name-day of several of their number, and their clatter, chatter and bonhomie radiated an atmosphere of tangible warmth and invitation.

At Klimatarea, one simply asks for the *mezé*, and a selection of starters arrives in dribs and drabs. *Skordhalia*, a pungent garlic dip, and spicy meatballs came first with the wine. Then we received some *aetherina*... small, crispy fried fish similar to whitebait... and a selection of other dips. The glory of the first wave was the charcoal-grilled squid, which that night became, and to this day remains, one of my favourite flavours. At Yiorgios' suggestion, we accompanied this with a Macedonian white wine which was crisp and cool and not apt to stay long in an uncorked bottle.

The party at the centre table tended to expand and contract as local people dropped in for a glass or two and wandered off again. During one of its migrations in our direction, Rex struck up a brief conversation with a couple of its adherents, which resulted in our glasses being filled with some retsina. The party also acquired at this point, whether by design or gravitation I know not, a blind accordionist and an acne-plagued youth with a bouzouki.

To Malcolm the Modern Music-Man, the presence of the accordion alone was an appalling development; as for the latter instrument, he would probably prefer to be attacked with a bazooka than a bouzouki. All his fears were confirmed when the duo opened the show by striking up a quavering, funereal rendition of 'Never on a Sunday', and he started drinking very fast indeed.

At about the time that our second batch of dishes started to arrive, the Greek couple who had been instrumental in our negotiations with the taxi-driver walked in, and sat down at the table next to us. Greetings and introductions coincided with the arrival of a plate of *barbounia*, succulent grilled red mullet, and in no time Thannassi and Vangelia were seated at the end of our table, tucking into the fish with us. I have since become aware that *barbounia* are highly prized (and priced!) in Greece, and a Greek is about as likely to refuse an invitation to partake of them as he is to emigrate to Turkey, but it was well worth the loss of a couple of fish. Thannasis, with much clicking of fingers, conducted a lengthy interrogation of Yiorgios, and issued a chain of commands which gradually materialised into a stack of plates in the middle of our table of every possible hue, bouquet and flavour. As for the wine, Yiorgios gave up fairly early on and just showed me where the fridge was, asking me to keep a tally of our consumption if at all possible.

Dancing began early. The waiters got the ball rolling, three of them linking arms across each others shoulders like the front row of a rugby-scrum and dancing the deliberate dressage-steps familiar to everyone who has seen 'Zorba the Greek'. The men of the party followed, hands clasped behind their backs as they swirled and dipped in slow-time. The odd plate began to soar though the air, and then it was everyone in for the hoe-down. Men and women, children and babes in arms formed rings, linked arms and undulated like a field of wheat in a force five. Malcolm cowered, but Rex and I got roped in along with Thannassi, Vangelia and another table full of tourists, and gleefully trod on the toes of people we hadn't even been introduced to. All service came to a standstill whilst the waiters provided special plates for throwing and enthusiastically showed how it was done. Children who would have been in bed hours before in Britain played tag round the tables and chairs, and in all my time in Greece to date, I had never seen a restaurant so free of cats and dogs!

Things settled down after a while, and the waiters resumed their duties. Then Malcolm, who had almost begun to enjoy himself again, was further brutalised by the onset of a succession of singers. The lugubrious, rather Arabic-sounding songs all seemed to be laments, although the word a*gapi*, which Thannassi informed us meant love, occurred almost every second word. Greek love-lives as portrayed in their music seem doomed to tragedy, although for Malcolm, the greatest tragedy was the music itself. He bore it badly, even before I announced my intention of singing myself.

I describe myself as a folk-ranter, and stress that I have no pretensions to musical excellence, or even competence. I sing in a key which a more talented musician than I (by no means a rare animal) once described as 'B demolished'. But I find that all lack of pitch, tone or rhythm can generally be concealed by the tremendous volume I am capable of producing. Wherever four chunky-knit Fair Isle sweaters gather round a Greenpeace T-shirt playing a guitar to nasalise a Celtic air, I am content to quaff my stoup, to Whack-foll-dee-diddle-oh with the best, and to stir, if not the souls of those within earshot, then at least the panes in the window-frames. After a certain quantity of ale has been disposed of by the audience, it is not entirely unknown for me to receive applause, at least when I stop. I have even been bought a pint, although Malcolm points out that the donor was no doubt aware that drinking it would otherwise employ my mouth. On the night in question, I was received with raucous approval by the Greeks. Malcolm said that if people of their musical taste enjoyed my singing, then he felt that that put it in a very fair perspective.

We ended the night in an establishment somewhat more to Malcolm's taste, a disco-bar. Thanassi and Vangelia bid us goodnight at the door, warning that the bar sold *bomba*, and adjuring us only to drink beer or wine. *Bomba*, it appears, is the local hooch brewed in the hills and coloured to resemble gin, rum, whisky or whatever. I stuck to wine anyway, but Malcolm wasn't about to be dissuaded from his rum and coke even by the threat of a chemically-induced hangover.

I spent a while trying to talk to a girl, which was difficult over the noise. It wasn't until I got her outside, however, that I realised just how much one can mistakenly assume in such an atmosphere. As I led her out of the door, I was under the impression that she was called Florence, that she was English and that we were going to another place called 'The Carousel', where someone played the piano. In the relative quiet outside, it transpired that she *came* from Florence, she *did not speak* English, and that she was going off to look for Marcel and Gianni. My presence was entirely surplus to requirements. Upon that cue, I strolled home, zig-zagging down the road to avoid submarines.

I didn't leap up out of my hatch for anything that night… I wouldn't have noticed if a brontosaurus had parachuted onto the foredeck with land-mines tied to its feet!

***

Motorbikes on the quay at Baltiza are a sure way of waking early. The previous night's carousing not withstanding, I was out on my foredeck by about eight-thirty. I did not feel anything like as bad as I deserved to, but I had a very dry mouth, so I set off aft for a drink. I discovered Rex soundly asleep in the cockpit and on descending into the cabin I found that this was not due to a desire for fresh air. There was a tousled blonde head on his pillow, and, given the amount of lipstick it was wearing, I would have been alarmed had it not been attached to a female. On the other side of the cabin, Malcolm snored in porcine contentment, and the table was littered with glasses, an ashtray and a brandy bottle. I was most intrigued to know what this was all about, but no 'accidental' noise I made roused them in the slightest, so after loudly making a cup of coffee, I clambered ashore to drink it and watch as the boats came to life. Then I headed to the Port Police for the weather.

Sign language had served me well in Hydra, so I tried the same approach in Spetsae. Here, an older Port Policeman with rather more stripes leaned his chin on his hand and watched me impassively whilst I went through my routine a time or two. Having let me continue long enough to begin to feel foolish, he then said, "The weather today will be light variable winds and smooth seas. The outlook for the next day is the same. There is always a weather map on the back of the Greek newspapers. You don't have to buy one, just have a look at the news-stand." Well, that solved *that* problem!

By the time I had helped a Dutch family to un-moor, done the day's provisioning, watched the same German perform a very similar departure to the one the day before in Hydra, had a coffee with a Danish couple, gone back to the shop to retrieve my coffee-mug, and returned to the boat, Malcolm had one eye open but was still snoring. Our overnight guest was showing signs of restiveness, but Rex lay as still as a log. I made more coffee, and started wafting it under the noses of all and sundry. There was still no sign of life that one could on oath have described as human or conscious, so I started flicking through the pilot book in search of a destination for the day.

I had just decided upon Kiparissi when a low growl of suffering issued from the cabin. Like a bear waking from hibernation to find his porridge gone, Malcolm rolled out of his blanket and sat up. He looked three weeks dead, pale and yellow-eyed, and held his head tenderly in both hands. He emitted, at regular intervals, low, feral groans of such shocking intensity that I was on the point of feeling compassion for the brute. Considering what sympathy I could expect if the roles were reversed, however, I said, "Serves you right. You were warned about the *bomba* in that place."

He looked up at me, face contorted with pain. I could see that he was considering a retort, but even the thoughts were far too loud for him. He let go another groan, and succumbing to pity, I gave him the coffee.

"And for God's sake, shut your eyes before you bleed to death," I added, just to add insult to injury. "You can tell me all about your night later." I indicated the blonde head opposite him, at which an expression of pure amazement flitted over his suffering features.

When she awoke, the lady was initially no better placed to account for her presence on the boat than the ravaged Malcolm. She came awake quickly and nervously, eyes flitting round the cabin as she realised that she was somewhere unfamiliar, before her own cranial disorder caused her shut her eyes in pain too. We were forced to await the leisurely awakening of Rex to shed some light on the matter, so I occupied the interval by making some nice, greasy fried eggs for all concerned.

"How thoughtful," grunted Malcolm when confronted with two yellow eyes staring at him out of a sea of oil, "...*Ouefs Amoco Cadiz*."

"Where's my boyfriend?" our guest suddenly demanded. An intriguing opening line, I thought. Even more so as the accent was definitely Australian, and the male of that species are not known for losing their womenfolk easily or with good grace. No answer appeared to be forthcoming, so the lady accepted a cup of coffee and made a half-hearted assault on her breakfast.

Malcolm spent an inconclusive few minutes sliding his eggs round his plate before finally trying a bite. His eyes closed tight, he offered to his lips a small piece of egg-white which was firmly rejected. He said that it made too much noise. Laughingly, I sold him an Alka Seltzer for two quid.

Rex, by comparison, could hardly have arisen in cheerier form. He wolfed his eggs, purloined Malcolm's rejects and sent those also to the happy hunting ground, and then looked on in a discreditably covetous manner as our guest slowly finished hers. Rex it was, apparently, who had lured the young lady back to the boat after she had had a bit of a tiff with her swain. However, it was Malcolm who had rather evilly dealt with the boyfriend when he finally arrived at the port in search of his errant partner. Rex related with relish the tale of how Malcolm had stood up, waved, and invited him to step straight on board... over the caique astern of us! He had clambered on board that vessel rather diffidently, but there had been little reluctance in his return to the dock; the Rottweiler, awoken in the middle of the night, turned out to be a decidedly anti-social creature, and young Lochinvar was off the boat again and almost across the road before his feet touched tarmac. Unwilling to try again, despite Malcolm's assurances that 'the dog was all noise...wouldn't hurt a fly', the timorous suitor paced the quay for a while, then headed for bed. Recollection of these events caused an interesting conflict of emotions in our overnight guest, who was spitefully amused and mildly remorseful by turns. Finally, in the logical manner of her kind, she left in high dudgeon to give her pusillanimous boyfriend a piece of her mind. I believe Malcolm still has her bra, if she should care to have it returned...

***

Unmooring was achieved by Rex and myself, Malcolm having crept back into the bed he had not in any real sense left. A taxi-boat or two buzzed about making gratuitous washes in the confines of the harbour, but there was little other activity to clash with our own. The windlass earned its weight in platinum-plated gold bars, hoisting from the depths a collection of anchors so densely entangled that we appeared to have levitated an ancient agricultural instrument. This the windlass did apparently effortlessly... apparently to me, at any rate, since Rex was the man grinding away at the handle! We unhooked the chains and anchors one by one where possible, but a couple of them were lobbed back into the uninviting depths still hopelessly dog-knotted to await the attention of someone more personally involved.

In passing, we could not help noticing a number of very odd implements with which some optimists attempt to moor boats. The Greeks favour grapnels, no doubt because four prongs are far easier to foul-hook than two, and thriftily retain the services of great, prehistoric stocked anchors which look as if they have already out-lived several boats. The yachts seem to have ever more space-age creations, made in alloy to make them lighter to lift; we were very grateful for this consideration. Then there are the do-it-yourself merchants... those who will never dream of using a mundane anchor so long as a disused traction-engine is close to hand. I hate those people with a passion they cannot possibly conceive of.

Our own anchor was easily found in this collection of unorthodox ironmongery by the process of doggedly following the chain, and since the size of the creek had precluded the do-it-yourselfers from throwing into it anything much larger than a Volkswagen Beetle, we were fairly soon on our way out to sea. Rex spent a happy ten minutes tearing bits of rope, tendrils of wire and assorted fishing tackle off the anchor before stowing it.

***

We found at the mouth of the creek that the wind was a light easterly, which solved the question of how to get to Kiparissi. The route is shorter to the east and south of Spetsae, then through the channel between Spetsae and Spetsopoula. There is a shoal in the mouth of this channel, however, which I was not keen to make closer acquaintance with and I had been searching for a good, seaman-like reason for taking the slightly longer, easier way through the Spetsai Strait, a reason that was likely to stand up to the penetrating scrutiny of Rex. The easterly wind was sent by some benevolent deity, and we ran goose-winged along the north shore of the island. Just as we came abeam of the entrance to Porto Xeli on the mainland side, the wind switched round to the west-north-west, and we had to beat out of the strait. Rex mooted turning and going back the other way, but a look over our shoulders showed another boat following us, still with the wind behind him. This phenomenon of wind blowing from opposite directions into a straight channel is not a rare one in Greece. We eventually worked out the reason, but at this point of the trip my lightening-quick thought processes had not quite made two and two equal an integer between three and five. We were to have a wet ride or two until the penny finally defeated the upwelling of dense hot air, and dropped.

As we cleared the strait, passing safely north of the little islet of Petrokaravo, the wind veered gradually until we were broad-reaching quietly towards the high, haze-softened line of the Peloponnese coast. From the corner of Spetsae, Kiparissi is roughly south-south-west and about seventeen miles distant. We could make out no features through the haze, so I took a rough shot at allowing for variation, conveniently ignored deviation, prayed that the compass was marginally accurate and opened a beer.

We were making, I suppose, about three knots for an hour or so. Spetsae receded over our port quarter, but we made no visible impression on the mainland on the starboard bow. The sun was out to play with a vengeance, and with the light wind abaft the beam, we idled along in a general south-westerly direction. With Malcolm below sleeping off his horrendous hang-over, the vote to play Beethoven's Sixth on the cassette player was carried *nem con*, and Rex and I drowsed, torpid and replete, lulled, nay, stupefied by the easy music of the opening movement and matching weather.

The weather continued to faithfully follow the mood of the music. Just at the instant of commencement of that part of the Pastoral Symphony which music *cognoscenti* would probably call the 'Fanfare Fortissimo in A Sergeant-Major' or some such thing, but which I call 'the first loud bit', our genoa was flung flat aback. The boat heeled sharply to starboard and slewed round to head north-west.

In the cockpit, Beethoven triumphantly soared to a minor climax of strings and woodwind as I shot off the port bench. I had been lying with my leg nonchalantly draped round the port sheet-winch, and this acted as a hinge to hurl me head-first through the insubstantial limbs of the cockpit-table into the cockpit sole. Deprived of whatever flimsy means of support it had once enjoyed, the table collapsed on top of me. Rex, by comparison, went absolutely nowhere at all… he was pinned across the throat by the mainsheet, whose unsecured traveller slide had rocketed across to the new lee-side, neatly garrotting him. Malcolm, it transpired, had not escaped unscathed either. Safe enough from falling out of what was now the lee-berth, he was pinned face-down against the back-rest cushion. In this helpless position, he received a full-ish bottle of Metaxa smack between the shoulder blades at high velocity.

My efforts to disentangle myself from the wreckage of the table were severely hampered. The lid of the thing was still hinged to the legs on the lee side, and it closed like a vice on me every time I tried to move. Rex's flailing legs delivered a shrewd blow or two, increasing in urgency as the mainsheet reduced his air-supply still further, and I was unable to get a purchase on anything to help me out of the cockpit bottom. Sadly, the uncomfortable truth is that I was constructed of such bounteous proportions that I just fitted perfectly into the moulded recess, with my arms and legs held rigidly up in the air. Every time I lowered my legs in an attempt to prise my buttocks up over the companionway-step, I was defeated by suction and a lack of leverage. My shirtless torso, lubricated by sweat, gleefully sealed itself hermetically into the fibreglass recess. When I was finally able to summon enough strength to break the suction and raise my buttocks up to the companion way step, it created a stupendous farting sound which, even in my state of dire extremis, set me giggling like an adolescent schoolgirl. From the sounds Rex was making, it sounded as if he was enjoying this lavatorial fanfare too, although I doubt whether he actually was. Strangulation, I would suppose, tends to concentrate the mind to the exclusion of even the most risible of innuendoes.

Having elevated my hips, I was able to rotate ingloriously through one hundred and eighty degrees and reverse onto the cabin steps, and thence to return to the cockpit in the guise of *Homo Erectus*. In my haste to reach Rex before he expired, I was a touch indelicate in my handling of the remains of the cockpit table, which reduced it to little more than kindling. It was a sacrifice which seemed worthwhile at the time, although when Rex got his breath back and began to blame me for the incident, I wished I had taken more care of the table.

The primary task of settling the boat on course again was achieved solely by the efforts of my good self. Rex seemed happy just to gasp and massage his throat, and Malcolm, it must be recorded with regret, contented himself with an ill-conditioned, blasphemous and defamatory diatribe directed at *me*, of all people. Had he not broken the fall of the bottle of Metaxa, I could cheerfully have wished his soul to the devil. The earthly remains of the cockpit table were consigned to the cave locker, Rex's lacerated throat was greased externally with antiseptic cream and internally with the juice of the Amstel fruit, and we sailed boldly onward.

***

The new wind built steadily from the south-south-east, which allowed us to make good a course close-hauled for Kiparissi. The wind continued to increase, slowly but steadily, and the sail gradually became a stirring experience. By the time we were close enough to the mountainous shore to make out the great bowl-shaped bay, *Nissos* was plunging briskly into short, sharp seas, carelessly chucking shovels full of refreshing spray over her port shoulder as she hewed a line of effervescence across the silk-blue Argolic Gulf. Even Malcolm was sufficiently moved by the experience that he emerged into the cockpit and gruffly muttered something about, "Having a go at this lark." With that, he took the tiller for the first time in the trip, and soon settled into the rhythm.

We entered the great bay of Kiparissi under full sail, because it seemed the only thing to do. The thought of tainting the moment with the sulphurous fumes of the Beast in the Bilge was less than appealing. However, my confidence was now tempered by hard-earned experience of the funny things that happen to a simple puff of wind when in the vicinity of Greek rock, and I kept a very wary eye on the water for the patterns that heralded the arrival of 'Poseidon's bullets'. Being suitably prepared for these hammer-falls of wind, naturally, was enough to ensure that they stayed away. I stood in the cockpit, one hand on the un-cleated genoa sheet and the other on the tiller, poised like a leopard for action with muscles a-tremble. (Malcolm took a moment or two to accept that it was actually my *muscles* that had been a-tremble, but I soon set him right.) However, as we entered the bay, the wind just died and the speed trickled away.

The bay of Kiparissi is about two miles across. It is fringed by a grey-white pebble beach, which is backed by a fertile, rising plain of olive trees and orchards speckled with the red roofs of the scattered houses. Then, nowhere more than a half mile back from the sea, there arises from this Arcadian slope a jagged wall of ragged, grey rock which towers up two to three thousand feet all around the bay. The sedimentary crags and cliffs are eroded and sheared into fairy-tale pinnacles and spires, streaked here and there with yellowish mineral stains. It is majestic, magnificent, absolutely captivating. Even now, years later, I am never quite prepared for the grandeur of Kiparissi. I think the most striking feature is the serrated ridge at the top of this mighty scarp; unsoftened by higher land behind, it is slashed across the skyline like a razor-cut. It has a surreal clarity.

The bay is as deep as it looks, and there is a pier at the village in the southwest corner but it is clearly a rather unprotected mooring. In the north and south-east corners of the great bight are small jetties in little nooks where the water is shallow enough to anchor. We selected Agios Georgios, the one to the south, as being better protected from the southerly wind. It was a happy choice. The little concrete quay is backed by a charming little chapel, and nestles into a snug little hook in the rocks. Water of an unreal blue and incredible clarity foxed me entirely... I let go the kedge anchor in what looked like a reasonable depth, only to end up hanging onto the bitter end of the rope as the whole lot gleefully snaked out over the stern-roller. Later investigation with the assistance of the echo sounder indicated that the water was over twenty metres deep... and I could see the bottom!

I heaved the kedge back up and dropped it somewhat closer in, on a steeply rising slope. It bit nicely, and considerably reduced the impact of the stem on the quay, which would otherwise have been substantial; at the crucial moment, the perfidious diesel would have nothing at all to do with an astern movement and stalled. Malcolm tied the bow to a post, I switched off the engine ignition buzzer, and that was that.

The clarity of the water, the heat of the day and the frequency of the beer through the voyage now culminated in a mass suicide attempt; as one man, we all leapt over the side into the crystalline water and disported our cetacean forms in the cooling bosom of the ocean. The water was colder than we had previously found, being deeper and fed by fresh-water from the mountains, but it was gloriously invigorating, and we frolicked with wild abandon for twenty seconds or so until our mighty bodies were exhausted: then we tried to get out.

"I thought," I said accusingly to Malcolm, "that I told *you* to put the swimming ladder down."

His reply, in essence, was in the plural, spherical and bouncy, and I felt lacked in helpfulness what it undoubtedly possessed in pith and terseness. We set about trying to get back on board.

Early efforts focused upon trying to levitate ourselves up the stern sufficiently to release the ladder. Malcolm tried to heave himself up with a finger-tip grip on the toe-rail, and did in fact lift himself high enough to raise one wanton nipple clear of the water. It wasn't far enough.

I tried next, several cunning attempts to climb sloth-like up the anchor rode being my strategy. On the second occasion, I got high enough to jam my finger painfully between the rode and the roller, but nothing further was achieved.

Malcolm and I then rested whilst Rex made his attempt. Kinetic energy was the key to his campaign, force, mass and acceleration combining in a sound, scientific approach to the problem. He intended to dive under water, then rise using his own buoyancy and power to soar out of the water in a graceful trajectory, high enough to catch hold of the pushpit rail. Malcolm and I used up valuable reserves of energy giggling at the demented sea-lion antics which ensued. Rex tried hard, I'll give him that. He refused to give up until, in one gargantuan effort, he surfaced rather physically between the rudder and propeller.

Next we had a look at the quay wall, but in a startling break with Greek concrete-pouring practice, it was as smooth as a baby's bum with no ledges or holes, and not a single protruding piece of wire or timber. That left the rocks, which were infested with sea-urchins below the surface and so eroded as to be sharply jagged at the waterline. As Malcolm put it, not even Reinhold Messner would be mad enough to attempt to climb up a sheer wall of knives infested by porcupines. The rocks were out. In desperation, I was forced to swim the forbidding fifty odd yards to a small beach, and then make my agonising, barefooted way back to the boat around the little bay. This was about quarter of a mile, over red-hot rocks and through scrub and brambles. I received no gratitude for this gallant feat, and so I enjoyed a restorative beer before letting the ladder down.

The squabble over the swimming incident did not run a normal course at all, and the gin bottle, for once, had little to do with the reconciliation. The scenery of Kiparissi Bay is such that even Adolf Hitler and Joe Stalin could have lapsed into companionable contemplation together beneath its soaring rock-faces. To hell with Geneva and Camp David, if you seriously wanted to get two people to agree on something, I reckon the job would be more than half done if you could just get them to Kiparissi. The man who could not agree to peace in those surroundings could safely be considered to be devoid of human sentiment of any value whatsoever, for the harmony and serenity of this bucolic bay would sooth a Viking berserker on an acid trip. It occurred to me that I would not despair of making even a jet-ski salesman repent his sins in such a place.

Rex had a look at the engine fuel, which seemed fine, and I then tried the perfidious engine again. It started immediately, with its usual eructation of smoke, as if nothing had been wrong.

"Running like a sewing-machine now," I commented.

Rex looked at me sidelong. "It might as well be a sewing machine, mate. We've certainly been stitched up with it!"

***

The obvious way to get into the village for dinner was to inflate the dinghy and paddle across, and by now we were intrigued to see what sort of craft dwelt in the orange bag in the cave-locker. The answer was 'a punctured one.'

When talking of inflatable boats, there are punctures and then there are punctures. Some of these punctures are tiny little affairs, elusive, whispering pinpricks which take patience, soapy water and cunning to locate, and moments to fix with a small patch. Others are large enough to be easily visible to the eye, and so are quickly found but rather more time-consuming to repair. The venerable dinghy that Spiro had given us fell into the very outside of the latter group; it appeared to have been repeatedly gored by an enraged unicorn. Even if Spiro had included a repair kit in the inventory, there was obviously no point in even thinking about re-assembling this sorry, shredded piece of latex. Once unrolled on the deck, it looked like the wreck of the *Hindenburg*. Sub-Lieutenant Warneford himself could not have done it in more thoroughly. Rex and I re-interred it in its shroud, whilst Malcolm went into a trance on the coachroof and called down the curses of the Gods of Angling (a potent and malign pantheon) upon the head of Spiro. We walked to town.

The walk around the south side of the bay is something over a mile, and very pleasant, but a moment's thought would have caused us to carry a torch for the way back. Life must be so predictable and mundane to those who are habitually fore-sighted: Rex, Malcolm and I will have no truck with it.

***

We reached the little village just as the sun's final blessing died away behind the soaring scarp, leaving a soft, grey-blue twilight in which to find the restaurant. Our search for somewhere to eat took us through silent, narrow streets between white-washed stone houses. We later found out that the main town of Kiparissi... itself really only a village... lies further up the hill. We had arrived in Paralia, which means the 'shore' or 'water-front'.

All is very well maintained in Kiparissi-Paralia. Even the houses closed up for the season are impeccably preserved, freshly painted, their gardens neatly trimmed. These are substantial houses, of classical proportion and very pleasing to the eye, rather larger than the majority of Greek town-homes we had become used to. Red tiled roofs and blue window frames flare against the sharp white walls. The houses are predominantly two-storey and many have an attractive local feature, the first floor is accessed by exterior stone stairs which combine with balconies and also provide a deep, arched porch for the ground floor. There is a substantial church and adjacent is a wonderful, tranquil cemetery which lies under a rearing rocky crag. It is accessed from the church over a charming little bridge spanning a dry river-bed... deeply symbolic of the transition from life to death... and on a moonlit night is a fantastic sight, the candles on the graves dancing like fireflies in the Stygian shadow of the cliff.

We finally found some life at the shop, a brief glance inside which revealed a few tinned goods, bags of staples such as rice, grains and sugar, some plastic-ware, and a mass of fishing-gear. Outside, several locals idly chatted away the quiet evening. The scene brought it home to us that, in a few hours lazy sail from Spetsae, we had passed from one world into another; from the cosmopolitan, lack-little world of the touristy Saronic, we had arrived in the harder world of the working Peloponnese; a place where tourism is for most people an irrelevance and daily toil yields the essentials of day-to-day existence but leaves little for luxuries. The people we met reflected this. They were dressed in working clothes of heavy cotton and serge, and were mostly bent and aged by their labour. They greeted us with grave courtesy, pausing in their stroll or backgammon game to watch us pass. It was quickly evident to us that the younger people, less attracted to the land and sea of their fathers, had moved away. We saw few people between twenty and thirty. I suppose that before long their place will be taken by holiday-home owners, and Kiparissi, tragically, seems doomed to change. No doubt there will be a noisy music-bar here soon.

There are two or three restaurants in Kiparissi, and we chose the oldest, close to the town quay. An early arrival is indicated, as there are very few tables, and your party will often share with another. There will be a set menu of one fish course, one meat course, and a couple of starters. If you want anything else, get back in your boat and head for a bright light elsewhere!

We took our seats at a table close to two American-Greeks who had come home to visit their Father's birthplace, and were offered *kokoretsi*, spit-roasted offal, and grilled *kolios*, which is a small Mackerel-type fish. With a kilo or two of the heady, heavily resinated wine and a leisurely local brandy to follow, it was a meal fit for the occasion.

Our neighbours were interesting people. Both first-generation Americans, their respective parents were born in adjoining houses in Kiparissi. One of them was doing rather well as a senior superintendent for an American shipping line, whilst the other was a sewer-maintenance worker from New York. Village ties that reached over oceans, continents and a yawning social abyss brought Alexandros and Makis back home every year to sit for a month in rural tranquillity, smoking contentedly together whenever their lack of common ground restricted conversation. Both had married city Americans, whom they left behind in the States; one visit to the hushed, pastoral paradise of Kiparissi had been too much for the city-gals.

Alexandros was a bit of an amateur historian, and it was through him that we were first introduced to the fascinating story of the Greek revolution against the Turks, which is very largely a story of internecine Peloponnesian politics and family feuds. We sat entranced that night as Alexandros effectively sketched the characters of 1821; the principled Demitrius Ypsilantis, the calculating Kolokotrones, the villainous Ali Pasha of Ioanina. What period of history can offer such colourful protagonists? The courage of Karaïskakis, the dash of Votsaris, the mountain obduracy of Petrobey Mavromichaelis, the high-flown hopes and desperate despairs of Byron. What fiction could conceive of belligerent Bouboulina's revenge for her fallen men-folk, the gadfly career of the alternately timid and gallant Mavrokordhatos, the hubris of patrician Kapodistrias? Can anyone, to this day, say whose side Odysseus Androutsos was on? Then, aside from the ethnic protagonists, who in Britain has ever heard of Frank Abney Hastings, or Sir Richard Church? Admiral Codrington's part in the battle of Trafalgar is long forgotten in his native England, and there is little public remembrance of Lord Cochrane, the lion-hearted black sheep of the Royal Navy. Admirals Heyden and De Rigny are long forgotten in Holland, Russia and France. All these names are commonly found on Greek street corners, however. The Greeks are not slow to acknowledge those foreigners who helped them win their freedom.

Alexandros was a gifted story-teller, and I formed an impression that I have since confirmed; he told his tale not in the idealised, clear-cut form which I suspect most patriots would have employed, but warts and all. The night ran fast past us as Alexandros, assisted by interjections from Makis and other locals, drew back the curtain of a hundred and fifty years and gave us a glimpse of the rich lore of the *epanastasis*, or revolution. He told of the glorious victories wasted by subsequent feuding, of the sacrifice in battle followed by avarice in victory. He told of promises casually made and more easily broken, of treachery hand in hand with honour, and of the occasionally unbelievable savagery of both sides.

The story is an epic one, of how an amalgamation of tribesmen, pirates, and mountain brigands, very loosely herded on an uncertain course by a blend of opportunist politicians and true patriots, now helped and now hindered by foreigners, funded by distant, principled philanthropists who imagined that they were restoring to glory the Greece of Pericles and Democritus, and assisted by the first steam-powered warship in history, eventually stumbled onto a road that lead to the birth of a proudly independent nation. It is story rich in colour, and Alexandros told it with flair. Part of the fascination for us was the immense amount of local involvement, because the Argo-Saronic area saw much of the action, both military and political. Having seen Hydra, her sons Miaoulis, Economou, Tombazis and Koundouriotis came more easily to life. Having sailed the Bay of Poros, the burning of the ships was more easily envisaged. My fascination with the Greek independence began that night and is with me still. It is a catalogue of tragedy, treachery, trial and triumph so rich with politics, war, scheming and loving, and studded with characters so vibrant, that it beggars fiction. If a syndicate were formed where Robert Ludlum wrote the plot, Bernard Cornwell the action scenarios, Sidney Sheldon the treachery and sleaze, John Grisham the politics, and Sven Hassel the violence, they couldn't match this for a tale. And for a cynic like me, of course, there is rich humour here too, in the Machiavellian intrigues of the protagonists and most particularly in the antics of the northern Europeans who became involved.

***

Oops! I got off on one there, didn't I? But let the reader not think that the book will now develop into a History. It goes without saying, of course, that all this background colour was ingested along with a reasonable quantity of the local wine, and thus we return to the common thread of our tale as a trio of optimists set out to find their way back to the boat, predictably tipsy, tottering... and torchless.

The sky was moonless but with some star-light, otherwise we would never have made it. As it was, it took us ages to negotiate the coast-track, which was wide enough but wound crazily along the cliff-face. We were only too aware, from the walk into town, that in places it lay a good thirty feet above the sea, and so we adopted a policy of moving very slowly and only along the inside edge of the road, keeping contact with the rock-face... a desperate measure, as the area is scattered with thorn bushes as spiky as Wellington's squares. As the gallant captain, point duty fell to me, so with Rex and then Malcolm holding on to my shoulders like gassed First World War soldiers, I picked my way with many a scream and stumble along the rubble-strewn edge of the track. By the time we could see the gleam of the candle in the church on our quay, the thorns had turned my right hand and forearm into a parody of an archery target, I had nearly sprained my ankle fifty times and, even inside my shoes, it felt as if my toe-ends had been kicked to bloody stumps.

With the candle in sight, our way home should have been straight-forward... but could I find the way down that bloody hill? Every promising downward slope seemed to end in an ominous black pit suggesting a precipitous drop of immeasurable extent, or in impenetrable thorn.

It was whilst thrashing about in one of these thickets that I lost about three years of my life. Sliding out of control down a slight, pebbly incline, I was appalled to see a shadow I had taken for a large rock rise up towards me of its own volition. It slammed into my thigh, sounded an alarm like a klaxon, and then rose past my ear like a rocket. I went down like a sack of spuds and attempted to reverse up the slope on all fours, but it fell on my back. With a few savage digs with its hooves, a frantic bleat, a sharp, rank waft of animal odour and a frantic clanging of its bell, the goat was off up the slope like a... well, a goat up a mountainside. I lay weak and cursing on the stony ground, unable even to smile at the pandemonium reigning further up the hill where the cloven-footed devil had met Malcolm head on. I scrambled to my feet, shaking like a leaf and cursing the beast to perdition as its bleating and the clanging of its bell receded upwards at incredible speed.

A bit more fossicking around led me onto the beach I had swum to earlier in the day, but no further. I could not for the life of me find the path back to the boat, and in any case I had had enough of the affair for one night. I announced my intention of swimming to the boat and returning with a torch. Even Malcolm divined that this was no time for a witticism, silently taking my clothes as I waded into the chilly water, cursed the sharper stones, and struck out for the candle-light.

Fortunately, I had not been tidy enough to pull up the bathing-ladder again after our afternoon swim, and so was soon heaving myself into the cockpit. I was somewhat non-plussed to find Malcolm already there, handing me a towel.

"How the bloody hell did you do that?" I demanded, with more than a little exasperation in my tone. Malcolm appeared a bit shifty about his reply.

"Er, well, just as you set off, I realised where the path was. Saw it, in fact. Like a drink? G and T, or a coffee and cognac nightcap?"

When Malcolm is as nice as that, something (other than the rollmops) is definitely rotten in the state of Denmark. Rex, ingenuousness personified, appeared in the hatch-way at that moment, and was gleefully happy to let me know what it was.

"Never believe it, would you. Malcolm rolls your clothes up, decides to put your wallet in his pocket for safe keeping... finds he's had a key-ring with a torch on it in his pocket all the time."

Even in a place as serene as Kiparissi, I find there are still some circumstances which make it possible to contemplate with relish the violent death of a fellow man.

***

Rex slept in the cockpit again that night, and we owe him a debt of gratitude for doing so. He excitedly woke Malcolm and I in the early hours of the morning, calling us outside. Ever fearing some emergency, I reacted like a good captain and yet again performed my impression of a Polaris missile leaving its silo through the fore-hatch, although beyond the re-appearance of the goat with vengeance on his mind, I could not think what ill could possibly befall us in this haven. In fact, Rex had called us to see the sunrise.

It was stunning. With the bay still deep in heavy twilight, the sun, still below our horizon, hit the top of the cliffs and lit them in a golden band. For several magical minutes, we sat and watched the glorious glow creep lower down the mountain as the bay became gradually lighter. A rare and memorable sunrise, and I speak as a long-time four-to-eight watchkeeper, to whom sunrises and sunsets are treated as an occupational hazard. I said as much.

"Thanks, Rex. That was rather special."

"Couldn't believe it myself when I woke up and saw it. Thought it was the Aurora Borealis, or something. Fantastic!"

Malcolm re-interred himself in his blanket.

"Thanks all the same, Rex, but next time you wake me up, try and have breakfast ready would you? Goodnight."

***

Midday the next day found the Good Ship ghosting idly south along the rugged coastline, with the destination of Gerakas in mind. A late start had been followed by a move to the town quay for beer, and I had telephoned Spiro's office to have a word about the reliability of the engine and the non-existence of the dinghy. I made the mistake of telling his secretary why I was calling, and was, of course, then told that Spiro was 'out'. Where he had gone was imprecise, but she felt sure he would be back by, say... Christmas? The secretary faithfully took a message.

"...And which boat you are on, Sir?" she asked.

"*Nissos*," I replied. There was a pause at the end of the line, just long enough, I would say, for a devout young lady to cross herself.

"And where are you, Sir?"

"Kiparissi."

There was a silence, which could have meant, 'Good, that's far enough away' or, possibly, 'Christ! The old tub's never got that far before... how the hell is he going to get it back?'

"Well, Good Luck!" she said doubtfully, and put the phone down.

I had then indulged in my morning ritual of looking for weather information, but Kiparissi has neither a Port Police office nor a newsagents, so we winged it again.

The pilot book does point out that the entrance to Gerakas is a touch tricky to find, and so I spent quite a bit of time quietly ensuring that I got it right. There are no lights or marks to go by, and I was reduced to carefully counting headlands as we passed them. All to no avail, I fear, because turning into a little nook in the rocks just where I calculated Gerakas should have been, I discovered an absolutely delightful bay... which was definitely not Gerakas. Fortunately, I had not said anything to The Motley, and so was able to pass this off as a planned swimming stop.

It was a glorious, un-inhabited bay nestled under massive cliffs and boasting the most perfect, cobalt-blue water over a clean pebble beach and bottom. The clarity of the water was unbelievable. Rex and Malcolm enjoyed it tremendously, but my attention was largely on working out where we were: it was either Vathi Avlaki bay or Ormos Strongilli, and depending upon which one it was, I either had to turn left or right on leaving to find Gerakas. Instinct said south, but then, instinct had brought me here in the first place. Science was at a stand… science is measurement, and with every headland looking the same, no log and a chart which looked like a camel's snot-rag, measurement was, to say the least, imprecise. That left art.

I have long held that navigation is an art rather than a science. You have only got to look at the number of mathematical imbeciles who have found their way around the world to realise that, and in fact the mystical haversine is actually nothing more or less than a mathematical con-job which avoids simple sailors having to decide whether to add or subtract. Navigation is more a 'feel', an almost tactile sense, based on experience, background knowledge and a sort of in-built course-and-distance register. I have always prided myself upon my grasp of this kind of seat-of-the-pants navigation, the ability to reduce navigational problems right down to fundamental and instinctive vector-plotting. Mind you, I was careful not to let Rex or Malcolm see me toss the coin…

Guided by 'heads', we turned south out of the bay and were duly rewarded twenty minutes later by finding a small light-structure on the coast. Snouting up to it, we turned a corner into what appeared to be a solid cliff-face, and found opening before us a superb rocky fjord in which nestled an idyllic little town. At first glance, you just *knew* it was going to be sleepy… somnolence simply leapt out and smacked you in the eye.

Gerakas lies along a stone quay on the northern side of the inlet, and edging up to this quay, we found it to be none too deep in the places we looked. A couple of hundred yards towards the entrance there is a much more professional-looking pier. It is almost as if someone thought they could get a real ship into this tiny bay… ridiculous! We were utterly gob-smacked by the folly of whoever had built it, since no ship of commensurate size could have entered the harbour, but grateful all the same. I put *Nissos* gently alongside near the root of the pier.

Arriving in mid-afternoon in Gerakas we found to be an unsettling experience. What at first appeared to be the idyllic peace of the place quickly seemed to be down-right spooky. Whilst Malcolm erected his rods and re-engaged in tiddlercide, Rex and I wandered down the quay into the attractive little knot of houses, which basked in the late afternoon sun without any sign of life whatsoever. Not a sound, not a soul, not a movement. Doors and shutters were closed, tables bare. The silence was uncanny.

All this, of course, we could explain plausibly by the fact that it was siesta-time; what really spooked us was that there were no cats.

'No cats!' I hear the reader cry, 'No *cats?*'

No Cats.

'Good God, man,' cries the reader who has never been to Greece, '...are you such men as to be intimidated even by the *presence* of a cat, never mind the *absence* of a cat! Have you no bowels, no steel in your spines at all? Have you no shame, to confess in public to Nilgatophobia? Fie!'

And, 'Good God, man,' cries the reader who *has* been to Greece, 'No Cats! What Tosh! No cats in a Greek town? Keep it at least *moderately* credible, will you? Shall we read next that Pleisiosaurs infest Staines Reservoir? That British railway companies actually read their own timetables? Intolerable!'

No cats.

I have only touched on it so far, but we had found that there were rather a lot of cats in Greece. In fact, I would go so far as to say that wildebeest never swept half so magnificently across the plain as cats did across urban Greece in the eighties. Like an omnipresent, furry sea, they undulated across open spaces, broke on the steps of tavernas and hurled themselves up the legs of restaurant chairs and tables, only to fall back into the groundswell. They lurked in the guttering and on the pergolas, and fell to earth from the trees like leaves in autumn at the susurrus of knife on fish-skin. They posed for photographs, mugged dustbin men, and attacked dogs. It was as if Greece itself wore a fur coat. A garbage truck going along the street trailed cats like the bridal-train of a princess. To put it in perspective, even Malcolm (who regards the indolent, haughty cat as the sole life-form of worth on the planet) thought that the cats in Greece were a bit much.

But we saw no cats in Gerakas. We saw nothing sentient at all. We crept warily along the lifeless quay, and then dared each other into venturing timidly up the stepped alleys until we emerged at the top of the town. The panorama of the little community lay below us, as pretty and impossibly colourful as a picture-postcard, and just as dead. The definitive still-life.

The pilot-book had mentioned some Mycenaean or Minoan ruins on the headland at Gerakas, and Rex and I stumbled happily about in the undergrowth for half an hour or so until we found them. Seemingly almost un-excavated, we found them on the top of a low cliff overlooking the entrance to the harbour and were entranced by the stillness of the site, by its scenic qualities, but mostly by the occasional traces of mosaic we found amongst its tumbled walls.

Despite being something of a history-lover, I had never previously felt a link to the past through stonework. Sculpture of the classical period also leaves me cold, possibly because so much of it is copied and seen around us in every-day life, possibly because I am an unregenerate barbarian. But that first piece of mosaic that I saw in Gerakas hit me full in the face with the impact of more than three thousand years. I think it is because it was in colour, whereas hitherto my concept of Ancient Greece had been in natural-stone monochrome, or in the two-tone style of their pottery. It was as though I was meeting for the first time in full colour people I had previously seen only in black and white photographs. I felt as if one of the inhabitants of Mycenaean Gerakas had stepped out of the ruins and shaken my hand.

The little inlet must have been a godsend to the ancients. It provided a safe harbour with a fertile hinterland, easily defended at the mouth and hell for an enemy to approach from any other direction. The daily land and sea breezes, as I had finally realised, blew down the coast in the morning and up the coast in the afternoon, which simplified trade, and the bad weather came mainly over the mountains, causing no evil swells. Only a bad north-easterly penetrates the labyrinthine entrance, and then the galleys could easily be hauled up into the soft mud of the lagoon at the head of the fjord.

***

There came a hum, never heard by the ancients, which grew to a roar that spilt the peace, and our friend the hydrofoil was with us again. Carving its virgin-white wake on the deep blue water, the gaudy thing curved around the southern headland and wound its way into Gerakas, still up on its stilts. It disappeared from view into the entrance, the engine note died... and then Rex and I heard a rapid hooting of its horn. We looked at each other in growing horror as each of us, independent of the other, reached an inescapable conclusion. There was only one boat in Gerakas that could feasibly be in the hydrofoil's way, and the only person on that boat was Malcolm. Lumbering into a cart-horse trot, I set off over the hill with Rex in gasping pursuit.

The only way that Rex and I are ever likely to win inclusion in an Olympic squad is if alcohol abuse gains recognition as a discipline (I had hoped, since each host nation is allowed to nominate one new sport, that something might have come of Sydney hosting the year two thousand games, but alas...) so it will come as no surprise to the reader to learn that we arrived far too late, and far too exhausted to be of any use. As we crested the hill above the village, the hydrofoil was already backing away from the quay, and the good ship *Nissos* was clearly seen to be untouched, but floating out in the bay. The figure of Malcolm, arms akimbo, stood in the cockpit, watching the retreat of the flying cockroach from our berth.

"Thank God for that!" I panted. "He's managed to anchor her!"

"How the hell did he manage that?" wondered Rex. "He's never driven her before."

We glanced at each other, shrugged, and ambled down through the town.

Despite the arrival of the hydrofoil, there was still no visible movement on the quay, and we were eerily reminded that 'necropolis' is a Greek word; however, just as we were on the point of leaving the place as being uninhabited, we finally encountered unmistakable evidence of life. As we passed under a low window with traditional louvered shutters, there came from within the unmistakable trumpeting of a thunderous fart, followed by a shrill cry of female outrage. This Petomanic fanfare both amused and reassured us, and appeared to mark the official end of the siesta. By the time we arrived back at the pier, a fishing-boat was puttering down the inlet, hydrofoil passengers lugged suitcases and a number of people strolled along the quayside.

Malcolm, it appeared, had not done quite as well as it had appeared from the top of the hill. True, he had removed *Nissos* safely and expeditiously from the path of the hydrofoil, but it appeared that he had done so by leaving all the mooring-lines on the pier and simply pushing the boat out into the middle of the harbour. The engine and anchor-winch both being entirely foreign to him, he was now drifting slowly out to sea on the afternoon breeze. To add insult to injury, when we arrived, he was standing on the foredeck apparently preparing his fishing-rod!

In Stentorian voice, utilising language of an unpalatably salty nature, I bellowed at him to stop messing about with his rod, let the bathing ladder down, and I would swim out to him. This, I informed him sharply, was no time for fishing. In reply, he ignored me completely, and, finishing his preparations, he lofted the rod and made a mighty cast round the forestay. To this day, he maintains that it was purely by chance that the large lead weight on the end of the line missed my temple by about a foot...

Rex, quicker than me to divine the intention, wrapped the line round a bollard and Malcolm then brought his vessel to port by standing inside the pulpit and reeling in on a meaty looking multiplier reel. *Nissos* kissed gently up to the pier to the delighted applause of several Greek promenaders, and Rex and I hopped on board with the mooring-lines and moved her down to the town-quay out of the way of further predatory hydrofoils.

***

With hindsight I applaud Malcolm for dealing with the situation in a manner fitting his own skills. Who is to say that a manoeuvre is wrong just because it is unorthodox? When I was a cadet, I observed in action one captain for whom the expected just never seemed to materialise. His powers of improvisation were acute, honed by years of (I now realise) entirely misreading the situation to start with! The most spectacular of his recoveries which I saw, however, was really not his fault.

We were entering Durban harbour, South Africa, one fine summer's day. Cooper Point and The Bluff slid by to port, the beach and then the sheds of the Point Berths to starboard. The telegraph stood at half ahead, the pilot had arrived on the bridge, the tugs were standing by off the berth at Salisbury Island, God was in his heaven and all well with the world. The captain lit a cigarette, and monitored progress contentedly.

"Stop Engine," ordered the pilot, and yours truly swung the heavy brass leaver to 'stop'.

169

"Stop Engine," I confirmed, and bowed my head to record this in the movement book. Before I could look up to confirm the engine stopped, the next order came.

"Slow Astern."

I acknowledged, and swung the telegraph back to 'slow astern'. I entered this in the book, glanced up to the rev counter, began to call out "Engine going astern," realised that it wasn't, and actually called out, "Engine still going ahead, Captain!"

There wasn't any doubt about it either; we could still feel the unbroken beat of the big six-cylinder Doxford thumping away below us. The third mate was onto the engine room phone like a terrier.

"We've given you Slow Astern, Chief, and she's still Half Ahead. Go Slow Astern, please." His face went a shade paler as he listened to the reply. He turned to the bridge-wing, and his voice was definitely up an octave.

"Engine won't stop, Captain!" The captain paused in the act of taking a cigarette from its packet.

All eyes swivelled ahead to the container-berths on Salisbury Island dead ahead.

"Oh, dear," muttered the captain, and lit his cigarette.

Things started to happen. The captain ordered hard-a-starboard on the wheel, then Full Astern on the telegraph. The pilot started gibbering into his 'talking brick', the walkie-talkie which linked him to the tugs. The engine room phone rang again, and the third mate informed us that the engineers could not stop the engine conventionally, so they had closed off the fuel; it would be about five minutes before the fuel in the system burned out.

Five minutes, by my reckoning, would see us half-way up Marine Parade, at the traffic-lights close to the old dolphinarium.

The ship was starting to swing to starboard, probably still making six knots even with the rudder hard over. On the port bow, water boiled under the counters of the two tugs. From their tall, yellow and green funnels erupted gouts of smoke and sparks, reminding some unoccupied corner of my racing brain that South African tugs at that time were still coal-fired, and they picked up way, heading for our port bow. We wouldn't have made it without them, our turning circle was too large for the harbour basin, and we would probably have steamed straight into Number Four berth on The Point. But the tugs caught us and, with great skill and panache, crushed their bow-fenders to our bow plating. We felt the gentle shudders as they took the weight... a very difficult thing to judge aright with both ships moving so fast, but both managed it without 'bouncing'... and then the sky blackened as they piled on the power to help us round. From the starboard side, another tug came ripping across the harbour to push our stern, but whether she ever made it or not, I cannot say.

Apart from the cackle of the pilot's radio, silence reigned on the bridge, there being nothing we could do but wait and see if we made it clear of the Point. And then the captain's voice cut calmly through the electric air.

"Three-oh, phone the engine room: warn them we may have a collision. The general alarm will be the collision warning. Cadet, call fore and aft. Warn them, and tell the mate to clear the fo'c'sle." He lit a cigarette.

Telephone buzzers sounded, and the foc'sle crew streamed aft along the decks.

"Cadet, call the galley. Tell them to take everything off the stove and go and sit down in the messroom. If I sound the general alarm, it means collision imminent. Three-oh, take the wheel. If we miss the Point, we're coming hard-a-port straight away to go out to sea through the channel. Prayer is very commendable, but we can do without it just for a moment or two." He indicated the Indian helmsman, who was evidently seeking divine assistance to the detriment of his steering, and then turned away and lit a cigarette.

We missed the Point, but by so close a margin that if there had been a ship moored there, we would have collided with it. The forward tug in fact *did* hit the dock.

We entered the channel and the captain took charge again.

"Hard-a-port, Three-oh. Midships. Steady. Take her straight down the middle. Cadet, let the engine room know, and tell the mate to go back forward and prepare to anchor." The captain watched the swing of the bows slow and steady down the channel, and lit a cigarette.

The engine-note finally died, the ship trickled anticlimactically out into the Indian Ocean, turned parallel to the beach on the last of her way and dropped anchor as she came to a stop. I looked around, full of awe for the cool skill of the tugs, the detached professionalism of the pilot, the sang-froid of the third mate and the unruffled calm of the captain.

The tugs had dog-knotted themselves together inside the harbour, the third mate was crossing himself at the wheel, and the pilot had his radio in his left hand and a cigarette packet in the other. As I watched, he tried to speak into the fag-packet. And the captain… he stood with a weary look on his face, and at his feet laid a heap of broken matches and seven unextinguished, unsmoked cigarettes. Me? I was still trying to push the telegraph lever past 'Full Astern' and onto the maker's nameplate.

The chief engineer, on being told later how close it had been, commented only, "Why all the fuss? Nothing to worry about. Navigators always miss The Point!"

The last word on the incident came over the VHF from Cooper Point Port Control in a strong South African accent.

"M.V. *Thames*, this is Cooper Point. Thanks very much for the visit, *Thames*, and don't hesitate to drop in again if you're passing."

***

Back in Gerakas, we tied up outside Ioannis's restaurant, which doubled as the very rudimentary village store. He was a cheerful chap with a limp and a son, Panayiotis, a gifted grouper- and sword-fisherman. Then there was a fish restaurant run by Takis, a bespectacled chap who spoke the best (possibly the only) comprehensible English in Gerakas. Angelo ran the Kavogerakas restaurant furthest from the harbour-entrance, a cheerfully balding, pot-bellied chap with a penchant for very short shorts and rude aprons. And finally, amidst the other establishments, there dwelt a splendid ouzeri. All were excellent establishments and, uniquely in Greece, they recommended one another! On reflection, why not? Life is evenly paced in this backwater, and once the village came to life there was no shortage of trade for all of them. We inspected the fish in each one over a beer, and found ourselves so spoilt for choice that a major policy decision resulted.

Hitherto, it had been our vague intention to see a few of the Cyclades Islands of Greece. Equally indefinite was the hazy idea of leaving the Peloponnese coast at Monemvasia, the next port south of Gerakas, and sailing overnight across to Milos and thence up the western Cyclades back to Athens. Now, however, there was a common consensus that we were perfectly happy on the Peloponnese. Rex was little inclined to make long voyages, I was intrigued by the history and heritage of the area, and Malcolm had learned from Panayiotis that this was the tuna season on the coast, along with the local recipe for catching them. All of us were happy amongst these hospitable pastoral people and rugged solitude of this coast, and none of us wanted to leave Gerakas with a restaurant untried. Moreover, no-one trusted the engine further than they could throw it!

Careful scrutiny of the pilot book over the evening ouzo provided the good ship *Nissos* with the first suggestion of an itinerary since we had taken over. It was duly agreed that the next day, we would go south the seven miles to Monemvasia for lunch on the morning north wind, and come back to Gerakas on the afternoon south wind for the night. Then we would head north to Leonidion and Astros, across to Ermioni, and have three days to get back to Athens from there. If the weather suited, we might then make a late dash across to one Cycladic island, probably Kythnos, en route back to Alimos, otherwise we would amble back via Poros and Aegina again. The lack of disagreement on this programme was a disturbing first for the voyage, and Malcolm suggested with evident distaste that we appeared to be bonding.

We dined at Ioannis's on grouper-fish soup and whiled away the night playing backgammon, to the amusement of the locals. They had never seen anyone play so slowly.

CHAPTER SEVEN

THE BACK NINE

In which we reach our furthest south, and our highest peak... Unwonted exercise... Running repairs... More night alarums... Northwards on the Arcadian coast... Athletic pusillanimity... The hunting of the Spiro... Spiro at bay... A traffic incident... A feat of navigation... A defeat of navigation.

After a night of blissful peace with, astoundingly, no occasion to leap out of my hatch, we arose the next day and put our plan into action. It worked unbelievably well, except that half of the sacrificial strip of the genoa came away from the sail en route, flapping around the foredeck and tangling itself industriously into the shrouds. Notwithstanding this, and underway before nine, we were in Monemvasia by ten-thirty, staring up in awe at the massive rock citadel. Hundreds of feet high it soars, this Gibraltar of the East, a sheer-sided monolith joined to the coast only by a slender causeway bridge and crowned by a fringe of Byzantine fortifications. We anchored stern-to the mole and walked around the south side of the rock to the town, wondering at the impossibility of assaulting such a fortress. About a mile along the south side, on a steep scree below the cliff proper, stands a most perfect walled Byzantine village in an impeccable state of preservation. Tourist shops lurk in its sinuous coils, to be sure, but detract little from the effect, and there is no traffic to poison the air with fumes or noise. Well, a donkey or two, which Malcolm proclaimed to be more offensive than cars in terms of both fumes and noise given off, but the point is that once one has passed through the twisting fortified gate in the town wall and left the camping-vans of the German tourists behind in the roadside, there is little to see here that wasn't – or couldn't have been –

here twelve hundred years ago. Apart, that is, from a few stereos and ice-cream machines.

From the back of the town a serpentine stairway ascends to the fortress proper. We did the decent thing, bit the bullet, and grudgingly, grumpily, lumberingly ascended the endless stone steps up the rock to the magnificent gate. Thence we climbed through the guard-house tunnel, up through the packed ruins of barracks, buildings, granaries, storage cisterns and finally came, veins bulging and hearts jack-hammering, to the church on the crest. Here we collapsed in the shade of an olive-tree.

"Bugger me!" gasped Malcolm.

"The fairest in the land couldn't tempt me at the moment," rejoined Rex. "You've got *no* chance."

Drawing in air like some multiple-stage, steam-driven Victorian mine-ventilation system, we lay prostrate in the shade of the tree, each affecting to the others that we were incapacitated by the stunning nature of the view rather than the ascent.

Recovered, we began to explore the ruins, which are a tightly-packed collection of tumbled-down houses, more-or-less intact walls and caved-in cellars or cisterns. Only the gateway and the church remain in good repair, the latter of which is a silent treasure of faded, candle-lit frescoes and icons of rich and complex execution. I don't know how old any of it is but it seemed fairly hoary to me, and even sceptical old mega-agnostics like us were able to lose ourselves in the history that oozed around the place.

Outside again, we walked around the back of the church, and whooaa! Steady, boy! This is not for the faint of heart. The church is built with its back to the sheerest drop on the north face of the rock, hundreds of feet straight down. Strangely enough, the repair of the rear wall of the church is not quite as meticulously maintained as the other sides... as Rex remarked, only experienced steeplejacks with parachuting experience need apply.

Back down in the town, lunch was taken in a leafy courtyard well used to catering to overweight culture-vultures who had played the giddy mountain-goat on the barren rocks of Monemvasia. Before even attempting to take any orders, a delightful young, brown-eyed waitress plonked down a litre jug of freshly squeezed, iced lemon juice on the table. We obligingly vaporised it for her.

We lunched well, the afternoon south wind worked, and we were back in Gerakas by five. By seven, I had nearly finished stitching the genoa back together. Trying to remove the dangling piece of sacrificial leach-cloth, I had given it an intemperate tug which ripped the stitching in two seams at the leech. The wicked old sun, which had sabred its way through the sacrificial strip in a mere ten seasons, had been no kinder to the sail-stitching beneath. Spiro, it appeared, was as unavailable to comment on the imminent disintegration of the genoa as he had been to discuss the unreliability of the engine or the evisceration of the dinghy. His secretary tried her best to be helpful, but was evidently rather less than comfortable with technical matters. When told that we had a problem with the foresail, she asked brightly whether we couldn't use one of the other three. When informed that the engine needed a new fuel-line, she informed us that there were some spare lines in the cockpit locker. If we had asked her for a grub-screw, no doubt, she would have supposed it to be an improper proposal for lunch-time. But she was so proud to have been of assistance that I left her in ignorance of her ignorance and thanked her kindly.

"My pleasure, sir," she replied happily, "...and before you move on, is there anything I can have sent out to you?"

Rex suggested a wreath.

***

Day nine opened noisily. The big ferry (the very one that, in my professional opinion, could not possibly have got into the harbour) got into the harbour. It performed the impossible with a minimum of fuss and, despite the churn and rumble of its engines, three such sound sleepers as we would probably never have known it had been there had it not serenaded the dawn with a prolonged blast of its thunderous whistle. Hearing this titanic, reverberating hoot so close whilst tied up in such a minute and peaceful harbour was as unexpected as a rousing chorus of *The Red Flag* wafting from the windows of the Carlton Club at one minute past eleven on Remembrance Day, and this time all of us made for the hatch. I leave readers to construct for themselves the vision of three under-dressed and panic-stricken hangovers in corpulent pink, all trying to get out of the companionway at the same time.

***

Day nine closed convivially in the port of Plaka, another charming niche in the mountains just below the picturesque town of Leonidion, about fifteen miles north. The wind theory held good, wafting us north in the afternoon with a gentle sea-breeze which did not over-tax our moribund genoa. Under the now familiar Wagnerian cliffs of the Eastern Peloponnese, we took our sundowners in the cockpit of a new friend.

Gerhardt, or Gerry to his friends, was a massive, greying bear of a man with sapphire laser eyes and a German accent that sounded like a panzer division driving through a muddy scrap yard. Taken prisoner by the British in 1945 at the tender age of fifteen, he had been a prisoner of war in Canada and, on release, had stayed for twenty years as a lumberjack. Now retired onto a fifty foot ketch, he had outlived two wives without visible regret and appeared to seek a solace which he found best in the company of young lady back-packers. At the time of our visit, three rucksacks hung from the belaying-pins on the rack at the foot of the mizzen and giggling, splashing noises floated up the companion way to indicate that three young ladies who had been washing in the sea for a week were doing terrible things to Gerry's fresh-water stocks. These tinkling, delicate, lively sounds roused the sap in a chap splendidly. The sun shone brighter, the air tasted better... it fair brought a lump to my groin, an emotion noticeably absent from my reaction to listening to Malcolm's efforts at personal hygiene in the Iron Midden.

Gerry had a pet amusement which required the participation of a Briton: he liked to introduce himself. Taking your outstretched hand in his own, a frying pan-sized affair which looked like a bunch of gristly bockwurst crudely sewn onto a male orangutan's jowl, he would look deep into your eyes with his ice-blue gimlets and say very slowly, in his incredible accent, "Hallo, I komm vrom Chermanee. My name iss Gerry." If the name caused the slightest hint of amusement on your face, he would slowly close his car-crusher grip on yours until the bones creaked and smile warmly, gently shaking your hand as he took an excruciatingly long time to convey how happy he was to meet you.

Gerry kept two Siamese cats on board. He explained that the reason was twofold; firstly they kept all other cats, any rats and most dogs off the boat by dint of being quite preposterously aggressive, and secondly he claimed that *in extremis* he would be able to use them to provide a little fresh meat on prolonged voyages. Perhaps he was jesting, but he *had* named them Kebab and Kutlet…

Leonidion is a farming town set in a sheer gorge carved through a towering coastal ridge of mountains. Fantastic houses and old mills cling to rock-faces and abutments, impossible paths lace the hillsides, and all is diffused and tinted blue-grey by the afternoon light. As the sun passes over and behind the peaks, the light, slipping down the hillside and oozing through the valleys, is constantly changing, thick, magical, slightly hazy, evoking myth and legend. A dragon flapping idly across the skyline would be entirely in keeping. Crags glower down on a fertile plain which reaches the sea in a long pebble beach, where the small, picturesque port of Plaka links to the world a community otherwise isolated by tortuous roads. In the port, the evening cool comes early as the sun dips below the mountains and we sat at Michaeli's taverna and ate a great pot of stewed artichoke hearts. An embodiment of peace was Plaka, although my snorkelling the next morning in the crystal clear, cool water of the harbour revealed a slightly alarming number of mooring cleats lying on the bottom. Evidently it wasn't always so serene!

***

Two days passed in a state of great contentment, brought about by easy sailing, womb-warm temperatures and mutual vilification. The sailing was made easy by the winds remaining gentle, and by my new-found comprehension of their diurnal patterns. I was as proud as could be with this self-made discovery, and passed it on willingly to anyone who wanted to know, and quite a few who didn't. I believe that I was starting to think of dropping a letter to Yachting Monthly, or even National Geographic, and a hydrographic note to the Admiralty hydrographic department when Malcolm quietly pointed out that the whole phenomenon was explained quite clearly in the pilot-book. Just as well, really, he opined; the world may have been quite at ease with Humboldt's Current, but he wasn't sure that it was ready for Blatchley's Wind.

We sailed north to Navplion. This elegant city, Greece's first capital and the scene of many exploits of the revolution, has nondescript modern suburbs, but the old town by the harbour is a superbly preserved juxtaposition of 16th century Venetian fortifications, 19th century mansions and large piazzas. Stylish shops, traditional restaurants and sprawling cafes teem with life under the Venetian fortress of Palamidi, whose battlements are casually draped around the fringes of terrifying cliffs above the town. The scene is overpowering; so is the smell of the harbour, so after a good lunch well away from the port we moved back to Astros for the night. Well, the smell gave us the excuse, but it wasn't entirely the reason. Each of us harboured the secret fear that if we had stayed the night we would have felt morally obliged to walk up the thousand-plus steps to the fortress... after Monemvasia we could, with some slight validity, claim that we could have done so if we had wanted to, but it would have been unconvincing. The excuse of the odour on the waterfront made us all feel just a little bit more secure.

***

Paralia Astros is a town on a narrow stretch of coastal plain between Argos and Tripolis. An attractive town with a castle at its summit, it would have been quite captivating at another time; however, at only a hundred or so feet in height, it seemed somehow lacking compared with the towering majesty of the previous days. Astros is a resort town for the Greeks, and judging by the acreage laid down to café terraces and restaurants, a very successful one in the season. We found, however, that in late October it was as quiet as a pathologist's waiting room. We bought excellent Tripolitsa salamis, local goat-cheeses and olives. Then Vangelis' restaurant in the main street fed us well on local produce, a much vaunted pasta and a fine sausage. The midnight eruption from the hatch was inspired by no more than a call of nature, and we left early the following morning for Spetsae again, with a weather forecast filched from the news-stand.

The morning north wind carried us to the Spetsae channel so efficiently that we were swimming in Zoogoria bay by mid-day, and by two the afternoon south wind set in firmly, so we carried on to Ermioni; it was a happy decision... the first person we saw on the dock was Spiro!

He evidently knew of our problems. He started down the pier to take our lines before realising who we were and, as recognition dawned, he performed

179

a spectacular double-take and body-swerve, and evaporated wraith-like into a restaurant. Rex and I dispatched Malcolm immediately to hunt him down whilst we tied up, but to no avail. He had evaporated... but we weren't too worried. The only other yacht in the port carried his logo, so it was fairly sure that patience would yield us the fox creeping back to his lair.

***

Ermioni is a functional farming, fishing and administrative town, built on a narrow spit of land with a harbour to the north and an open quay to the south. My enduring impression of the town is of the massed ranks of elderly men who patrol its docks and litter its kafenieons, all telling their worry-beads with an intensity that causes a permanent clicking-noise which, in other places in Greece, one would attribute to cicadas. Although it is one of the very ancient towns of the Argo-Saronic and has some relics in the harbour, Ermioni has lost some of the natural charm it may once have had under an avalanche of flat-roofed cement buildings, but it is a friendly and comfortable place. Prices are much less tourist-driven; it is a good place to take stores and has no shortage of restaurants. The tavernas on the south quay are a beautiful place to sit and watch the sun set over the Peloponnese. However, we had a Spiro to ensnare, and so we lingered in the harbour. Selecting an advantageously positioned ouzeri, we settled ourselves to wait.

I am no professional when it comes to 'setting up a stake-out', as I believe it is called. No doubt the S.A.S. would have dug a burrow out of solid rock with their teeth and lain in it, distilling fresh water with a cigarette lighter and a condom, eating worms and defecating into baked bean-cans to pass the time, but we take our pleasures in other ways, and made another culinary discovery: the *pikilia*. This is, literally translated, a 'variety', and is a large plate of mixed hors d'oeuvres. They vary in ingredients from place to place, and the ouzeri to the right as you come off the Ermioni quay is a worthy practitioner of the art. A large oval plate appeared laden with stuffed bacon rolls, fried cheese and marrow croquettes, meat balls, prawns and anchovies nestled amongst tomato, cucumber and stuffed vine leaves. Taramasalata, tsatsiki and humus are dotted in between. Cool retsina from the ubiquitous tin jugs... it was a very pleasant way of doing a stake-out indeed, but there might be something to be said for the S.A.S. method too, because we all but missed the dark form that flitted from shadow to shadow, elusive as a bat.

Once brought to bay, Spiro, to be fair to him, was no eel. There was a brief initial 'My dear boys, I had *no* idea...', but he sensed that it wasn't exactly convincing in the light of his furtive behaviour. He swapped our dinghy for the one on his boat, glancing over his shoulder as he did so. It appeared he was skippering a group of American charterers, whom he understandably did not want to involve in a discussion of the faults of one of his boats.

He promised to buy us some tools for the toolbox in the morning, but as far as the engine and genoa were concerned he confessed himself to be powerless to help. He could send a new sail from Piraeus, he said, and he could call a mechanic from the same source; but it would involve a day or two delay. Would we not prefer to continue? Naturally, he would not hold us responsible for any problems, and he would be pleased to offer a discount on a future charter to cover any inconvenience... in the mean time, could he buy us a drink? Yes, he most certainly could! But as much as we enjoyed the drink, Spiro had the better part of the deal as it moved us away from the quay where his Americans were re-embarking. Spiro kept a beady eye on them, carefully counting, and evidently there was one short because he manfully maintained a flow of small talk, which was largely complimentary about charterers who did not make a fuss about minor problems, whilst furtively scouring the quayside. He really did not want a chance meeting between us and his charterers, and I wondered what was not working on their boat. When at last the errant client returned to the boat, Spiro was so relieved that he picked up the tab for our whole meal! At our last sight of him that evening, he was marching down the quay to his boat from whence a forceful female voice informed him and the world that, "The goddam pump in the goddam john came off in my goddam hand *a-goddam-gain!*"

There was one other incident in the night. The now inevitable porpoising out of the hatch was this time occasioned by a fracas on the quay. Poking our heads out of our now customary vantage points, we found a group of fishermen carrying a struggling figure towards a large fishing caique. The reluctant was evidently rather drunk, and he bellowed and raged, kicked, struggled and spat at his tormentors; but they stoically took little notice and carried him to the caique, where they threw him with a great one-two-heave technique over the bulwark into a pile of nets on the deck. Then two men sat on the drunk, and the rest cast the caique off, got underway and steered out of the harbour. As the ranting of the man and the beat of the engine died away, Rex wondered aloud. "What the hell was all that about?" he asked.

"Maybe it's his turn to be the bait," replied Malcolm, and with that we went back to sleep and never did find out what lay behind it all.

***

The holiday was now at a late stage, with the end clearly in sight three days ahead. Whilst waiting for Spiro the night before, we had decided that, as the forecast (gleaned from the back of a newspaper) was benign, we might after all try to reach Kythnos, just to be able to say that we had reached the Cyclades. The day dawned clear, and as still as only the morn of a long trip in a wind-powered form of transport can well be.

We arose early, but Spiro had preceded us… there was a small handful of tools on the fore-deck and not a sign of him or his boat. As we wriggled out of Ermioni harbour, there was some slight movement of air, but this was evidently generated by the furious whirling and clicking of the fifty-odd sets of worry-beads which had dragged their owners down to the quay to see us off. It looked sufficiently promising to a blind optimist like me that we hoisted the mainsail as we cleared the little jetty, but five minutes on our way we could see that there wasn't a breath outside. The horizon lay indistinct between a glassy blue sea and a soft blue sky. The port of Hydra was a spatter of white on a fuzzy, ochre hump to starboard. The diesel pulsed like the muffled bass drum of a military funeral, and trailed an ostrich-feather of mourning black from the exhaust. We churned on our way down the Hydra Strait with the mainsail slatting idly, towing Malcolm's trawl-warp, at the end of which lurked a nightmarish lure that resembled one of those reflective balls one comes across in discotheques, hung about with a lethal arsenal of hooks.

***

The trip to Kythnos held little attraction for us if it was to be attended throughout by the pounding of the engine, so we decided to make Tselevinia

Island the decision point; we would see if there was any wind at that point, and then either sail on for Kythnos or abort the Cyclades idea and motor up to Poros, an island we felt we could very happily revisit.

All the way up the strait, it looked increasingly certain that Poros would win the day, but the will to see at least one of the Cyclades was strong, and so when Poseidon tempted us with a wafting northerly zephyr, we stilled the engine and carefully unrolled the temperamental genoa. It filled willingly enough, and *Nissos* leaned gently away from the mild force of the breeze, the water chuckling past her as she settled into her rhythm. I laid her about ten degrees to windward of the course for Merikhas and found that she trimmed out onto a fairly close reach. We had already found that *Nissos* liked this point of sail very well indeed with regard to balance, although it was not her 'greyhound' point by any means. She settled down, nodding sedately into the very long, low northerly swell and stretching her sheets until they matched the strain. We settled down ourselves, finding the neutral point on the tiller where it needed only a nudge every now and then and levering the tops from the ubiquitous brown bottles.

Rex belatedly set to work writing postcards. To avoid complications, he had bought twenty of them, all exactly the same, a view of the ruins of Delphi. On the backs of these, he inscribed 'Here's something else I haven't seen. Cheers, Rex', and added the addresses. Malcolm dozed in the shade of his waxed hat, apparently sound asleep apart from one hand which ceaselessly tweaked at his fishing line and the other, which periodically fed his mouth a long, gurgling slurp of beer.

I dozed too at the tiller. Balm, beer, a slice or two of Tripolitsa salami. The day was not quite as warm as the previous one, probably due to the northerly wind, but it was still very pleasant indeed. Almost ahead, the hazy spike of Agios Georgios Island appeared and slowly waxed, and I began to look forward to crossing the shipping lanes.

Like hedgehogs and rabbits, I have a fascination for crossing busy thoroughfares. On big ships, I can soon tire of watching empty ocean wastes roll monotonously past eighty feet below my bridge windows, but in traffic I come alive. The Philip Channel off Singapore at four o'clock in the morning is a perverse joy to me; making sense of the myriad of lights, trying to judge which side to overtake so as to hit the next corner right, dodging the optimists who ply across the busy waterway and the nutters who delay switching their lights on until they are right under your bows, and the delicious, masochistic uncertainty of never knowing which of the mass of ships around you is the one on the VHF calling the pilot, and so liable to suddenly sheer across the traffic-lane to get to the Eastern Boarding Ground. Or how about Buzzards Bay on a foggy summer Sunday afternoon? Here, every American with the wherewithal leaps into a sailboat or a growling, water hurling gin-palace and starts playing Russian roulette with the ships clearing the Cape Cod Canal. Gibraltar, Dover, the Skagerrak and Kattegat, they all have their tingling pleasures, but what can equal midnight in the Gulf of Suez, with every north-bound ship a bit late on his schedule going hell for leather to make the morning convoy through the canal; cutting corners, giving way to no man, oil-rig supply ships and fishing-boats wheeling freely across the melee... Oh! Sublime!

At times like these, the VHF comes alive with terse calls of:

"Ship on my Starboard side!"

"I am flashing a light to you."

"What de bloody hell you dooin', man?"

"Filipino monnnkeeee!"

"Channel six for Greek Music!"

And once, unforgettably, "I pray for your soul in heaven, friend. On earth, you are finish contract!"

Most of it is unnecessarily abusive, but occasionally one hears some subtle and delightful barbs which make the rest of the carrier-wave pollution almost worthwhile. It shouldn't go on, but it does, and however much I may disapprove of the annoyance caller or the crude abuse-monger, I would lie in my teeth if I said that I *totally* abhorred the practice. Many a long watch has been lightened and made memorable by a Channel 16 *Bonne Mot*. Naturally, I would never *dream* of doing such a thing myself...

Yachties, in general, miss the meaning of a lot of this chit-chat. The significant conversations as far as I am concerned are the cosy little chats which start with something like, "Ship on my starboard side..." and develop into a friendly discussion about who will keep out of whose way, with everyone calling each other 'Sir' and apparently behaving with punctilious rectitude. The very model of well-ordered traffic control to the untrained ear, these little confabs frequently show to the professional that the correspondents have scant knowledge of the collision rules, or of their responsibilities. They also lead to some splendid Keystone Kops situations when a ship, having agreed in fine detail who will do what to keep clear of another, suddenly realises that she has been talking to the wrong ship altogether… a ship perhaps thirty or more miles away! The situation is still no closer to resolution, and the protagonists are five minutes nearer to each other, which could be three miles for ships on approaching courses. Supposing that this dodgy nonsense started when they were six miles apart, which is fairly typical, then by the time they realise their error, they are five minutes away from sending another gaggle of Lloyd's underwriters plummeting off Tower Bridge. Far better had that five minutes been spent getting on with the business of avoiding one another like professional mariners, each secure in his own complete knowledge of the Collision Rules.

Oops! Soap-box again! But it is pertinent to touch on VHF abuse at this juncture, as we shall shortly hear.

The traffic-separation scheme approaching Athens from the south is not one of the most rewarding in terms of traffic encountered, but neither is it at all bad. We had good sport with a conveyor-belt of ferries bound for the Cycladic Islands, and quite a close look at an Egyptian cement-carrier (Malcolm insisted that the officer on watch had rather a lot of fillings, and Rex claimed to have noticed a scratch on his spectacles). A Greek Navy destroyer bustled past us in splendid style, stern down and making a fine rooster-tail as she hurried home for tea. She was a touch elderly, and so still retained the towering, sweeping elegance of a day when warships were built to make the taxpayer think he had really got his money's worth. What a glorious, brave picture she was as she hewed her high-flung, foamy furrow across the crumpled blue silk of the Saronic. She was flying her ensign from the gaff on her after mast, so as is my wont in such cases I courteously dipped my ensign to her… I am frequently accused of being a bit of a bull-merchant for this, but it gives me a simple pleasure. You see, I only have to lean back and lift the ensign staff out of its socket, but the little chap on the destroyer has to leg it like the devil from the bridge to get to his ensign, with a snotty officer-of-the-watch egging him on every inch of the way. I rarely bother with warships, which fly their ensigns from the gaff at the back of the bridge… not the same sense of achievement at all.

After the destroyer, there was a quiet spell which made me think that the fun was over for this crossing of the lanes, but then on our port bow there appeared a fuzzy blob which gradually materialised into a very large tanker. A quick glance through the guardrails showed that she was on a steady bearing, so I settled back to see whether she would do the proper thing and keep clear of us.

After a while, during which the tanker stoically stuck to his course, Malcolm cleared his throat and said, "Yeah, well, let's just go round behind him, Eh?"

"Hang on a mo," I replied. "We've got right of way. He'll come round in a minute or two."

"You have faith in that, do you?" enquired Rex, who levitated slightly from his indolent slouch along the cockpit side-deck and momentarily removed his snout from his wine-tumbler. I nodded. The tanker, high in ballast, grew, and grew, and remained neatly bisected by the second stanchion from aft just to make it quite plain that we were on collision-course. She was painted a rust-red colour, with a cream superstructure.

"Well, she doesn't seem to have read the same regulations as you, Ahab," said Malcolm. "What say we just get out of her way, and avoid impeding the progress of International Commerce, eh?"

"I very much doubt if we would impede it much," muttered Rex sepulchrally. "No more than a dragonfly could impede Concorde, if you ask me."

"He's not so close yet," I breezed. "'Bout four miles. He'll alter at about three."

"And if he doesn't?"

"Oh, I'll just bang her about on the other tack. No worries. It's actually quite hard to hit another ship at sea. Think of it as a vector-plot… "

Rex became alarmed at that.

"Bugger that! If you're relying on mathematics to keep us out of that thing's way, I'll go swimming now! I've seen you trying to work out whose round it is… three people and yours only comes round once every five!"

"Hark at him," I jeered. "A very brave man. Wouldn't shout if a shark bit him!"

"It is rumoured you believe that Arithmetic is someone who has respiratory attacks!"

"Sez who? The man who thought Pythagoras's theorem was something to do with Hippopotamuses!"

Rex brayed a sardonic laugh. "Actually, it's Hippopotami. Which is…"

"…A bloody silly thing to be talking about ten seconds before being battered to death by the original blunt instrument!" Malcolm completed the sentence for him. Rex looked thoughtfully at the tanker for a moment.

"Yes, it doesn't really have a sharp end, does it? What are all those numbers on its bow?"

"Draft marks," I informed him, "To show how deep she is in the water."

"Mmm. Eighteen. Metres, I dare say? Or would it be fathoms?"

"Metres…" I said.

Malcolm thrust his face into mine.

"Turn around, Bligh!"

"Just a minute," I said, "This is a bit off, this bugger not altering for us. I'll just give him a call on the VHF."

"Like hell you will! You turn this thing around now, or I'm going home!" growled Malcolm. The logic of this statement escaped me entirely, but I swallowed my pride.

There are many twee little rhymes to help sailors remember the rule of the road, such as

"When you see three lights ahead,
Starboard wheel and show your red"

or

"In danger with no room to turn,
Ease her, stop her, go astern."

I learned a few of these from books, or at college, but the only one I ever was told actually at sea went:

"Here lies the body of William Day,
Who died insisting on his right of way,
He was right, he was right, he knew all along,
But he's just as dead as if he'd been wrong!"

(Actually, that's not the only one I learned at sea, but the one about what to do when you see three lights in front has no place in a polite publication such as this).

I put her about. I eased her into the wind, and the jib backed gently. The main slatted briefly, then filled and *Nissos* hove-too as sweetly as one could wish. We gazed up as Leviathan thundered by, wallowing in her wake as she passed. *Then* I reached for the VHF.

Putting on my most outraged and British voice, I seized the mike and berated the lackadaisical navigator of the tanker. I scorned his manners and knowledge of the rules, begged leave to doubt the quality of the lookout he kept, cast aspersion upon his tutors and his alma mater, called down the wrath of the righteous upon his head, and informed him of a few hitherto unpublished facts regarding the relationship between his parents.

Even by my standards, it was a good rant, and I was confident that this Foreign Luigi or Manuel had been well put in his place as I completed my call.

I would have been surprised to receive any reply at all, and from the tanker I didn't. But someone else had heard my tirade, and a few moments later a very recognisable Geordie voice called me by name, and requested me to do something anatomically challenging with my head.

It took me a moment to re-wire my jaw, after which a spirited conversation got under way on a working channel. I hadn't seen Geordie, who was driving another tanker about twenty miles to the north, since college, but he hadn't forgotten the sound of my voice!

*****

Late afternoon found us trickling along to the north of Agios Georgios Island, which is the approximate half-way mark between the Peloponnese coast and the Western Cycladic islands of Kea, Kythnos and Serifos. The wind was all but gone, and around us great patches of mirror-bright water signalled the apparent end of the day's sailing, but we were in no hurry to unleash the beast in the bilge, and took to gambolling in the sea. Alternately leaping in and towing behind on a long mooring-rope (an article with which *Nissos* was not over-equipped), we sported and lazed the halcyon afternoon away.

A touch of coolness creeping on towards dusk was initially attributed to the sun setting, and we had towelled off and stowed the bathing ladder before realisation dawned that the temperature drop was a result of a new wind setting in. The initial euphoria which greeted this development faded somewhat upon perceiving that the wind was coming from the north-northeast, which made it a hard beat to Merikhas. Said euphoria continued to dissipate rapidly in inverse proportion to the rising velocity of the wind. By five thirty, still fifteen miles dead to leeward of Merikhas, with the wind gusting towards a six and the boat double-reefed and plunging to windward into violently short, sharp little seas, I very much doubt whether even the most painstaking search of the *Nissos* would have revealed sufficient euphoria to fill a eunuch's codpiece.

I was personally not too bothered at first. To be sure, the boat was heeled hard over, making very heavy weather of the wicked, short seas and throwing great sheets of water into the cockpit, but the water still had a slight warmth to it. Equally surely, the wind direction and a crabbing leeway meant that we now had to put a tack in to make Merikhas, but so what? But then slowly the coming of night put a chilling edge into the flying water. The wind veered another killing half-point, and all enthusiasm for the Cyclades evaporated like good humour in a plane crash. A swift perusal of the chart showed the mainland port of Palaeo Fokkia to be a comfortable reach to the north-north-west, and we slammed the boat over onto the starboard tack, eased sheets and raced away into the dying light.

The wind held slightly forward of the beam at a stiff-ish five and the seas slapped and slammed under the turn of the bilge, occasionally piling up high enough to tumble over the weather-rail onto the braced and resigned helmsman. It was a hard, wet sail, made almost brutal by the still-developing beam sea, but once freed off the wind, *Nissos* ran as I suspect rarely she had run in a long time. She seemed almost to be awakening, recalling a technique long disused. At first hesitantly, and then with growing confidence, she tucked her port rail just above the water, stretched and strained her rigging to the point of comfort and equality, and fled across the darkening seas.

The luxury of a speed-log was not for her, but we later worked out that she had run two hours at almost seven knots. She handled the belligerent seas with authority, swooping along the line of the lesser and vigorously shoulder-charging the more presumptuous with her bluff tumblehome, whilst huddled on the windward side of the cockpit her crew knew by turn power, impotence, exhilaration and inundation. It was a magnificent sail.

A notable incident occurred whilst Rex and Malcolm were below trying to make sense of the chart. Yours truly, leg braced across the cockpit against the heave and surge of the tiller, was alternately staring hard forward to find Ghaidouronisso light and ducking with eyelids clenched against the flying spray. Suddenly I received a ringing blow on the side of the head and simultaneously heard a loud 'Crack!' Falling from the windward rail, I pushed the helm down and *Nissos* shot up into the wind.

In the instant of falling, I believed that the backstay had broken and hit me. I had no idea whether I was hurt or not, but was desperate to get the boat head to wind before the mast came down. Prostrate upon the bench, I held my head, pushed the tiller a-lee and bellowed for Rex and Malcolm to let the main halyard go. As they struggled up the companion way, I thought the better of letting the main halyard go, as the sail sheeted in would support the mast, and quickly had Rex furling the genoa and Malcolm heaving in the mainsheet. The genoa rolled in thunderously and reluctantly, the mainsail flogged, the boat bucked wildly, and above the confusion I noted three things. The first was the completely intact backstay. The second was a frantically flapping, beating thing by my foot, which leapt and spasmed like a weightlifter's heart suddenly ejected from his chest by a supreme effort. The third was an overpoweringly strong smell of fish.

I had been hit by a flying fish! And I can assure those of you who have not shared this notable experience that it is a rough business. I was sufficiently disoriented by the shock and the humiliation of the assault that I so lost my senses as to pick the wretched beast up and hurl it back into the sea... not only did I deprive myself of the ultimate vengeance of eating it, the creature even lived to tell the tale. We gently re-set the reefed genoa and got underway again, with Malcolm and Rex now totally oblivious to the sailing conditions, united in mirth at what Rex christened 'The affair of the ICBM, or Incontinence-Compelling Ballistic Minnow'.

***

Whatever lights exist to guide one into the bay of Paleio Fokia may have been working that night, or they may not. Against the backdrop of bright lights ringing the bay we could distinguish nothing, and so feeling our way into the bay was the sternest test of navigation of the entire trip. With the sky obscured by cloud, there was no starlight to show the hills at the ends of the bay, and the lights ashore destroyed our night-vision if we tried to make out features to landward. The wind raced off the land, throwing spray into our searching eyeballs, and our hopeful scanning of the seaward side revealed no fishing boat returning home to guide us in. The idea of heaving-to until dawn had little to recommend it in the short, nasty sea, and I did not fancy sailing all the way to Poros or Aegina in the dark, so... time for Captain Chaos to perform his miracle!

The echo-sounder, hitherto almost unused, now came into its own. The British Admiralty chart (might as well give Hydrographic Office publications a plug, then they might do the same for mine) was clearly marked with a ten-fathom depth contour, so with the engine on, sails furled and Rex on the tiller, I seated myself at the chart-table with sounder and chart and ordered a course of East. Malcolm was posted to keep a lookout ahead, and particularly to starboard as I expected to strike soundings on the south side of the bay. After a wait that seemed horribly long, the little whirling red blips firmed up at ninety feet and crept backwards around the dial to sixty. I ordered a course-change to port, and, surely enough, the water got deeper again! A touch back to starboard... shallower. In this tortuous manner, we edged our way into the bay, steering great crazy loops along the coast as we tracked the contours. As we did so, I sketched a rough approximation of our course and speed made good on the border of the chart until I had enough to match the drawing to a section of contour, and from this position we set course across the bay for Palaeo Fokia mole. In triumphant mood, we located the mole and dropped anchor at one in the morning, just about three boat-lengths off in its lee. With a comfortable night's sleep now in prospect, Malcolm and Rex were more than obliging in their compliments over the post-arrival brandies, and I went to sleep content, with my reputation as a navigator thoroughly vindicated. Soundly I slept, never thinking that something else was already half vindicated: the First Law of Nautical Recreation, which had just engineered an unwitnessed triumph, was gathering a mighty throng to attend our berthing in the morning...

***

We were not exceptionally well provisioned for living aboard *Nissos*, and so when Rex and I awoke it was an easy and unanimous decision to put the boat onto the quay straight away and breakfast in one of the tavernas ashore. It was a cool but brightly sunny morning. The clouds scudded raggedly across the sky trailing fleeting patches of shade, driven by the hard, northeast wind that blew off the beach onto the inside of the mole and on out to sea. The inside of the quay was occupied by fishing-boats, but there appeared to be a space or two and, despite the wind direction, there was no bad motion. Leaving Malcolm to sleep, we quickly hoisted the anchor and motored inside the little sickle-shaped harbour. We prepared two anchors forward, as we would be mooring on the windward side of the quay, and as we passed the end of the breakwater I noticed that the time was ten minutes to eight.

From the seaward side of the mole, there had appeared to be several spaces on the quay. On arriving inside, however, most of the 'gaps' were occupied by small boats not visible over the wall, and I had quite a job to hold *Nissos* steady into the wind as we looked for a place. There were no other yachts in the place, just fishing boats, and being rather loosely moored in the Mediterranean style, each gust of wind swung them from side to side so that gaps opened and then closed just as I lined up on them. After chasing a few of these mirages, I decided to make my own space, and selecting a spot that appeared clear of the leads of other anchor lines, I had Rex drop the bower anchor. Then I crabbed to starboard a bit and dropped the kedge in a classic open hawse, and began to fall back to the quay whilst Rex paid out the chain and warp. Our manoeuvres had attracted the attention of the ten or so fishermen who sat on the breakwater, and as the second anchor dropped, I noticed that net-mending ceased, pipes were stoked, and the audience settled back in the front row. This should have warned me.

I reversed back straight and true for an obligingly open gap, but just as I approached the bows of the adjacent boats, *Nissos* stopped abruptly. For an instant, I thought she had struck bottom, but then she sheered sharply to starboard, and I had to leap to the rail to stop us hitting the bows of a solid looking caique. The reason for this was soon explained. Rex announced that he had come to the end of the kedge warp. On the quay, the fishermen had bunched together close to us, and were emitting spurts of smoke as fast as the wind ripped them away.

Restrained from leaving the rail by the need to keep us from damaging the caique's paintwork, I directed Rex around the boat in a search for a rope to extend the kedge-warp, but in vain. She was no floating chandlery, was our *Nissos*, and we had only the two short lengths used for securing the stern. I cursed myself for re-reeving the Genoa halyard, toyed for a moment with the heinous idea of committing some atrocity with the free end of the mainsheet, forgot all about the genoa sheets and decided to go back out and lift the kedge. Rex started heaving in the anchor lines, but to no avail. It is amazing how far you can't go when your anchors are hard in forward and your prop is tangled in the anchor-line of the boat astern! Nothing for it but a swim, and about fifteen fishermen saw me strip and enter the water. At least twenty saw me emerge some minutes later, triumphant but minus my watch. A plastic strap is no match for a suddenly de-tensioned rope, it appears.

As the now free stern of the boat was beginning to swing towards the caique on our port side there was no time to dive for the watch, and by the time I regained the helm, half-naked and blue in the chill wind, there were some thirty fishermen on the quay and others were hastily downing their ouzos at the cafes and hurrying across the road.

Rex could not get the kedge anchor up.

Things were beginning to get a little wearing, and I was perchance a trifle short in asking him to use the anchor-winch. We needed to remove the chain of the main anchor from the windlass so as to leave it free to recover the kedge, and the instructions I gave were terse, pithy and ringingly clear; nevertheless, it seems that Rex was unable to assimilate all the information in the format given. In particular, I am quite clear in my own mind that he is in error in suggesting that I failed to give entirely clear directions as to how to secure the free end of the chain of the bower anchor. What the cause of the misunderstanding was I cannot truly say. I can only here record with what deep, deep disappointment and even chagrin I heard the vigorous rattle of chain followed by a splash so smug and self-satisfied that it was as if the Aegean Sea had belched in appreciation of this juicy morsel.

About forty fishermen and a wife or two heard what I said, but I assumed from their indifference that there were numbered amongst them no speakers of modern, idiomatic English.

It was warmer back in the water than it had been out of it, which would have been a welcome development if it hadn't been so bloody deep. The first dive located the end of the chain, but only at the moment of expiration and it was the act of a lunatic to try to surface with the leaden links in hand. I lay gasping with an arm through the swimming ladder for an ice-age or two before trying again with a genoa sheet. At the third attempt, I retrieved the end of the chain, which I advised Rex to attach to his genitalia, as further loss of the bitter end would in one way or another result in the confiscation of same.

By the time Rex announced that he still could not get the anchor up, wives about equalled fishermen on the quay and some children were hurrying from school. I went forward to show him how to work the winch properly, but it instantly became clear that even our mighty windlass was inadequate for the task. We were hooked into an anchor chain the size of which eloquently explained the complaisance with which the fishermen regarded the safety of their own boats. As I entered the water a third time, it seemed to me cruel that a bus should disgorge another platoon of milling voyeurs.

Well, we freed the kedge. And we ascertained that the main anchor was dug in on its own, not also embracing the bath-plug chain of the Mediterranean. And we backed into our place on the quay.

And the main anchor-chain wasn't long enough either.

The stern swung round, Rex and I were both fully occupied holding off the boats to port and starboard, and impasse had been achieved. So I called Malcolm out to give us a hand. Now, I was aware that he was awake and about the arcane rituals which pass with him for ablutions, but I had not appreciated his state of dress, nor the stage his toilette had thus far achieved.

Malcolm, as I believe I have previously mentioned, sleeps in what the Egyptian who sold it to him would call a galibeya, but what anyone else would call a green-striped nightdress. In this he now emerged, with an imitation pearl-backed hand-mirror (the only mirror on the boat) in one hand and a suspicious looking hairbrush in the other. With his ten-day stubble and shoulder-length hair in disarray, the effect was that of the most raddled drag-queen yet imaginable, and the keen interest of the massed phalanxes of spectators amplified instantly at this new development. Ignoring the chatter of comment and glee along the quay as best I could, I positioned Malcolm at the rail and extended the anchor chain with the abused genoa sheet, completed the mooring in silence, killed the engine, and without a look or a word back at my crew, stalked ashore. A path through the watchers cleared automatically for me as I stomped along the quay.

Half way along, a young lad with a net on a long pole handed my watch back to me. It was ten past ten. The lad obviously expected a consideration for this deed, but his life was saved by a kindly old man with a magnificent moustache who led him away and explained, presumably, that this wasn't the moment.

The first three things I drank at the cafe were large Metaxa brandies, two of which appeared courtesy of the fishermen. Malcolm and Rex took a look or two through the door before venturing to sit at a table near, but not quite next to, mine. It was almost lunch-time before they ventured to sit on the opposite side of my table, and history (but not my memory) records that by two o'clock, half the village appeared to have joined us for a rollicksome lunch. They made us very welcome, the people of Palaeo Fokia, and at no time mentioned my discomfiture.

But I've never been back.

CHAPTER EIGHT

THE END OF THE BEGINNING

In which we enjoy one memorable sail, and suffer another... More history... The final haven... Reflections on the odyssey... Hello, not good-bye.

The morning we left Palaeo Fokia was the penultimate day of our charter. The wind was still a sprightly and, by now, cold north-easterly, but the sun shone fiercely between ragged sheets of cloud, the air was crystal clear and almost painfully bright. There was no temptation to try one last time for the Cyclades against such a wind, but equally there was no hurry to be back in Kalamaki a day early and most certainly no inclination to stay a day longer in a port where we had been the focus of so much hilarity. The island of Aegina lay again invitingly down-wind, and we determined to visit its main harbour this time. Faced with real weather for a change, I turned accordingly to real sources for my forecast... eschewing Port Policemen and newspapers, I consulted the people who know. If, as the fishermen forecast, the wind went south on the last day, this would leave us an easy 18-mile reach back to Kalamaki.

Having gone to bed early, we were up early, but not earlier than our fan-club. We almost disappointed a largish crowd who came to see us off, but Malcolm is nothing if not an entertainer and contrived to drop both a fender and then a boat-hook during our departure. I politely declined to have anything to do with his plan of reversing into the spider's web of moorings to retrieve them, and the fan-club got a moderate chuckle out of Malcolm's high-headed, spasmodic dog-paddle. They probably still talk about our antics in Palaeo Fokia.

That sail, under double-reefed main and a very cautiously set genoa, was one of the sparkling mementoes of the trip, a tearing, swooping, whooshing roller-coaster of a ride across endless ranks of white-plumed rollers. Rex and I shared the tiller, and Malcolm alternately photographed the scene and produced handsome sandwiches and hot toddies. Early hangovers were soon dispelled by a judicious combination of brisk air, exhilaration and drinking chocolate laced with Metaxa, and we came early and euphorically round the north of Aegina to fetch the harbour by about twelve o'clock.

Even allowing for our popularity rating in Palaeo Fokia, I was disconcerted to see the massive crowd which greeted us in Aegina. The whole island appeared to have turned out to watch us moor in the blustery conditions; young, old, fit and frail, all dressed to the nines, they surged along the quay beneath a virtual canopy of national flags. For an instant, the suspicion crossed my paranoid old thinking-muscle that the Mayor of Palaeo Fokia had been on the dog-and-bone to his counterpart in Aegina with the news that the circus was coming to town. After a moment's sober reflection, however, it was clearly ludicrous to think for a second that the throng was eagerly gathered to observe whatever enormity of nautical incompetence we were about to commit. This was October 28th, *Ochi* day, the national celebration of the day on which Prime Minister Metaxa told Mussolini to go and fly a kite in 1940. The crowd were not, of course, waiting for us, but they might as well have been because the celebrations had not yet begun, and so we were an unwitting warm-up act… and, of course, just because you *are* paranoid doesn't mean that they are *not* out to get you.

The story would probably begin to get a touch tedious if, at this point, we had made yet another irregular mooring. We did not. Working like a well-oiled team of… well, at any rate, a well oiled team… we neatly put the boat bows-to in one of the two spaces available. We even drew a murmur of appreciation from the crowd, and a nod or two of approval. So why, as I elbowed my way to a vantage point to view the parade, did I feel a sense of foreboding; why did there linger above my brow an image of the sword of Damocles; a nameless dread of custard pies still to come? Uneasily, I watched the parade.

It was a very colourful affair. Junior school children paraded in the national dress, the young boys in their white kilts, hose and bright caps and the girls in long dark skirts, embroidered bodices and coifs. Older school kids marched, inexpertly but earnestly, in blue-and-white, and youth groups such as scouts and guides followed in uniform. Two crashing, blaring brass bands oompah-pahed energetically not quite far enough apart, and over every unit of the parade fluttered the gold-fringed national flag of blue and white. Little of the spectacle was expert, or even competent, but there was no doubting the sincerity or the patriotism of those involved or watching. I have seen like celebrations around the world far better stage-managed but infinitely less meaningful, and the strongest expression of this came as a small naval detachment marched past, arms shouldered and bayonets fixed. Applause broke out, old ladies blew kisses and flowers were thrown. As their standard passed, I removed my cap as a mark of respect, and was rewarded with smiles from the crowd around me. Several muttered *Bravo!* and an old man gave me *Efcharisto*, the beautiful Greek thank-you.

The parade having passed by, we attempted to repair to a restaurant, but were unable to cross to the shoreward side of the street. The parade came back again, this time bearing at its head the gorgeously attired clergy, an ornate crucifix and a towering icon. Once past, the multitude wheeled in confusion and marched past again, bearing the eclesiastical contingent back to their church. The narrow back streets of the island town do not permit the parade to make a circuit, so as it reached the end of the *paralia* it had to do a flip-turn which involved breaking up and being completely re-assembled. After the third fly-past it finally disbanded, just sort of dissolving by common consent half way along the front. Bedlam ensued as costumed children sought proud parents, family groups sought cohesion and absolutely everyone milled feverishly in search of a restaurant seat.

We were fortunate in this last respect, as our unit integrity was already established, and found a table outside a Mr. Lekkas's chicken shop. We were offered a choice of drinks, beer or wine, and chose the latter, which took a considerable time to arrive in the pandemonium. Placing an order for food, however, was beyond us. All pleas for a menu were brusquely ignored by the whirling waiters, and we would probably have just drunk our drinks and slipped away had not an unsolicited avalanche of food suddenly arrived at our table. A waiter bearing a massive tray above his head swept it grandly down to table level, adroitly fended off an importunate cat and an enterprising dog, and made a gesture of offerance. We made a gesture of acceptance, and instantly relieved the tray of its burden. We could barely get all the dishes on the table.

It was a feast. Grilled chicken, succulent inside and brittle without; juicy Kondosouvli; a piece of grilled liver which would have made the gods weep. A crisp salad of cabbage and olives and oil, another of lettuce and tomato; *horta*, the spinach of Greece, a plate of beetroot with garlic sauce, some lamb chops... why, even our modest appetites were put to shame, and we commented admiringly on how well the Greeks did themselves on feast days.

A lone stranger meandered through the throng at a late point in our meal and, unable to find a seat elsewhere, he requested (in excellent but heavily accented English) the spare seat at our table. We not only gave it to him, we also begged him to help us finish off what we had left... I doubt very much if we had eaten a half of what was on that table. He accepted with alacrity, paying his way with another order of wine and thus proving himself an agreeable chap. Where did he come from? He gave a quick glance either side. Well, he lived in Greece now, but came from Italy actually. But no need to shout it out loud today, you understand. His name was Marco, and he was a doctor in Athens.

He did enquire how it came that we had ordered so much food: Had part of our party not arrived? We told him the tale. He wiped his lips, and his eyes sparkled with humour, although he was far too polite to laugh aloud.

The tray, he explained, had been a sample of everything the restaurant had to offer, a sort of living menu from which one was free to take or leave what one wished. He had no doubt that the restaurateur would be most gratified by our rather sweeping endorsement of his product...

Conversation ambled lazily around the subject of Greece and Greeks in general, and Marco, eighteen years in Greece and married to a Greek, was able to enlighten us considerably. We chatted a little about the independence (of which we now knew a little), about the Balkan Wars (of which we knew nothing), and finally about the Second World War participation. A bit of a military historian was our Marco, he took evident pleasure in explaining how, in 1940, Mussolini had mustered a powerful mechanised modern army in Albania and arrogantly demanded of the Greeks the right to march through their territory to the then Italian islands of the Dodecanese. The popular myth is that the Greek Prime Minister of the time, one General Metaxa, relied with an economy of language rarely found in the prolix world of diplomacy. The telegram said simply *'Ochi'*... No! As it happened, Mussolini had not waited for the reply... his troops were already across the border, but to no avail. Outnumbered and lacking almost everything in the way of mechanisation, modern armament and training but stiffened by national pride and their Prime Minister's robust reply, the Greek army fought the Italians to a stand-still in an appalling winter campaign in the mountains of Pindos and then, in the spring, drove them back over the border and half way across Albania. Marco showed no national discomfort in this. He was a staunch socialist, and felt no more association with Mussolini and the Fascists than he did with Martians.

He went on to tell us of Hitler's invasion of The Balkans to save the face of his bellicose ally, and the long, hard retreat of the Greeks, Australians, New Zealanders, Indians and British to the bitter evacuation of the Peloponnese at Kalamata and the vicious fight for Crete. He told us of the Greeks in exile who fought at El Alamein, and at sea in submarines and destroyers. And he expounded a theory that the Greek defeat of Mussolini and the British retreat through Greece was the turning point of the war. Hitler coming south, he opined, delayed the invasion of Russia for two months, which meant that the Germans were halted outside Moscow by the winter of 1941. The Greek defence of Epirus, he considered, meant that the Soviet Union was safe and the war was lost for Germany. For three staunch Englishmen such as ourselves, brought up on a diet of the Battle of Britain, El Alamein and D-Day, it was a thought-provoking theory, and one which we were a little amazed to find held a certain amount of water.

****

In the late afternoon we ambled back to the boat. The restaurants were emptying but the kafenieons still did a roaring trade, and we elected to sit in the cockpit to drink coffee and observe humanity passing by. The wind had decreased a little but was still fresh and boisterous, and we wrapped up against its chill. Malcolm, below in the cabin, was looking through our papers and making sure that the plane tickets were safe. Just as Rex was sloshing a generous dollop of Metaxa into my coffee-mug, Malcolm's face appeared at the hatchway with a bloodhound-like look of puzzlement. In one hand he held a guide book, in the other an airline ticket.

"It says here," he said, brandishing the guide book, "…that *Ochi* day is the 28th of October."

"That's right," I agreed.

"In that case, Bligh, we've got…" he looked at the ticket, and then at his watch: "…Just less than nine hours 'til our 'plane leaves."

"No, no," I reassured him. "We fly on the 29th."

"Indeed we do, Bligh," he agreed, "…at Two A.M. in the morning."

There was a silence. So horrified by this development that I even failed to berate Malcolm for his tautology, I took the ticket and read it carefully. I read it twice. I opened my mouth. I shut it again. Then I called for the charter agreement, which I also read carefully (for the first time). There could be no mistake. The boat was due back in Kalamaki in one hour, our flight was in eight and a bit hours and check-in time was one hour earlier. The Nemesis I had felt on my shoulder when we arrived in Aegina had duly unmasked itself; having skied gloriously down wind all morning, we now had to thrash back dead against it, with darkness falling soon and very little time in hand.

Thirty minutes later, following a hurried phone call to Spiro's office, we were battling our way round Kolonna point on the north-west corner of Aegina and setting sail for a filthy fourteen mile beat dead to windward.

Oh, that trip. The wind blew relentlessly from the north-west, and although there was not enough fetch for a swell to develop, it drove a short, steep, stopping sea into which we slammed violently every few moments. With the mainsail hard in and flattened by a reef, we motored about twenty degrees off the wind and were relentlessly whipped by spray and deluged with solid water. The boat pitched and reared alarmingly, sometimes stopping dead as she ran head on into a wave or dropping into a trough with an appalling crash. Then she would fall off the wind and slowly pick up way again. Every time she pitched thus, the engine coughed, died a little and our hopes died with it, and then it would surge back to life. I prayed to any gods listening, ancient or modern, terrestrial, aquatic or heavenly, monotheistic or polytheistic not to present me with a blocked fuel filter or an airlock. The light faded early under the racing grey cloud and left only a smudge of sunset over the hills around Corinth, and our nav-lights alternately soared and plunged, throwing their red and green glow back from the oncoming seas. No one spoke much that I remember, if at all. We all felt thoroughly miserable and disinclined to talk, and anyway any open mouth collected a pint of salt water before it could utter much.

Rex did most of the steering, coached by me not to let her come too close to the wind where she would not make way. Malcolm crawled about inside, trying in the mayhem of flying personal effects to pack our bags. I navigated, alternately peering to windward in the flying spray to pick out lights and then lurching from the cockpit to the chart table to try to identify them on the chart. Apart from the light on Tourlos, the east end of Aegina, none of it made sense as the bright lights of the Athens conurbation swamped the coastal lights on the Attic shore. There was absolutely no chance of finding the green flashing light at Alimos. I could remember it from our departure but it wasn't on the chart, and, in fact, Alimos Marina itself had been built since the chart was printed, so I was aiming for an area marked 'Hellenikon', which I believed to be the airport. Eureka! I stared to windward, dashing spray from my eyes and blinking furiously against the spray, and sure enough I saw an airliner angle up into the sky from the airport. Alimos lay a little north of the north end of the runway by my reckoning, so every time a plane took off, I had an approximate land-mark.

Finally, with the lights of the Bay of Phaleron reaching out to embrace us, we felt the seas begin to ease a very little as we came into the lee of the land. As far as I could make out, we were to the south of the marina, as the planes were rising steeply slightly to port, so as soon as we got a flicker of a sounding on the whirling depth sounder, we went onto the starboard tack and angled shallowly into the coast. Every time a bit of air went under the boat, the sounder leapt to zero depth and alarmed, and we held our breaths waiting for the grounding, but then the trace would retreat back round the dial and we breathed again. Rex and I were soaked to the skin under our waterproofs and chilled to the marrow to boot, whilst inside the boat Malcolm, glowing a rosy red from the temperature generated by his activities, the engine and the lack of ventilation, sweated copiously and was scarcely drier.

It seemed that we were almost on the root of the mole at Flisvos when suddenly, in the corner of my eye, I caught a flash of green against the orange glare of the street lighting and traffic on the Glyfada highway. We had almost past it when I saw it, and we swung in gratefully. The seas died away to nothing, the wind gusted, and we dropped the main as we turned to head south down the concrete channel we had left two short weeks and a long lifetime ago. The wind was on the beam as we ran in. Even with the main down, we heeled a good ten degrees, and I realised that the wind had picked up quite a bit since we had left Aegina.

Finding our berth was a nightmare, even with Spiro shouting and waving from the end of the quay. Every time I headed towards him, I found another quay between me and him and had to reverse across the wind out of another dead end laced with anchor lines, but eventually we made it. The mooring should have been hideous too, with the marina crammed full of boats this late in the season and mooring warps running everywhere, but of course there was no one watching. I backed the old boat up to the narrow gap and, regardless of the wind on the bow or the yawing of the other boats, she ran back straight and true and wriggled her stern into the gap like a ballerina shimmying into a pair of tight jeans. I swear she did it herself... glad to be home, I guess.

It was 10.00 p.m. We had made the trip from Aegina in just under five hours, which had seemed like five days, and now we were faced with a lightning packing session and cleaning the boat whilst handing her back to Spiro. We had three hours to get to the airport, we were a good half mile from any chance of a taxi, and not withstanding our gargantuan meal at lunchtime, we were all ravenous. Spiro weighed up the situation, and smiled wolfishly. As we feverishly crammed damp woollies into straining bags, and squirted off the worst of the salt in the minuscule shower, he pointed out that we were five hours late arriving back, and the boat still had to be cleaned and refuelled before we left according to the charter agreement. However, he told us that if he could be assured that no mention of any of *Nissos*'s ah... *deficiencies* would be raised with the charter brokers in England, that we need not bother about the cleaning and refuelling, could leave the sail as it was, and he would drive us to the airport and stop for a bite on the way. He had us, and he knew it. We took back our deposit and signed a happy little document which Spiro just happened to have a copy of. It was in English, and was all about what a lovely time we had had, how happy we were with the boat and service, and how soon we would beat a track to the door of 'WundaWave' yacht charters again. Then Malcolm and Rex squeezed into the car and, as Spiro piled bags in on top of them, I stood for a few moments on the quay, looking down at the drab little boat we were leaving.

She lay nodding quietly, her mainsail still awry and ballooning occasionally in the wind; ropes and gear and a huge bundle of laundry cluttered her cockpit. Under the orange lighting, her reverse counter faced up to me with her black plastic stick-on name barely visible through the dark grey exhaust soot. She looked even more jaded than when we had first seen her.

By now I knew all about her dodgy genoa, her paintball-range interior, and her asthmatic engine. Leaving her should not have been any sort of a wrench. But I had also seen her reach twenty four miles in less than four hours with just a light hand on the tiller in seas which would have had many modern boats yawing and skidding like a rodeo mount. I had felt her putting her yeoman shoulder to a stiff blow, and doggedly make her ground, and I had lazed at her tiller as she trickled serenely through cobalt seas, beneath powder-blue skies, to ports of spectacular peace and striking beauty. The engine could have been said to be a worry, in about the same way that the assassination of the Arch-Duke Franz Ferdinand could have been said to have caused a spot of bother, but she had housed us and moved us around quite adequately during our holiday. She was undoubtedly equipped to only a very basic standard, and equally certainly a bit sluggish in light weather, but *Nissos* had taken us about two hundred and fifty miles around the traps in a couple of weeks. Whatever her failings, she had certainly been ours for a peppercorn rent, and I reflected that, for the price we had paid, we could have no real complaint. There was something else, too. She had been a 'lucky' ship.

Almost all ships I have sailed in, great or small, have had a distinguishing character. One tramp cargo boat I sailed on was a supreme sea boat, inadequately powered but a gentle mover in the worst of seas. I have always thought of her as a dancer. My first ever ship was a fighter, a doughty, tough and unlovely ship with an unconquerable heart. She was not an easy ship, on her I worked as I rarely have done again before or since, but she was a very successful ship; I respected what she stood for and I was proud of having sailed in her. Some while ago, she passed me in the Singapore Straits making nineteen knots in her twenty-fifth year. The worst ship I ever knew was by some way the happiest, and I stayed with her an amazing fourteen months. My first command was a very old lady, an ageing supertanker with many of the marks of age on her. She was past her best, but whenever something was going to go wrong, I always knew. She told me. Even in the dead of night, I was always somehow already alert when the phone-call came, or the lights went out. She remains in my mind as the only truly *honest* ship I have sailed in. And *Nissos* was lucky. Oh, not in the sense that things went well... they didn't. We had ended up with egg on our faces in public far too much for comfort. But in the sense of serendipity she had been a pearl beyond price; she had introduced us to superb scenery off the beaten track; had led us to stray into the paths of warm and interesting people; had delivered us to fine food and drink in a land which is often maligned for its cuisine. I don't think I could have hoped to go to Greece any other way and so quickly found something of the true country. Somehow, I doubt whether I could have done it in another yacht, either. That may be illogical, but boats are illogical, and when you look at the returns for the expenditure in purely rational terms, so are the people who sail them. I suddenly found it very hard to walk away from *Nissos*, and felt an absolute heel for not at least stowing her sail properly. I quietly bade her a private farewell and thanks, and wished her good luck.

***

Spiro chattered away as we bumped back along the partly made quay and up to the main road. The content was rather complimentary; with our signed affidavit safely in his pocket, he was disposed to be quite frank about the condition of *Nissos*, and he felt that congratulations were in order for managing to navigate her. He had been amazed to hear that we had gone as far as (and come back from) Monemvasia, and was very fulsome in his appreciation of our last minute dash back from Aegina. Most clients, he confided, would have left the boat on the island for him to collect. He actually *listened* whilst Rex explained about our engine problems, muttered appreciatively as I described how I had worked out all about the wind patterns and complimented Malcolm as he blatantly took any credit going for our choice of route.

"Remarkable!" he cried. "I doubt if any of my clients this year have had so much out of a two-week rental."

He was true to his word about the bite to eat, and we stopped for half an hour in a small souvlaki shop for a last plate of gyros and a carafe of very good retsina, during which Spiro kept up our flow of high-spirited reminiscence by prompting and sincere, avid interest interspersed with admiring comment. He even hinted, not too subtly, that if I ever felt like coming to work in Greece, he was looking for someone…

However unpleasant the last sail had been, there was a definite sense of achievement at having made it. Testosterone was battling with adrenaline for the right to course through our veins, and it was only as we were saying good goodbye to Spiro at the airport that I came down to earth long enough to realise what he had achieved.

"Well, I can see that you will *definitely* be back, lads," he beamed. "Here is my card…." He distributed two or three of his business cards to each of us, "…and be sure you call me first. I'll make you a *very* special deal!" He unzipped the bag of wedding dresses one last time, slammed the jeep into gear and shot off. Of course, he didn't *really* cry "Hi ho, Spiro", and a Suzuki two-stroke jeep cannot rear on its hind legs and whinny before galloping away in a cloud of dust. But all three of us thought it had.

I looked at Rex. Rex looked at Malcolm. Malcolm looked at me.

"You do realise what he's just done, don't you?" I asked.

"He's just sold us another holiday," agreed Malcolm.

"And not only that," said Rex. "He isn't even going to lose the commission to the booking agent next time, 'coz we are going to book it direct with him."

"We'll probably get the same bloody boat!" wailed Malcolm.

"Undoubtedly," I nodded. "And we'll take it, too, because we will feel a bit clever, like we are cutting out the middleman. We might actually even save a bob or two."

"He's probably just made three customers for bloody life!" chuckled Rex, shaking his head in bemusement.

We stood grinning for a moment, and them Malcolm smiled his vilest smirk imaginable.

"I wonder what he says to French and German charterers about Brits?"

We shouldered our bags, and marched into the obscene yellow-ish glow of the airport.

Inside, humanity surged. The cool outside air was just a memory in the fug, created by a heaving maggot-box of people queuing for the various check-in counters. We fought our way to the appropriate trail of blow-torched humanity, and as we disconsolately kicked our baggage forward, I heard all about me the loud summaries of Greece as others had found it.

"It's not like Tenerife... I don't think we'll come again..."

"We were in Chaos. That's on the Turkish coast..."

"I quite liked it, but it's *so* bloody *foreign,* innit?"

"Adonis said he'll get me a job in his brother's bar next summer...Oh, he's *lovely!*"

"...Foods always cold and the chips are *awful!*"

"The beaches are all gravel, not sand...."

"Mykonos was full of poofs...dunno 'ow they wear all that leather in this 'eat."

"Well, its worse than Spain, innit? Yer can't understand Dagoes, but these don' even write the same as us..."

It suddenly hit me that I didn't want to stand in this airport and be jostled around by this herd. And I didn't want to get into a cramped little aeroplane with them. I most certainly had no pressing need to find myself, tomorrow morning, in Manchester airport on a cold, foggy morning in the latter hours of October, waiting for a train that probably wouldn't arrive until November. It further occurred that, whilst waiting for said mythical train, I would have ample time to reflect that the forecast for Athens tomorrow was sunny. And then, with blinding clarity, it struck me that I didn't have to. I still had two months leave, a pocket full of travellers' cheques, and absolutely no commitments. I shook hands with an astounded Malcolm and Rex, commiserated with them on their business obligations at home, walked out of the airport and hailed a taxi. Behind me, an airliner roared into the sky.

***

The next morning at eight thirty, I telephoned Spiro. By ten thirty, having had a coffee with him, I was back on board *Nissos*, furling her mainsail. At two P.M., I was on a bus crossing Parnassus on its way to the Corinth Gulf port of Galaxhidhi, where Spiro had a boat stuck. On Sunday morning, replete with a breakfast of *koulouria* and Greek yoghurt and with a thermos of laced coffee and a packet of cold bacon butties to hand in the cockpit, I unrolled the genoa of a Sunfizz 40 into a fresh westerly and squared away for the thirty-something miles to the Corinth Canal en route to Alimos. The air was not very warm but the sun fairly blazed. Ragged white clouds scudded over Parnassus and Delphi, the air was as clear as only mountain air can be. Spiro had four more boats to be brought back to Kalamaki from Corfu, Rhodes and Kos, which would keep me busy for a while. I donned my headphones, switched on my walkman, and listened to the first lesson on my Greek language course tape.

I couldn't have been happier.

POSTSCRIPT

That was twenty five years ago, and many things have changed in Greece. There are far fewer cats; the charter-yachts are mostly brand-new; the airport has been replaced by a gleaming and efficient marble-trimmed edifice; Athens is surrounded by a modern tangle of motorways which writhe through a jungle of industrial architecture and advertising hoardings reminiscent of suburban America. A stunningly modern metro system has been grafted onto the creaking old 'Elekrikos' railway, and modern trams slide sibilantly through the streets of Athens. Credit-card machines, the internet and mobile phones, all pure science fiction when *Nissos* cruised, are now ubiquitous. The Euro has replaced the Drachmae, and there is a new urgency to Greek life in the city which is increasingly indistinguishable from anywhere else in the Western world. Greeks have staged and starred in a spectacular Olympics, which even their kindest admirers might have thought unlikely not too long ago. Credit has arrived, bringing a flood of new cars and boats and buildings, and immigration is now a major influence. Climate change has brought more humidity and changed the weather patterns. Many harbours have been extended or built and of course congestion in high tourist season has increased. Above all, prices have changed... Greeks are now struggling to cope in the post-Euro world where prices have more than doubled and wages have remained static.

Interspersed with the trappings of the march of progress, however, there is still much to be found of old Greece. Fast food has arrived, but has not seriously challenged traditional restaurants; the bouzouki joints and kafeneions still thrive; financial difficulties do not repress the national impulse to sing, dance and offer hospitality whenever the opportunity arises. The alphabet has not yielded significantly and over all the blue-and-white flag of Greece is still proudly flown by all and sundry.

As you move away from the Athens conurbation towards the Peloponnese, the combined affects of European investment, 'globalisation', the touch of the Olympics and the twenty-first century fade rapidly, and the old Greece quickly becomes even more manifest. The rural areas are very largely as they were when Theseus walked these shores on his way to Athens; the bays and harbours are busier but still very accessible; the innate hospitality and '*filoxenia*' are to be found everywhere; tavernas and kafeneions are still very affordable and one is never hurried at one's table. Most significantly, Greece and Greeks retain their distinct character... flamboyant, original, passionate and infinitely interesting. The trail of the *Nissos* could perfectly well be followed today with a reasonable hope of finding things much as we did.

Some more specific things have not changed. One, I am delighted to say, is *Nissos*. Now in the caring ownership of a Greek family who have refurbished her and use her privately, she is still plying the Saronic and looking good. Another is Spiro, ever youthful and now a firm friend of many years. Pan can still be found marshalling the yachts in Hydra, Petros still runs his kafeneion in Poros, although sadly Sotiris was taken from us last year. In Hydra, 'O Kipos' is no more but birds and pigs still turn on the spit at Lekkas's chicken shop in Aegina. And finally there is me... twenty-five years on my Greek odyssey continues. Since this beginning, I have sailed many thousands of miles through the islands and around the coasts of the Eastern Mediterranean, and my daughter has been born in this enigmatic and beautiful land.

GLOSSARY

Anchor – Intended as a means of finding your boat where you left it, this useful item is primarily a conversation piece. If you have three yachties in a room, you have five opinions on anchors. Some people favour the sorts which are light and easy to lift – these people are dangerous lunatics who should be confined for their own good. What you need is a behemoth with lots of teeth and attitude.

Anchor-chain – Attaches the anchor to the boat. In the Mediterranean, you want lots of it, and none of this nonsense about rope being just as good.

Back-stay – A wire which is attached to a very strong point at the back of the yacht and runs up to the top of the mast. It supports the mast from behind, and is an essential safety feature when urinating over the stern.

Bitter-end – The very last link of the anchor-chain. The one you *really* don't want to let go of.

Boom – A spar which attaches to the mast with a hinge. Its purpose is to extend the mainsail aft from the mast, to control the angle of the sail to the wind, and to tension the foot of the sail; its perverse delight is to batter the unwary about the bonce.

Bow-sprit – Devilish device on more traditional boats – a large spike sticking out of the front to extend head-sails, stays and anchor-leads. Fine at sea, but a liability in small harbours. *Nissos* didn't have one, thankfully… who knows what sort of trouble we could have got into with one of them!

Cap-shroud – A wire which is attached to a very strong point on the deck and runs up the side of the mast to the top. Half-way up it passes over the end of a small spar called the Spreader. Its purpose is to support the mast from the side, and other vital uses are as a hand-hold when entering the boat in a state of impaired equilibrium or a support for the shoulder when urinating over the side.

Companionway – The main entrance and exit of the cabin to the cockpit. This is usually a steep climb down 2 or 3 steps to the cabin-floor, and the steps commonly form the cover of the engine compartment. It is protected from the elements by a sliding hatch-cover over the top and by wooden hatch-boards that slot in to the vertical side. Effectively, the yacht's front door.

Echo-sounder – A gadget which sends a sonic signal out of the bottom of the boat and times how long it takes to come back. By a simple sum allowing for the speed of sound in water it takes an educated guess at the depth under the boat. Often complicated by the fact that a signal leaves and takes so long to come back that it returns after the next signal has been sent... resulting in indications of shoal water where none should be and subsequent myocardial dysfunction. Works equally well on dolphins, fish, and air-bubbles, with the same result.

Engine – A contrivance which works on the principle of squeeze-bang-blow to convert money via fossil fuel into approximately equal portions of noise, smoke and forward motion. The clever little thing also makes something called 'Amps', which are the preferred bed-time snack of batteries. Variously referred to as The Iron Top-sail, The Beast In The Bilge, and That Bloody Monstrosity, it is more properly referred to as an infernal construction engine.

Fender – A sort of strong balloon on a rope which is hung over the side to prevent hull-to-hull contact with adjacent boats or quaysides. Frequently wrongly tied on, and consequently lost.

Foot – A) The bottom edge of any sail.
    B) Something Malcolm rarely does with the bill.

Forecastle (or fo'c'sle) – The forward part of a ship, the scene of derring-do with ropes and anchors.

Fore-sail (or Head-sail) – Any sail which sets forward of the mast, supported on its forward side by the forestay.

Fore-stay – A wire which is attached to a very strong point at the front of the yacht and runs up to the top of the mast. It supports the mast from forward and is used to set the genoa or jib. It also acts as a shoulder-rest for urinating off the bow, and supports hammocks.

Galley – Sailorese for 'kitchen'. Outwardly simply jargon, but there is in fact a distinct delineation between galleys and kitchens. Food which would never be acceptable from a kitchen is commonly highly esteemed when created in a galley. Examples are sardines in condensed milk, sautéed corned beef in onion brulée and the eight-day curry.

Gang-plank – What you get when you don't have a passerelle.

Genoa – A species of fore-sail commonly fitted to modern yachts. It is attached at the luff to the forestay, and extends aft of the mast. Very powerful. Often abbreviated to 'Genny'.

Genoa-sheet – Rope which extends from the free corner of the genoa to the cockpit and controls the angle and shape of the genoa. Due to the power of the genoa, it requires a winch to adjust it. Often abbreviated to 'Genny-sheet'.

Genoa-track – A sort of railway and car with a pulley through which the genoa-sheet passes on its way to the winch. There is one on each side of the boat. It is used to alter the shape of the genoa to suit the wind, and to keep curious crew busy when the skipper needs a few minutes to think.

Gin-Palace – Large motor-boat of the opulent variety. Much loathed by sailors for running generators in idyllic bays, occupying large chunks of harbours, creating huge washes which spill one's curry, and costing a lot of money.

Gooseneck – The hinge at the front of the boom.

Gybe – The act of turning the stern of the boat through the wind so that the sails change from one side to the other, the principle feature being a rapid movement of the boom across the top of the cockpit. Divided into two categories, 'intentional' and 'unintentional'. Both categories are further subdivided into 'controlled' and 'uncontrolled'. An intentional, controlled gybe is much appreciated by sailors; an unintentional, uncontrolled gybe is much appreciated by mast salesmen and occasionally undertakers.

Gypsy – A sort of gear-wheel in the windlass or anchor-winch which grips the chain.

Halyard – Any rope which pulls a sail up the mast and tensions the luff of the sail. Main-halyard for the main-sail, genoa halyard for the genoa. Something logical at least.

Hatch – An opening Perspex window in an aluminium frame set in the deck of the boat to allow light and ventilation in and scared yachtsmen out.

Heads – Sailorese for 'toilet'. Derives it's name from the 'catheads'– a place up by the anchors on old sailing ships which was designated for the purpose of letting it all hang out. Due to the size and complexity of plumbing in yacht toilets, this old tradition is undergoing an enthusiastic revival.

In Irons – See Tacking

Jib – A fore-sail smaller than a genoa. Most charter yachts have only a storm-jib, a very strong, small sail for extreme conditions... and no way of setting it due to the existence of the roller-furling.

Kedge – An anchor which is dropped from the stern of the boat, instead of the bow. Used when mooring bow-first, or when desperately trying to stop, it is also sometimes transferred forward and used to make an open-moor... this is defiance of the rule that if a yacht can't lie safely to one anchor, then elsewhere is the place to be!

Keel – Lump of hopefully aqua-dynamic iron attached to the bottom of the boat to a) minimise lee-way and b) keep said boat sunny-side up.

Kicking-strap – A rope pulley which tensions the boom downwards. It is used to control the shape of the main-sail, and to keep idle hands busy when they might otherwise be peacefully employed denigrating the skipper.

Lazy-line – A thin rope, frequently covered in marine growth, which connects a permanent mooring to the quay so that a visiting yachtsman doesn't need to drop his own anchor; he simply backs-in and pulls the lazy-line up until he has attached his boat to a large ground-chain and in the process covered himself in slime, slashed his fingers to the bones on barnacles and transformed his gleaming yacht into a kelp-bed.

Leach – A) The trailing edge of any sail.
      B) Description of Malcolm in a bar.

Life-Lines – A sort of fence around the sides of the boat to stop the inhabitants falling off. It is made of wires stretched tightly between the pulpit and the pushpit, supported at intervals by posts called stanchions. Also serves to attach fenders to.

Log – Gadget which measures distance travelled through the water, and calculates speed. Mentioned here in absentia only, as *Nissos* didn't have one.

Luff – A) The forward or leading edge of any sail.
      B) The act of coming closer to the wind until the front of the sail collapses. If persisted in it will lead to a 'tack'. When done deliberately, a recognised way of slowing down or moving up-wind; when done accidentally, a recognised way of annoying the hell out of the skipper.

Main-hatch – The sliding hatch over the companionway.

Mainsail — The sail which sets aft of the mast. In a conventional rig like that of *Nissos*, it is attached to the mast by the forward edge or 'luff' and to the boom by the 'foot'.

Main-sheet — The system of blocks and line which controls the angle at which the boom lies to the mast. In gybes it can rocket across the cockpit, and since it is close to the crew it can become highly importunate.

Mud-Weight — Substitute for an anchor used almost exclusively on the Norfolk and Suffolk Broads — just a big weight, like the ones Tom always hits Jerry with, on a rope.

Open Moor — Dropping two anchors a little way apart in order to give support to the bow from two sides. Very secure mooring, but it requires skill to execute and skill *and* luck to recover afterwards. Usually only attempted in the Mediterranean by the most desperate of skippers, due to the unbelievable amount of ironmongery in Mediterranean harbours.

Passerelle — A neat little gang-way, frequently with a tidy rope hand-rail and sometimes even lights, which extends from the stern, or sometimes bows, of a yacht to allow the crew to walk ashore. Not mentioned in this book, because *Nissos* didn't have one.

Pawl — A sort of tooth on the windlass or anchor-winch which only allows the winch to turn one way, to stop the chain running out again when heaving-up. To drop the anchor it has to be lifted up.

Pulpit — A tubular frame, usually stainless-steel, which wraps about the forward side of the yacht as a means of projecting the life-lines round a person working on front of the boat. Named because of its resemblance to a pulpit.

Pushpit — The same as a pulpit, but at the other end of the boat. So if one is called a pull-pit, the other must logically be…

Reefing – The act of reducing the area of one or more sails in order to stay alive when the wind gets stronger.

Roller-furling – A nifty device somewhat like a café awning, which makes it easy to set and reef or douse the genoa. A sort of tube, which fits around the fore-stay with a reel at the bottom, it winds in a 'furling-line' as the sail is rolled out and when the furling-line is pulled back out it winds the sail back in again. Most of the time.

Rope-clutch – A devilish enticement… a lever attached to a toothed jaw which holds a rope under tension. Very easy to apply, and very hard to release when you really, really need to!

Sacrificial strip – A strip of material sewn on the leach and foot of the genoa to protect it from ultra-violet damage from the sun when rolled up. On *Nissos*, it had already comfortably passed its name-sake condition.

Tack – The side from which the wind is coming and a deciding factor in who is to blame when sailing boats collide. The vessel is on the tack *opposite* to the side on which the mainsail is. Logical? Look, I didn't make this stuff up, I'm just passing it on!

Tacking – The act of turning the boat so that her bows pass through the wind so as to change from one tack to the other. This is another opportunity for the boom to have a go at the crew. If this is done accidentally with the genoa still secured on the other side, the boat will be 'taken aback', an ungainly position wherein the skipper's gin and the crew's blood are likely to be spilled. If the boat is not going fast enough she stalls head-to-wind, when she is said to be 'in irons'.

Taken-aback – See Tacking

Tiller – A glorified lever which steers the boat by transmitting the helmsman's errors to the rudder. The arcane nature of sailing makes it inevitable that to go left, one has to push it to the right.

Topping-lift – Rope leading down from the mast-head to the outer end of the boom which supports the free end of the boom when the mainsail is lowered.

Traveller – A device fitted close to the helmsman consisting of a sort of railway and car which adjusts the position of the lower end of the main-sheet. In the hands of the expert, a powerful tool for trimming the main-sail; in the hands of the inexpert, a finger-guillotine.

Up & Down – Another manifestation of arcane sailing jargon. On a sailing boat, everything reverses itself depending which side the wind is on. 'Up' is used to mean 'towards the side the wind is coming from', and 'down' the opposite. Also, as the tiller goes the opposite way to the rudder, one must put the helm up to make the boat go down, and vice-versa. When the boat changes tack, up becomes down. Sometimes the wind is dead astern, so it doesn't work at all. To further clarify the matter, people also use 'up' and 'down' to mean heave-in or slack-out on various thingamabobs. One may also hear both 'up and down' used together when heaving up the anchor, to indicate that the anchor chain is vertical so the anchor is directly under the boat and about to break-out. I hope this has cleared up any confusion.

VHF – Very High Frequency radio… a piece of electronic equipment which develops one's vocabulary and self-confidence. Users instantly begin to use words such as 'affirmative' and 'negative', or phrases like 'please advise your location' instead of the sadly proletarian 'where are you?' They are also instantly able to confidently use words they don't understand, such as 'roger' 'radio-check' and 'wilco'. There is no embarrassment at this as they cannot see their audience. An indispensable aid to confusion.

Winch – A thing like a barrel with gears inside powered by a removable handle inserted in the top. You wrap a rope three times round it and wind the handle, which gives you sufficient mechanical advantage to pull in sails, mooring ropes, very large fish, etcetera… an indispensable device which has made sailing accessible to the indolent.

Windlass (or anchor-winch) — A winch mounted on the fore-deck for the sole purpose of releasing and recovering the anchor. Love and cherish this machine... its wellbeing is utterly crucial to the success of your Mediterranean holiday!